A WAY OF LIFE

Sheepdog Training, Handling and Trialling

Bwlch Taff with his daughter Lyn. (Neville Pratt)

A WAY OF LIFE

Sheepdog Training, Handling and Trialling

H. GLYN JONES talks to BARBARA C. COLLINS

FARMING PRESS LIMITED
Wharfedale Road, Ipswich, Suffolk

Acknowledgements

Grateful thanks are due to the following:

The International Sheep Dog Society for help in the clarification of certain points mentioned in this book.

Eric Halsall for his contribution to Chapter 11, the provision of some photographs and his Foreword.

Working Sheepdog News for permission to use material first published as a short series of training articles.

Gillian Hubbard for the information on hereditary eye disorders in the Border Collie contained in Appendix 1.

Ann G. Owen for the veterinary information contained in Appendices 2 and 3.

Katy Cropper for the diagrams.

Diana Rimmer for the cartoon in Chapter 11.

The many people who responded so quickly to my requests for photographs and information about their dogs.

The anonymous photographers who were impossible to trace but whose contribution has been considerable.

First published 1987, reprinted 1988 and 1989

Copyright © H. Glyn Jones and Barbara C. Collins, 1987

Distributed in North America by Diamond Farm Enterprises,
Box 537, Alexandria Bay, NY 13607

British Library Cataloguing in Publication Data

Jones, H. Glyn
   A way of life: sheepdog training, handling and trialling.
   1. Sheep dog — Training.
   I. Title   II. Collins, Barbara C.
   636.7'3   SF428.6

ISBN 0-85236-166-1

Phototypeset by Galleon Photosetting, Ipswich
Printed in Great Britain at Butler & Tanner Ltd, Frome, Somerset

Contents

Diagrams

Foreword

By Eric Halsall

TEACHING, NOT TRAINING, a collie dog to use its inbred wisdom for shepherding is the secret of Glyn Jones' great success with working collies. There is a subtle difference though few realise it. It means taking the time and interest to understand the particular characteristics of each individual collie and to foster them to perfection. It is a slower process than the more common and accepted ways of training collies, but it is lasting and, if the dogs have the flair, makes trials winners, if not, good and reliable workers around the farm.

Dogs respect the interest which Glyn Jones takes in them—and they try to please. 'Each is an individual and must be recognised as such,' he says. Dogs respond to a man who takes the trouble to know them and, though few people have the knack to get inside a dog's mind like Glyn Jones, this book details the way to go about it.

Glyn's methods are singular and not easy to write down; read with a receptive mind, they will produce dogs which are skilful, willing and contented partners in the craft of shepherding. I have been privileged to know all the top handlers of working collies in my time but none can match the teachings of Glyn Jones. I rate his views the best and I am pleased to have persuaded, even threatened, him into sharing his methods in this book.

It was on the mountainside above Glyn's home in the Clwydian range that I pondered the information and methods which are set before you in the following pages. They are methods which taught Gel to listen and to use his own method—that trait which is akin to genius in the working collie—and to win the Supreme Championship of the International Sheep Dog Society, the greatest sheepdog honour in the world. They taught the sometimes temperamental Bracken to discard her feminine foibles and join Gel in the winning of the Welsh Brace Championship—and to stay unbeaten in five television 'One Man and His Dog' contests. They taught the handsome, tricolour Taff to win two Welsh National Championships and Reserve Supreme title whilst he was still a youngster. They taught Hemp, a dog who loved to run the mountain, to win the International Farmers Championship.

Glyn's methods have taught many collies to enjoy their work, to shepherd sheep with skill, to win countless trials prizes and, really more important, to improve the general management of farmstock in many parts of Wales—and much further afield, for Glyn has taken his advice, on request, to the New World.

My musings on the mountain above Bodfari were interrupted when my own collie, Gael, came to say it was time to go. I stirred and together we walked down to the farmstead at Bwlch Isaf, the home of the wisest dogs in the world—from whence came this book.

Cliviger, 1987

Preface

By Barbara C. Collins

I FIRST MET GLYN JONES several years ago after my husband, Tony, and I moved to live in an isolated farmhouse in North Wales and rapidly became immersed in the absorbing hobby of breeding and training Border Collies after Tony was given a bitch puppy by one of our neighbours, another well-known handler, Meirion Jones. Until that time, we had watched sheepdog trialling on television and the occasional trial on local fields, recognising the names of some of the better-known handlers but unaware that we would one day be fortunate enough to count them as our friends (and adversaries on the trials field). The generous advice and encouragement we have been given by all the sheepdog people we have met, firstly in Wales and later including handlers 'across the Border', has been of incalculable value to us both and eventually resulted in the pair of us leaving our respective professional jobs, Tony becoming an avid sheepdog trainer, triallist and part-time shepherd whilst I took over the magazine *Working Sheepdog News*, and those, combined with breeding sheepdogs, are now the pursuits which fill our lives.

It was while Glyn and I were working on a series of articles for the magazine that the subject of a book on training sheepdogs was raised and, although in the background for some time, the idea did not begin to mushroom until the spring of 1986. By this time there had been an enthusiastic response to the articles already written, there was a publisher interested and a method of working together had evolved which was producing results, so we decided to take the ram by the horns and collaborate on the writing of this book. I have always enjoyed writing and this interest, combined with the growing knowledge of the sheepdog world which I was gathering as my work with the magazine progressed, provided me with the motivation to tackle what was to prove, in the event, quite a formidable, although enjoyable, task. Added to those factors was the inevitable one of the need to earn a crust of bread, so my motives were not purely altruistic!

My part in the book has been to record on paper, and edit, the facts which Glyn so ably talked about in the many conversations we had in the compiling of the necessary data. The method used was to record our discussions initially on tape and I would then type out the salient facts, putting them in some sort of logical order before further refining was attempted. Glyn's quicksilver mind, wealth of knowledge and 'grasshopper' technique in conversation made this an interesting experience, to say the least! One minute he would be training a young dog, the next minute he would be winning the International Sheep Dog Trials, then to dogs of the past, then brace work and on to choosing puppies—rather like a series of potted chapters, all in the space of about five minutes. However, as each section of the book was discussed and a reasonable first draft had been achieved, there would be reading, discussion and editing until the final contents were agreed, at least long enough to go on to the next part. Once the book was complete, we carried out a final edit and found that we had managed to finish our task without a cross word having been spoken from start to finish—quite an achievement for two people who both have minds of their own and like to get their own way most of the time.

A great bonus, for me, has been that I have been able to get to know Glyn, his family and his dogs so well in the months spent in the preparation of this book—months which have involved much laughter, a lot of hard work and occasional argument—and, after assimilating all the information the book contains, I now feel that I should be able to train my own sheepdog—I will certainly find the many trials I watch to be of increased interest and fascination now that I have a better understanding of this absorbing pastime, having learned so much from a man who is an acknowledged master of the art.

Pwllglas, 1987

Introduction

FOR SOME YEARS NOW I have been running classes on training sheepdogs in the British Isles and have also run training 'clinics' in Canada and America when I have been in those countries to judge trials and enjoy the marvellous hospitality which I have always experienced there. Many people have been suggesting to me, over the past few years, that I should write a book on training sheepdogs but, although I feel strongly that experienced handlers and trainers should be prepared to pass on their knowledge and training methods in order to enable others to achieve success, I never did anything about putting pen to paper—like all farmers, I love my busy, outdoor life and would never be able, or prepared, to spend hours of my time writing when I could be outside working around the farm, training my dogs or running classes to help others to train theirs.

However, things change and my desire to share my experiences, joys and sadnesses and the knowledge I have gained over the years began to force me to think again. My ideas about writing also altered when I discovered it would be possible for me to talk and somebody else to do the actual writing (I'll talk the hind leg off a donkey if the subject is sheepdogs, their handlers and trialling) and, now that the book is finally completed, I can only hope that the contents will be of help and interest to any reader who enjoys involvement in rural life and with the working sheepdog, be he farmer, shepherd, handler, spectator or armchair enthusiast. The experienced handler may find it interesting to criticise and compare my training methods with his own, the novice will be able to use the book to plan his training programme, and spectators who either go to watch trials or sit in their armchairs watching trialling on the television will, I am sure, have their enjoyment greatly increased if they can gain a wider understanding of what the training and handling of these lovely, intelligent dogs entails and how it is done by at least one handler.

Since I was a very small child I have been amongst Border Collies, having been born into a Welsh-speaking family where sheepdog handling was part of family tradition and our everyday lives. In this book, I have criticised some of my father's methods of training and I have no doubt at all that my daughter Ceri will criticise some of my methods as she progresses with the training of her young dogs in years to come. My book will, perhaps, act as some sort of yardstick for her, and others, to start from, using what they feel is good and discarding what they find does not work for them. As long as dog handling and sheepdog trialling exists there will be a need for criticism and change to help it to develop and grow and, although I accept that all change is not necessarily for the better, it is impossible to progress in anything in this world without change from time to time—without it, things stagnate and the sheepdog world, together with agriculture in general, has seen so many changes in the last fifty years that it has become a necessity to be able to adapt in order to survive.

I think that, in addition to putting in a lot of

hard work with my dogs, I have had more than my fair share of luck over the years in a trialling career which has brought me moments of joy, sadness, laughter and great fun. My dogs have brought me into contact with some remarkable people, they have taken me to the other side of the world and have brought people from many countries to visit us at Bwlch Isaf. My wife, Beryl, and I have exported puppies to many countries including our most exciting (and exhausting) project to date—the export of thirty-four registered Border Collie puppies to the Falkland Islands shortly after the Falklands war.

Another area of luck for me was that I was the first handler to be asked to train a young dog for a television series to be featured by the BBC—the youngster I used for that purpose was Glen, and I now run a son of his in Bwlch Taff who, although he has not won the Supreme Championship, has come very close to it and has done so well for me in his trialling career. Glen and I had great fun doing that series of programmes and it enabled me to meet people who have since become household names—personalities such as Phil Drabble, author, country-lover and conservationist, and Eric Halsall, author, journalist and commentator, who is mad about sheepdogs and has written several books about them in addition to giving me much encouragement to produce this book.

I was also lucky enough to win the International Supreme Championship at the Centenary International Sheepdog Trials when they were held in Bala in 1973—one of the best moments of my life. Not only had I achieved my major ambition in winning the championship, I had also won it on home ground in Wales where, at the very first trials to be held at Bala one hundred years before, the Welsh had suffered the ignominy of having a Scotsman winning the championship, so I felt much as the cricketers must feel when they win back the 'Ashes'! The history books will record that a Scotsman won the first trial at Bala but that a Welshman won the Centenary trials there so I feel that we are now quits with

our Celtic cousins. Mind you, I might have been the champion for that day but one of the things about reaching the top is that the only way to go from there is down, and you can be at the bottom of the heap when you run in your next trial, a handler and his dog only being as good as their last run.

I have been most fortunate in having a wife who has been prepared to put up with me and my dogs for the past twenty-six years—without her backing I would never have been able to spend so much time with my dogs and she is the one who deals with the breeding side of things so competently. I would never pretend that there have not been times when we have almost come to blows over the dogs but, by and large, we have got through the good and the bad times together and we are still in partnership, so, again, I consider myself a lucky man.

In the writing of this book, events from my earliest days kept intruding to such an extent that I realised they were as much a part of the development of my own methods and ideas as other factors which have influenced my thinking up to the present day. I therefore decided to start the book with a chapter based on these beginnings in the hope that readers will find it of relevance and interest before going on to the more extensive content about training. Throughout the book I have referred to the dog in training, be it male or female, as 'he' for the sake of clarity, and there is no intention of any bias towards one sex or the other—the choice of a dog or bitch being purely a matter of personal preference for the handler concerned.

It only remains for me to say that, if some novice, having read my book, sets out to train a young dog of his own, he does not need a lot of cash to set about it. By purchasing, or breeding his own puppy and then working through the various stages of training as outlined in the book he will certainly have a first-class farm dog and should be able to reach trials standard if he so wishes. If that novice should one day win the National or the International Sheepdog Trials, just have fun at local trials or be content to improve his handling and training of his farm dog, I feel that my methods will have been worth recording. He will have a lot of fun, happiness and some heartbreak. He will gain many friends and lose a few but, at the end of the day, he and his dog will be the winners because they will have learned, and done, so much together.

H. Glyn Jones
Bodfari, 1987

THIS BOOK IS DEDICATED TO MY WIFE, BERYL, AND DAUGHTERS, CERI AND RHONA.

CHAPTER 1

Early Days

My roots in North Wales

DRIVING THROUGH SOME of the loveliest countryside in North Wales, I always feel a great sadness whenever I pass through Pwllglas village and come to the handsome stone arch with great wooden gates which is the main entrance to Nant Clwyd Hall—the stonework is modern but the pieces of stone with which the arch is constructed were taken from the place which I still remember with love and sadness, the place where I was born—Efail y Plas (Derwen Hall Smithy). Driving for a further mile or so, I eventually come to a turn to the right and, particularly if I am alone, I rarely manage to resist the urge to turn into the lane, over the old railway bridge and then the little hump-backed bridge over

The sad heap of stones.

the river Clwyd. I park the car at the side of the road, climb over the wooden gate which is now fastened with a piece of wire and I am back home, the memories flooding back as I look at the places where the house, smithy and outhouses used to stand. All that is left of the old stone buildings is a small piece of the 'ty bach' (little house), which served the family as the outside lavatory, and the crumbling walls of the building where the cattle and other animals were housed during the winter.

The piece of wire to which my mother used to attach her clothes-line so many years ago is still there round the trunk of the great oak tree which stands in the paddock where the back of the house used to be, and I can still see her, reaching up to secure the other end of the line to the pine tree on the opposite side, the clean clothes drying in the wind and sun, and the fresh smell as she folded the washing and put it into the basket, ready for ironing the next day.

Turning my back on the sad heap of stones, I look across the small piece of field which runs down to the river and there are the fruit trees which my father planted, still standing, weighed down with blossom and springtime fragrance, and the years roll away—I see myself as a young boy, running down to the river bank to 'tickle' the trout, splashing around in the water with the dogs, picking the watercress which grows in such profusion on the opposite bank, slipping on the stones on the bed of the river and falling into the icy cold water, picking the ripe fruit and watching my mother making jam in the kitchen with wasps everywhere to sting the unwary.

Sitting on the river bank over fifty years later I listen to a cock pheasant calling for its mate, the chuck-chuck of a moorhen, the sound of the river bubbling over the stones, a songthrush singing its head off from its perch in one of the fruit trees, and the only thing which seems to have really changed is the appearance of the river, which has silted up over the years and is now almost devoid of fish life. Gone are the thousands of brown trout with bright orange spots along their sides which were so easy to catch, and also missing is the green growth of water plants on the river bed which used to provide feed and shelter for the teeming freshwater life that pollution has inevitably destroyed. The river's sparkling, clear appearance belies the ravages caused by so-called progress, although salmon and sea-trout (or sewin as they are called in Wales) still return to the river of their birth to swim up to the spawning redds nearer its source.

A hundred yards beyond the far bank of the river there is now a wilderness where the railway line used to be. When I was a child, the steam trains ran up and down it regularly. The drivers all knew my father well, and when their trains were carrying coal, they would gather speed just before the smithy, hoot a greeting and then slam on their brakes just before reaching the bridge. The sudden jolting this caused meant that lumps of coal would come cascading off the great heaps in the wagons, landing by the side of the railway and later picked up by the children and carried back to the house in bucketsful. Standing on the railway bridge now, I can still see all this happening and find myself laughing at the knowledge that so many families living near the railway line in those days had an almost inexhaustible supply of coal! Strangely, a chugging steam-train did not seem to interfere with the peace of the countryside, perhaps because on that part of the line the trains usually moved fairly slowly and were not like the huge steam locomotives used on the main lines.

A familiar sight along the railway was the

Efail y Plas as it was in my childhood.

gangs of men involved in continuous maintenance of the line; they would walk along one side of the rails, knocking in the wooden chocks which held the metal rails in place, then walk back along the other side with the same regular rhythm, securing the lines before moving on to the next section. As this was a continuous, ongoing task we all got to know these men very well over the years. As children, we had the job of collecting firewood daily and heaven help us if we ever picked up one of the wooden chocks to increase our load. My father would spot it and the offending child would be sent smartly back to the part of the railway where he had found the piece of wood and would leave it there ready for the linesmen's next visit.

Looking down at the river also brings back a memory of the great, noisy hisses of steam which billowed across the surface when the red-hot bands of metal which my father had welded around the big wooden cartwheels came into contact with the water which was used to cause quick cooling of the metal and contraction to provide a really tight fit. These were special days for the children, with a huge bonfire lit and, in its very hot centre, small raised circles of bricks on which to rest the various-sized metal rings. The wooden wheel would be ledged on a sort of tripod with a big peg coming up through the middle and a screw which was used to keep the wheel secure. Then two or three men with open metal hoops would lift the white-hot metal ring and place it over the wooden wheel, and as quickly as possible the wheel would be released and allowed to roll down the slope into the river. There would be this enormous 'whoosh' as hot metal came into contact with icy water and, all being well, the metal band would shrink and fit snugly on to the wheel. Occasionally things went wrong and the metal band would split with a colossal bang and hurl itself about—highly dangerous if anybody was foolish enough to be standing nearby, but providing great excitement for the watching children. The wheelwright's art is a very exact one, entailing detailed knowledge, measurement and skill, and when things went wrong my father would be so mad about it that we would make ourselves scarce.

There was no electricity in those days, no running water, no inside sanitation at Efail y Plas, and, of course, no television to provide instant entertainment. It might seem that life consisted of nothing but hard work but it really wasn't like that at all. In a way, you never started work and you never stopped, it was just part of one's everyday life to carry the water from the spring, to clean and refill the oil lamps, to sit enthroned in the 'ty bach' with the door half-open and look at that magnificent scenery (and how many modern loos are there which can offer such a pastoral view?). Whenever we went out roaming the woods and fields, we never returned home empty-handed, as we always picked up suitable pieces of wood, carrying the ever-increasing load on the return journey to add to the stack in the old outhouse and never looking upon this as 'work'. The gamekeepers all knew who we were and there was never any unpleasantness or accusation of trespass as there would be nowadays—they knew we were up to no harm and left us to our own devices. Muriel, my middle sister, is still unable to resist the urge, whenever out walking, to pick up pieces of wood lying on the ground to carry home for the fire—a piece of her past which is still with her as mine is with me.

Collecting water from the well was another task which was allocated to the children, and we had a system of taking the buckets up the path to the well on the way to school in the mornings and, on our return in the afternoon, filling the buckets and carrying them into the house. Again, not really work, but part of the pattern of our lives.

If I walk towards the smithy from the bridge, I come to an old hedge—this was the first hedge which I laid and I was very proud of it at the time. I was about seventeen years old when I did it and I can still see the evidence of my work all these years later, my sense of belonging being reinforced by the memory. I still enjoy watching the craftsmen of the present day when they are laying hedges round the fields—a real craft and still thriving, as hedge-laying competitions at many present-day rural agricultural shows demonstrate.

The seven acres of land which formed part of the smithy smallholding in the old days are still lush and green and the landowner's sheep find it to be tasty grazing, their lambs frolicking in the sunshine where we used to play as children. I firmly believe that the old place, where a large family has been reared, where

Looking towards the river and bridge from Efail y Plas (1986).

there has been a lot of fun, sadness, much happiness and some tragedy, has soaked this all up and somehow preserves it in the present. Whatever is done to the old place now, there will always be for me an indefinable amalgam of memories there, in that sheltered spot by the river which seems to cry out to me, 'I am still here, build another house for me so that I can be lived in once again'. And believe me, if I was a millionaire and had the opportunity to buy those seven acres, I'd snap them up in a flash, build a house in the traditional style of the area and hope that, after my death, it would again be filled with a family of children who could enjoy all that this lovely place has to offer and feel privileged, as I do, to have been a part of it.

A family tradition

I have always felt that I was born to follow in my father's footsteps as a trainer and handler of sheepdogs. My father, whose ideas and methods of training were very, very different from my own, learned about sheep and sheepdogs from his mother, who lived in a little cottage called Foel Ganol in the mountains above Cyffylliog, Denbighshire (now the County of Clwyd). This cottage has become a weekend holiday house now but, at the time my grandmother lived there, she worked as a shepherdess on nearby Fron Farm, and the outstanding memory I have of her is her whistle when she was working with her dogs. Such a whistle it was—something for a young boy to emulate and practise in privacy. I never achieved a whistle of her standard and I am sure that she would have scorned the use of the flat shepherd's whistle so widely used today. So, my grandmother was the first generation to handle working sheepdogs, my father was the second, I am the third generation, being a farmer and a sheepdog handler, and now the tradition is being carried on by a fourth generation in the person of my daughter, Ceri, who has been running dogs since the age of seven.

In addition to being a sheepdog handler and trainer, my father was a very able blacksmith, a poacher par excellence, a trainer of poacher's dogs, a beekeeper, a drinking man and a marvellous shot—in short, he was a real 'character', steeped in the lore of the countryside in which he had spent his whole life and which he loved. He was a Welshman who spoke little English, he had a marvellous sense of humour, was a great story-teller and could tell jokes with a straight face; he had a quick temper but never bore malice, he worked and played hard all his life, and there is no doubt that he was a major influence upon me, particularly in my early childhood and adolescence. Without him, my life would probably have taken a very different, far less turbulent course—and I would never have known the trials and tribulations of becoming a sheepdog breeder, trainer, handler and trials enthusiast.

An early start—my daughter Ceri with Moss.

Being a blacksmith, my father was kept busy all year, with much of his time spent repairing the threshing machines which were an essential part of farm life at that time. This meant that there was always a continuous stream of men visiting the smithy, which was a favourite meeting place for sheepdog handlers and, of course, poachers. There would be drinking sessions at night after the day's work was finished and the talk next day would be of the pubs and the poaching of the night before. Poachers would share their knowledge and vie with each other, telling tales of their escapades, embroidering each incident, with fish, pheasant and rabbits always growing larger in the telling and in the imagination of one small boy sitting agog in the background, praying that nobody would realise it was long past his bedtime. These men would egg each other on to go and poach in areas where the keepers were known to be keen of eye and meticulous in their duties, providing additional excitement in an already hazardous pastime and increasing the status of any poacher who could prove that he had managed to get in and quickly out with his quarry without being caught—which was, after all, the main aim of any poacher (and essential, as discovery would mean the loss of one's livelihood and home, both of which were provided by the estate).

Father always had dogs around the smithy, with one or two more favoured ones being part of the family, and, of course, there would always be poaching dogs such as his tremendous lurcher, Black, amongst them. Lurchers were the best dogs for poaching and they were produced by crossing a greyhound with a Border Collie—the greyhound for his speed and the collie for a thick, warm coat, stamina and brains. These dogs were about the size of a greyhound but were much more versatile and were greatly sought after.

Every sheepdog that my father trained for trials was also taught to retrieve—an ability which was put to good use during shooting days on the estate; and because he trained dogs for poachers as well as sheepdog handlers,

he was well patronised, both kinds of dog being in great demand. Surprisingly, as far as I can remember, being taught to retrieve did not seem to interfere with a sheepdog's ability to work with sheep when required to do so.

When teaching a dog to retrieve, Father or the boys would skin a rabbit and stuff the skin with grass (it looked surprisingly life-like and lasted longer than a dead rabbit), and the children would be sent to drag the stuffed rabbit along the ground to make a scent-trail before hiding it somewhere. It was quite a challenge to try and find hiding places which the dogs would not be able to locate and I don't think that we ever were successful.

My father with two of his favourite dogs, Jaff and Meg (circa 1948).

Father always started a dog's training indoors in the shoeing part of the smithy. To teach a dog its sides he would have one of my brothers on the end of a long rope attached to the collar and me on the end of a second piece of rope on the other side. Then he would tell the dog to 'Go away' or 'Come bye', each boy pulling the rope for the appropriate side until the dog's reactions became automatic in response to the given command. Father required blind, unquestioning obedience from his dogs, never allowing them any freedom of thought or action once they had begun their training, when life became very serious with no fun. Even when out walking with Father the dog would have to walk close to heel all the way and there was never a 'That'll do' to signify the finish of work and the opportunity to play. This method was not thought to be cruel in the days when everybody's life was full of harsh realities and only the tough nuts survived—it was the same for both man and dog but, nevertheless, it was not long before I was beginning to question Father's methods and, with my own dogs, to look for training methods which included reward and play and also encouraged the dog to think for itself.

Of all poaching activities, the most exciting of all, to my mind, was when we went poaching for fish in the dead of night, the soft whispering voices of the men, the inky blackness, animal sounds, owls calling, the sound of the water and our hearts' beating. Father, whose eyes were watching the river all the time, knew exactly where the fish, big sea-trout, would be lying, and he would put a light over the water only long enough to gaff the silver fish which had been taken completely by surprise.

Then we were off, moving swiftly and quietly to elude the gamekeepers, who must have known what was going on but never managed to catch us. Of course, *the* most exciting place to poach fish was from the deep pools in the river Clwyd where it ran near to Nant Clwyd station—that was where the gamekeepers lived, and presented the challenge of taking an eight-to twelve-pound sea-trout from under their very noses. I was brought up in this fraternity of poachers, first as a listener to tales of derring-do, then as a watcher and, eventually, at about ten years of age, as a participant—and I think that there is nothing, to this day, not even sheepdog trialling, which compares to the sheer heart-bursting excitement of going out so many years ago with my father and his lurchers for a night's poaching.

Early days at sheepdog trials

My father was also a trials enthusiast and, as well as training on the smallholding at the smithy, he would take his dogs with him whenever he walked to the 'Fox and Hounds' in Pwllglas (a regular occurrence), training his dogs on everybody's sheep on the three or four farms along the three-mile route before finally arriving at the pub. Wherever my father put his cap, there the dogs would lie until it was time to go home. Such was the total obedience of these dogs that if somebody took Father's cap, the dog would go with the man who had the cap! In particular, I remember a grand little bitch called Jess—you could not move anything of my father's without her following it.

Forty or fifty years ago there were far fewer sheepdog trials than there are today, and for my father and his mate, Jack Ellis, trials day was a real day out, each trial being a great event and providing a sort of mini-holiday for men who worked long hours and had little leisure time. The pair of them would set out in Jack's little Austin 7 and I swear that that car knew every public house on the way to every trials field in North Wales!

Trials were usually held on a Saturday and, as soon as I was deemed old enough, I was allowed to go along with Father and Jack—the two men sitting in the front of the little car and myself in the back with the dogs, the frequent sorties into the pubs on the way providing more space, albeit temporary, for me and the dogs to stretch our legs. They were marvellous days out with a lot of laughter and hair-raising near-accidents occurring as the pub crawl went on, eventually arriving at the trials which were held in places where they have now become well established over the years—Llangollen, Llannefydd, Glyn Ceiriog, Ruthin, Denbigh and Pentrefoelas.

I remember once, at the Pentrefoelas trial—the judge was Canon Owen from Corwen who used to do a lot of judging at that time—Jack Ellis had a dog called Mick, and it was very

At the Pentrefoelas trial. Front row from left to right: Ifor Jones, John Jones, T. O. Jones. Back row: Canon G. Owen, Garnet Jones, J. D. Evans, Mr Evans, J. T. Jones, William Jones, Ted Jones, John Pugh.

unusual for Mick to do anything much at a trial, really, but on this particular day, he did very well until he reached the pen. Then the dog started to run round and round the sheep and the pen, so Father shouted to Jack, '*Stop* the dog.' Jack walked back to where Father was standing and yelled, 'You know perfectly well that I *can't* stop the bloody thing.' Canon Owen was using a shearing bench as his judge's seat and he fell off it, laughing at the pair of them arguing about whether Jack could stop his dog or not. I doubt if this sort of thing would happen at a trial today as we tend to take things so much more seriously now—both the competitors and the judges. Also at the Pentrefoelas trial on the same day, John Pritchard's bitch, Fan, a real greyhound/lurcher type, marked a rabbit which had hidden in the dry-stone wall at the side of the field, so John went over and took part of the wall down to get the rabbit out. If you did that now you'd be up in court for damage to property.

Another day I remember well was when I went to the new trial at Nannerch with Father, Jack Ellis and six dogs—all in the Austin 7, with Dad sitting in the back to keep the dogs from fighting. As usual, there were several stops at the pubs lining our route, both Father

and Jack getting so merry that when we arrived at Nannerch my father said he wasn't going to run, Jack said he couldn't, so I ran my dog and won the trial. I had £30 in my pocket on the way home and what a journey we had—Father and Jack decided to travel back over the Clwyds via the steep mountain road which comes out at the back of Llangwyfan. Jack was driving and Father was controlling the hand brake—the most memorable ride I have had in a car in my whole life.

As a youngster, I was much more interested in dogs, farming and country pursuits than in academic education, and it was, therefore, inevitable that, on leaving school at the age of fourteen, I should start my working life at Rhewl Bach Farm. I lived in as a member of the family and while I was there I bought my first dog and learned a smart lesson. I heard that a man in Llanfair Dyffryn Clwyd had a dog to sell so I cycled the three miles from the farm to see this man. He told me that the dog was a marvellous worker, extolling its virtues and saying that he was sorry that he had no sheep at present and so could not show me the dog working. I accepted the man's word about the dog's ability, bought it and took it back with me, only to find that he was useless with sheep and the only good thing he ever did was to go down every rabbit hole he could find. Needless to say, ever since that day I have never bought a dog without seeing it work first.

Four years later I left Rhewl Bach and went to work for Mr Griffiths who had taken over the tenancy of Derwen Hall. This was my first working contact with somebody who was not Welsh, and in the time I spent working there, I was introduced to ideas and a type of farming quite different to anything I had known before. One thing which greatly improved was my command of the English language, as I had not learned much of it at school, everybody being Welsh-speaking in the local community.

It was while I was working for Mr Griffiths that I began to take a really serious interest in training sheepdogs and I bought my first registered pup, arranging for it to be sent down from Scotland to Nant Clwyd station—the cost was £3, including the rail fare, and that was a lot of money at a time when I was only earning fifteen shillings a week. However, when the puppy, Jaff 6966, eventually arrived from Scotland, my Father said it was too good for me to ruin so I swopped Jaff for Meg, a little bitch of my father's who worked well enough for me but was not going to win trials. This was another lesson learned and I decided to buy myself another good puppy, determined to keep it for myself this time. I saw an advertisement in the *Farmers Weekly* and bought Glen 6967, a grandson of J. M. Wilson's International Supreme Champion Glen 3940 and bred by R. W. Brick out of his bitch Wyn 6050. Glen was delivered to the station for the sum of £5 and he turned out to be my first serious winning dog. It is from that time that the incurable disease known as 'Sheepdog Trialling' really began to get a hold on me and it has continued in its acute form ever since.

Turning points

When I purchased Glen 6967 in 1949 I was twenty-two years old and I decided that I would attempt to train and look after him in my own way and not rely on the methods of others. Looking back, it is difficult to recall exactly how my approach to training has changed and evolved in the ensuing years, but I do remember that I made a conscious decision to use methods which were totally different to those of my father except for the few areas where we were in agreement, such as always ending a lesson on a happy note.

Father would never groom a dog—it was just not done—nor would he ever show his dogs any affection, many working sheepdogs in those days being grossly undervalued, as the working horse and the milking cow were considered the most important animals on the farm at that time. Over the years I have seen a great change, with handlers showing more affection for their dogs and looking after them better, grooming and a well-balanced diet now being part of routine care. I have heard some people say that we are spoiling and pampering the working Border Collie but you only have to remember the bedraggled appearance and poor condition of some of the trials dogs of the old days to realise that, rather than spoiling the dogs, we have developed a better understanding of their physical and psychological needs. There have, of course, always been handlers who cared well for their dogs but there were far fewer then than there are now.

On the trials field today it is rare to see a dog that is not well looked after and rewarded with praise and affection. If you do happen to see an ill-cared-for dog, he sticks out like a sore thumb and, hopefully, once the handler is aware of this he will be spurred on to care for his dog better in the future. I believe that sheepdog trials have done much to improve the lot of the working sheepdog and will continue to do so.

As I had Glen from a puppy, we were inseparable and spent all our time together, becoming great companions and workmates, with a relationship built up on mutual trust and respect—and to this day I still believe that this is the best way with any dog when it comes to training. You get to know each other so well in those early days that when the time comes to start training in earnest you both start off on a much better footing: the dog has learned to listen to you, understands you and notices every intonation of your voice. This means that, when training starts and things are not going right, a change in your tone of voice is all that is needed to make the dog take notice. Compare this approach to buying in a young dog at, say, nine months of age—he may have been left for long periods on his own, may not even know his name, and that essential basic bond between dog and handler has not been established. It takes much time, patience and a different approach to train these dogs and is, generally speaking, less rewarding for both trainer and dog.

As with every puppy I have kept for training since that time, I took Glen with me everywhere I went so that he came to accept me as the pack leader, his number one in every situation he encountered. He was soon eager to work and very early on demonstrated a remarkable natural ability to stop on a sixpence, gradually developing into a handsome, black and white, rough-coated dog with a somewhat 'creeping' style, a lovely line and good tail carriage when working. Recognising

that Glen had great natural ability, I also realised that it was up to me to harness that ability with careful training if he was to achieve his full potential, and that I must avoid methods which would produce a robot-like response in the dog, giving him little chance to use his brain.

Glen's training progressed well, based on a system of reward, and I learned fast myself. I had to find ways of training which would avoid direct confrontation with the dog, as I realised that if you try to *make* a dog do something (rather than *encourage*), he will inevitably take up the challenge and try to win the battle—the worst thing that can happen when training dogs. It is important to recognise early development of bad habits and to nip them in the bud without making an issue of it—a real art and one which I am still trying to perfect.

By the time he was eighteen months old, Glen had won the Open Class trial at Nannerch and had also come first in the Open Class at Ruthin trial (I rode there on my bicycle with Glen sitting on the crossbar). I was over the moon with this success, partly because it was such a prestigious trial and also because the

PEDIGREE OF H. GLYN JONES' GLEN 6967
Rough-coated, black and white dog. Born 12/4/49

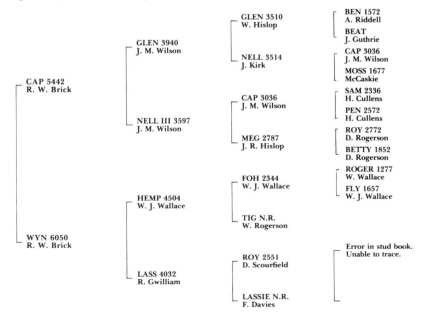

		GLEN 3510 W. Hislop	BEN 1572 A. Riddell
	GLEN 3940 J. M. Wilson		BEAT J. Guthrie
		NELL 3514 J. Kirk	CAP 3036 J. M. Wilson
CAP 5442 R. W. Brick			MOSS 1677 McCaskie
		CAP 3036 J. M. Wilson	SAM 2336 H. Cullens
	NELL III 3597 J. M. Wilson		PEN 2572 H. Cullens
		MEG 2787 J. R. Hislop	ROY 2772 D. Rogerson
			BETTY 1852 D. Rogerson
		FOH 2344 W. J. Wallace	ROGER 1277 W. Wallace
	HEMP 4504 W. J. Wallace		FLY 1657 W. J. Wallace
		TIG N.R. W. Rogerson	
WYN 6050 R. W. Brick			
		ROY 2551 D. Scourfield	Error in stud book. Unable to trace.
	LASS 4032 R. Gwilliam		
		LASSIE N.R. F. Davies	

prize money was £25—a small fortune to a young man whose weekly wage was thirty shillings—the prize money represented several months' wages to me.

Glen's greatest moment came when, at the age of two years, he won the Shepherds Class at the 1952 Welsh National at Swansea, earning us a place in the team to represent Wales at the International Sheep Dog Trials held later that year at Inverness, where we both watched Dai Daniel's winning run in the Supreme

called Roy, and the other was a dog by Jackie McDonald's marvellous little black and tan dog, Mirk 5444, who ran in the International Supreme Championship at Inverness in 1952, gaining fifth place. Unlike his father, Mirk never even looked at sheep and was quite useless! Sadly, both Glen and Roy picked up some poison somewhere and died—an utter disaster which left me with Mirk who wouldn't work and therefore with no dogs to work or enter for trials. I never did find out where the

A Border Collie in first-class working condition—a later Glen (92091), sire of Bwlch Taff.

Championship with his dog, Chip 4924.

After running Glen for two seasons and doing so well with him, I had built up an excellent relationship with him and I was looking forward to the future with him as I felt that, at two and a half, he had still not reached his full potential. Then, as so often happens in life when things are going really well, tragedy struck. At the time I had Glen, I also had two other young dogs. One was another excellent work and trials dog, an unregistered sheepdog

poison came from because we did not use rat poison on the farm on which I worked and the dogs had been nowhere else where they could have picked it up.

When Glen died I was so heartbroken that I had no stomach for starting all over again and I gave up the dogs altogether, leaving Wales to live and work on a farm in Cheshire where there was a herd of milking cows, the only dog being a German Shepherd. The farm was owned by three spinster sisters and their

A group of well-known Welsh handlers in the 1950s. Front row from left to right: Griff Pugh, Ifor Jones, Selwyn Jones, R. H. Williams, unknown, Alan Jones, Gwynfor Pritchard, Gwynedd Thomas, John Jones. Back row: D. Daniel, Mr Matthews, Bill Miles, W. J. Evans, E. L. Suter, unknown, unknown, Hywel Williams, Ted Jones, John Evans, Huw Davies, unknown, John Pritchard, R. E. Pritchard, J. H. Roberts.

seventy-year-old brother and they were all very good to me. I lived in, learning all the time and finding farm life in Cheshire quite different to farming in Wales which, up to this time, I had thought to be the only good farming area in the British Isles. The land on the Cheshire plain was very rich and fertile, providing a comfortable living for its farmers, in sharp contrast to the hill farms of North Wales where it was difficult to eke out an existence.

Whilst in Cheshire I must have been missing my dogs more than I cared to admit and it was probably inevitable that, eventually, I would be unable to resist the challenge of training the German Shepherd dog, not as a sheepdog but as a guard dog, before returning to work on the farm at Efenechtyd in North Wales which I had left in such sadness three and a half years before.

Return to Wales and back to sheepdogs

Immediately upon returning to Wales I went back into dogs and have never been without Border Collies from that day to this. I bought

Nap, a son of J. M. Wilson's Whitehope Nap, who turned out to be a smooth-coated killer, and Tweed 12324, who was a son of J. M. Wilson's Bill 9040 (the International Supreme Champion in 1954) and turned out to be a fantastic dog for work, trials and breeding. At the same time, I had a dog in for training called Moss. Moss 18885 belonged to R. H. Williams, Bryn Polyn, St Asaph, who was one of the top handlers in Wales at that time. I felt honoured that he should ask me to train his dog for him, only to be very disappointed when he rejected the dog at the end of the training period as a 'no-gooder'. He told me that I could keep the dog, and Moss subsequently turned out very well for me and won several trials. I also bought a bitch from Cecil Holmes—she was Wendy 13195, the bitch who, together with Moss and Tweed, founded the Bwlch line of Border Collies which my wife, Beryl, and I have developed, breeding and training registered Border Collies during the twenty-six years of our marriage. When Beryl and I were first married we lived in Pwllglas and I continued to work at Plas yn Llan until we were eventually able to rent a small farm, Bwlch Isaf, Bodfari, which we later bought and where we have lived and worked ever since.

As none of my dogs would work for Beryl when I was away, she decided to get a dog for herself, and that is when her interest in breeding Border Collies really began and the Bwlch line came into being. The dogs which we first used as sires were Moss 18885, Tweed 12324 and, later, Glen 92091, who was the father of my daughter Ceri's dog Bwlch Taff 113243, a son of Bwlch Bracken 74660. Wendy and Moss were the parents of our next Wendy 23844 who was mated to Tweed, and we kept a bitch puppy from this litter—Sheba 33229. Moss, Tweed, the two Wendys and Sheba all appear in the pedigrees of the Bwlch dogs up to the present day and I find it very interesting that I can see a lot of Moss in seven-year-old Bwlch Taff. Sheba proved to be one of the best bitches I have ever had for work, trials and breeding, and her granddaughter, Bwlch Bracken, had a very successful breeding, working and trialling career before her retirement— she is now fifteen years old, enjoying life on the farm, and, until recently, clearing fences and gates with the abandon of a two-year-old.

My daughters Ceri and Rhona with Sheba in 1965. (W. E. Jones)

A flexible approach

After my return from Cheshire, I had started to train dogs again for myself and also for other people. As my practical experience increased I gradually realised that every dog is different, necessitating a flexible approach when planning individual training programmes—an

PEDIGREE OF H. GLYN JONES' TWEED 12324
Rough-coated, black and white dog. Born 21/3/56

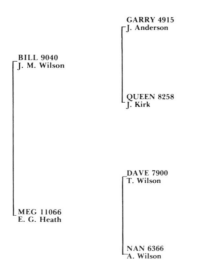

GARRY 4915
J. Anderson

BILL 9040
J. M. Wilson

QUEEN 8258
J. Kirk

DAVE 7900
T. Wilson

MEG 11066
E. G. Heath

NAN 6366
A. Wilson

GLEN 3957
S. Banks

GLEN 3510
W. Hislop

NELL 3514
W. Hislop

TIB 4458
S. Banks

SPOT 3369
J. McDonald

LINT N.R.
C. Scott

SWEEP 3834
W. J. Hislop

GLEN 3510
W. J. Hislop

NELL 3514
W. J. Hislop

LASSIE 6711
A. McCudden

CAP 3036
J. M. Wilson

TIB 2819
T. Brotherstone

DRIFT 4380
J. R. Millar

TAM 3465
J. Purdie

NORA N.R.
A. Carmichael

MEG 5623
D. Young

MONTY 3823
Illingsworth

JED 4770
Young

DRIFT 4380
J. R. Millar

TAM 3465
J. Purdie

NORA N.R.
A. Carmichael

CHARM 4020
Houston

CAP 3036
J. Wilson

FLOSS 3945
W. Wardrop

PEDIGREE OF H. GLYN JONES' WENDY 13195
Rough-coated, black and white bitch. Born 28/2/56

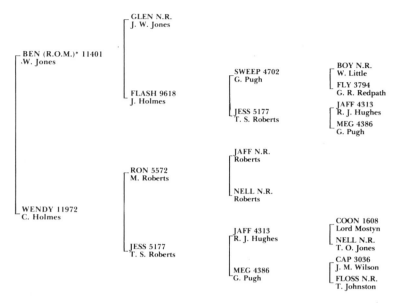

* Registered on merit

important discovery which has been continually reinforced from that day to this.

I soon found that, when training other people's dogs, I was spending much of my time correcting faults which had been allowed to develop between the time of birth and when the dog came to me for training. There were also other factors which lessened the enjoyment of training these dogs and probably also reduced the effectiveness of the training, i.e. if you take a dog to train for somebody else and are being paid for it, you want to get the dog trained as soon as possible, (a) to keep the cost down for the owner and (b) to release you to start training another dog. In addition, the strong, basic bond of affection and respect between the trainer and the dog is not present and can take a long time to develop sufficiently to produce a good working relationship. So the time came when Beryl and I decided to keep some of the puppies we were breeding to provide me with young dogs to train which had been home-reared, with early training initiated in the house and around the farm without the puppy realising that his training had, in fact, begun from his first, early days. Some of these puppies would later be sold on as farm or trials dogs and some remained with me to form my workforce and trialling partners throughout the years. I have occasionally bought young dogs in for training since that time but they have been in the minority.

CHAPTER 2

Choosing a Dog

THE OLD SAYING, 'You can't choose your relatives' is very true but you *can* choose both your friends and your dogs and, when involved with sheepdogs, three of the best friends you can have are your bank manager, your veterinary surgeon and your solicitor. I always remember when these thoughts first crystallised in my mind—it was after winning the Rembrandt International Trials at Ruthin with Gel (a now defunct trial which was then sponsored by Echo Jewellery of Ruthin). I was asked to be the guest of the Managing Director at a Rotary luncheon and it was not until after I had accepted the invitation that he suggested I might like to make an after-lunch speech. Never having made a speech in my life, and being in a position where it was impossible to decline, I agreed with some trepidation and wondered what on earth I was going to talk about until I contacted a friend of mine who is a solicitor. He said to me, 'Nobody can write a speech for you—all you have to do is to enjoy your lunch and then simply stand up and talk about the subject you know best—dogs!' When I stood up to make my speech, I saw that my bank manager and veterinary surgeon were also amongst the guests, so I based my speech on my dogs and these three friends of mine and, as predicted, I *was* able to talk enough to keep the audience interested.

I find that I like some dogs a lot more than others (as with people) and I always do better with those which I really like right from the start. I think it is necessary to remember that, if there is a clash of temperament between the

dog and handler, it does not necessarily mean that the dog is no good—he may do extremely well with a handler who has a different personality and approach, so this is one of the factors which should be considered when problems occur and particularly if you find yourself not liking the dog as his training progresses. As time goes on in your training and handling of dogs you will find, as I have done, that you will look for certain traits and characteristics which you have seen in other dogs you have trained successfully in the past. In a recent discussion at an Agricultural Training Board class (see Chapter 12) two young farmers were both saying of their own

My most treasured Welsh trophy—the Llanrhaeadr yn Mochnant trophy first won with Wendy and later with Spot, Roy, Gel and Lad.

dogs, 'This is the type I like.' Each was saying exactly the same thing about two dogs which not only looked different but also had totally different working styles. The interesting thing was that the two collies were litter brother and sister although their owners were not aware of this. Not only had these dogs been brought up by entirely different people, they were also *naturally* different to each other.

I firmly believe that one can, with experience, pick out traits in dogs from particular lines, even going back many generations. In the line which Beryl and I have developed (strongly based on Wiston Cap) it is possible to recognise a Wiston Cap type of puppy at a very early stage, one that not only looks like his illustrious ancestor but also moves and thinks like him. In my book, Wiston Cap was a marvellous dog, full of intelligence and innate ability, and I will never forget the first time I saw him working—I watched his run in the qualifying trial with his owner, Jock Richardson, and also, on the final day, the run which won the International Supreme Championship, and it was beautiful to watch. Latterly, it has become fashionable in some circles to denigrate Wiston Cap but I am convinced that he was one of the greatest dogs of all time and that any breeding problems have been caused by overuse of him as a stud dog, often to bitches whose owners did not give sufficient thought to suitability of lines. Too many people who should know better will take their bitches to a dog because he is an International, National or good Open trials winner, *not* because the line of the dog is compatible with that of the bitch. An additional factor has been that some breeders fail to check back at least five or six generations on both the sire's and the dam's sides to ensure that there are enough outcrosses in the lines before making a decision about mating.

I think that when you find a line of breeding which is right for you and is providing the type of puppies/dogs which you like (either as breeder or purchaser) you should stick with it. If you are breeding, you should try to keep to a

Jock Richardson with Wiston Cap. (Scottish Farmer)

pattern or breeding plan if you can—this is not easy to do and I would be the first to admit that, in addition to careful planning, there is always a measure of luck involved in the process. If you breed your own puppies, I think it is always easier to keep a bitch of the type you like because you can introduce a dog which you like, with compatible lines and characteristics complementary to, or balancing, those of the bitch. Then you will have a whole litter of pups from which to choose the one(s) you wish to keep. When buying a pup from another breeder one should always have a firm opinion as to the type of pup required and then not swerve from that until the right puppy appears. Never rush it and never buy one which falls short of *any* of the criteria you have set yourself.

PEDIGREE OF JOHN RICHARDSON'S WISTON CAP 31154
Rough-coated, black and white dog. Born 28/9/63

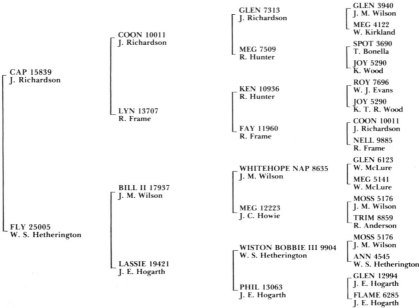

Whilst the experienced sheepdog handler will already have formulated his own ideas on how to choose a puppy for future training for work, and some to go on to sheep dog trialling, the novice handler invariably asks, 'How do I go about choosing a puppy in the first place?' and I will put forward my ideas on this subject in the hope that this will be of help, particularly to this latter group.

Doing your homework

Before even going to look at litters of Border Collie puppies, do your homework and do it well. Part of the homework for the novice is to consult your vet because you are going to need help and advice from your dog's doctor. He will be able to advise on vaccination programmes, diet, general care, and will inevitably be involved at some point in the well-being of your dog. Particularly if your eventual intention is to compete in sheepdog trials, go to trials and watch the dogs working, ask questions about the dogs which take your fancy, find out if their progeny are working/trialling, ask for advice from good handlers and learn as much

as possible before making up your mind. You will find that, if you demonstrate a real interest and a thirst for knowledge (and you are a good listener), all sheepdog handlers will be prepared to give you information about their own dogs—and the dogs of others—and, whilst naturally biased towards their own favourites, they will be able to give you sound counselling about the various breed-lines. In addition to this, there are now several very sound books on the market which include this sort of information and can offer fairly unbiased advice and information—so, in addition to travelling and talking, you should read round the subject, using several different sources of opinion. There is a list of recommended reading in Appendix 6.

Once you decide which breed-lines interest you most and which *you* feel will be the best one(s) from which to choose a puppy, you then need to make a decision as to the type of puppy you want—coat length and colour, personality, bitch or dog, a pedigreed dog (registered with the International Sheep Dog Society) or unregistered—always bearing in mind that you will need to have a registered dog to compete at the level of National or International standard. When considering the merits of registered pups versus unregistered it is important to remember that there are no checks on the eyes of unregistered stock (and their forebears) and that you are not able to trace the bloodlines sufficiently to ensure that inbreeding (the biggest common factor in inherited genetic disorders) has not occurred. I am not saying that the unregistered dog is no good! Many of them are first-class farm workers and some win trials which do not stipulate registration as a prerequisite for entry. But I *am* saying that if you are going to make a big investment in training a dog for work and/or trialling, then the odds against problems occurring are shortened when buying a registered pup.

Do not take too much notice of people who say that it does not matter what a sheepdog looks like as long as it works—there has never been a first-class dog yet which did not look good, and always remember that, if your dog or bitch is used for breeding at some time in the future, you will want both looks and brains. Everybody has differing requirements so be prepared to wait to get the puppy which you think will suit you and which meets the various criteria you have set. *Never* allow sentiment to sway your judgement when choosing a puppy—whilst this can often be a sound way to choose a pet dog, as many people can testify after giving a home to a homeless dog from an animal shelter, it is definitely *not* the way to choose a dog which is needed for high standards of work and sheepdog trialling.

In preference to going to a breeder who offers cheap pups which have not been particularly well reared, it is better to go to one who is known to rear first-class pups, even though he may charge a little more. This can be cheaper in the long run as properly fed pups from vaccinated and eye-tested stock are less at risk of disease and eye disorders; they are also likely to be more inquisitive, lively and outgoing, with better adapting ability when moved to strange surroundings.

Decision time

At some point you will find yourself looking at a lovely litter of puppies from parents you like and a breeder who is known to bring young pups up to be sturdy and healthy. The moment of decision is at hand! Personally, I think that when choosing your pup you should take your time and just stand and watch the litter for a while. Then pick the pup which pleases you most and which you like the look of. It is

This one's mine! Ceri with Bwlch Bracken and her puppies by E. Wyn Edwards' Bill. (Bee Photographs)

essential that you like your puppy right from the start as it is going to be with you for a long time, and if you do not like it 100 per cent you will not get the best out of it and neither you nor the dog will give each other sufficient reward to make it worthwhile to go on with training. The puppy is from an intelligent and sensitive breed and he will soon sense your feelings and respond accordingly. If this is your first Border Collie pup, I think you would be wise to choose one which tends to stay with the group, watching you with his head on one side, listening to you and weighing things up. Don't take the one which runs off to hide in a corner (that is giving way to sentiment—you feel sorry for it), and don't take the very bold one·which runs up to you before the others—he could be the one with a very well-developed 'leader of the pack' instinct which could cause battles with the handler (who should be the pack leader) during training.

It could be that, although the litter is from the lines you favour and the pups are basically sound, you find that there is not a particular one which takes your fancy. If this is the case *never* feel that you are bound to take one away with you simply because the breeder has taken the trouble to spend time while you look at the puppies. Any good dog breeder, although he may be disappointed, will understand if you leave without taking one of his pups, and you can always go back again if you change your mind!

Assuming that you have reached the point where you have found your puppy, there are one or two points to look for and some questions to be asked before sealing the transaction. It is a good idea for the novice to take along a list of these requirements to ensure that none are missed out in the excitement of having a future champion to take home with you. Remember that you and the pup have fallen in love with each other and we all know what falling in love can do to one's faculties!

What to look for

Straight back legs Watch the puppy as he moves about, particularly as he moves away

Spoiled for choice.

from you. His back legs should be nice and straight, there should be no sign of cow-hocks (hocks turned in and toes turned out) and his hips should move smoothly and freely.

Good bone The legs should be sturdy, with good, sound bones of medium length. Poor bone, bowing and enlarged joints could be a sign of rickets caused by poor feeding. Although the progress of this disorder can be reversed by a suitable feeding programme, you want your puppy to be sound right from the start. Paws should show no signs of soreness and there should be no dew claws on the hind legs.

Jaws Look closely at the puppy's mouth, checking that the teeth are clean and sound. The top set of teeth should fit closely over the bottom set. If there is any sign of an overshot or undershot jaw do not, on any account, take the puppy as this is a congenital defect which can affect the dog's eating ability and can be passed on to progeny if you breed.

Hernia Hold the puppy with his back towards you, support him with your legs and look carefully at the abdomen—this should be firm and clean and there should be no lumps in the groins or in the region of the umbilicus. Whilst occasionally a hernia will resolve itself as the puppy grows, the vast majority need surgical treatment to correct—all additional expense and risk.

Scrotum If you are buying a dog puppy, make sure that both testicles are down in the scrotal sac. If they are not, there could be problems with breeding later on.

Fleas While you have the puppy on his back, look at the soft skin on his abdomen and in the groins—if he is infested with fleas, there will almost certainly be small, telltale red spots where he has been bitten. Severe infestation can cause sores on both the abdomen (where they are easy to see) and on the body (where they are more difficult to see because of the density of the coat). (Also see Appendix 2.)

Sheep ticks Puppies can be infested with sheep ticks if the mother has been carrying them; they are to be found on the body and can be felt as small, hard nodules embedded in the skin. They are a blood-sucking parasite and, if the body is knocked off, the head can remain embedded in the skin and be a source of infection. (Also see Appendix 2.)

Ears Turn the ears back and look inside— they should be clean and free of smell. Small amounts of wax are sometimes visible but this should not be excessive.

Eyes The eyes should be clear and bright and there should be no evidence of soreness or infection. The very young puppy's eyes will be blue but they have usually begun the change towards brown by the time they are ready to leave the mother. Check that the colouring is the same in both eyes, as some dogs have one brown eye and one blue eye (these are often referred to as wall-eyed dogs). I find I can never take a fancy to a blue-eyed dog, always going for brown eyes, but this is a purely personal preference, so take your choice.

Healthy, bright-eyed pups.

Questions to ask the breeder

1. Has the puppy been wormed? When was this last done? All puppies should have been wormed at least twice by the time they are eight weeks of age.

2. When was the bitch last vaccinated? Has the puppy been vaccinated against parvovirus disease? In view of the rapidly increasing incidence of parvovirus disease in the British Isles (and in other parts of the world), it is important that the bitch has had adequate vaccination cover prior to the birth of the litter. It is now possible to have the bitch's blood tested, prior to whelping, for the immunity levels which she carries, and the vet can then advise the breeder at what age the puppies should be vaccinated. Providing the pups have suckled early and have had their fair share of colostrum (the first milk the bitch produces) they should have some immunity to parvovirus, and many breeders are now having puppies injected at around eight weeks of age with a recently introduced vaccine which provides almost 100 per cent immunity until the pups are sixteen weeks old—by which time they should have had their full course of injections and have full immunity for one year. (Also see Appendix 2.)

Taking an unvaccinated pup from an unvaccinated bitch is fraught with hazards and should be avoided. Some breeders and farmers will tell you that this is an unnecessary fad and that they never have their dogs vaccinated and have never lost any with parvovirus disease or any other disease. All I can say is that they will live to regret their irresponsibility and lack of care. If the pup you choose is over three months of age and has not been fully vaccinated, it is advisable to ask the breeder to have him vaccinated (you will have to cover the cost of this) and keep him for you for the time this takes—usually between two and four weeks (most breeders will agree to do this if you offer to pay the feed costs). This is necessary because an unvaccinated pup, put under the stress of a change of home, possibly preceded by a long

Real 'class'. Ted, son of Ceri's Bwlch Taff and Ted Jones' Kate.

journey in a car and strangers around him, is more likely to pick up any infection which might be lurking in his new surroundings. Remember, however clean you keep your dogs and their living accommodation, infection can still strike and it is better to be safe than sorry.

3. What is the age of the litter? The majority of breeders will keep a litter for about eight weeks before selling them. This gives time for the pups to develop their self-confidence; they are fully weaned, eating well, active and enquiring and ready for adaptation to change. I think that it is too young for Border Collie pups to leave familiar surroundings at the age of six to seven weeks but there will be many who would argue this point. Beryl and I have tried various feeding regimes over the years and find that the pups which do the best are those where weaning on to very small amounts of minced

meat starts at a very early age, two weeks being the norm, with three weeks the latest limit, and we leave the pups to suckle from the bitch for as long as possible, even if for only two or three minutes towards the end of the seventh week. This depends to a certain extent upon the number of pups in the litter and adequate feeding programmes for both bitch and pups. I think that puppies which are weaned completely from the bitch by the time they are around five weeks old lose the comfort of their mother's teat far too soon in life, and this can affect their stability and personality later on.

4. Have the parents of the litter been eye-tested and are they free of congenital eye disorders? The two main inherited eye problems in the Border Collie are Progressive Retinal Atrophy (PRA) and Collie Eye Anomaly

(CEA) (both of these conditions are described in Appendix 1). It is also a good idea to check the eye-test history for three to four generations back, particularly if you think you may wish to breed from your dog/bitch at a later date. This is quite simple to do: if dogs have been run in the National and International trials they will have been eye-tested as a requirement of entry; otherwise the Secretary of the International Sheep Dog Society, Chesham House, Bromham Road, Bedford MK40 2AA, will be able to provide you with the information.

5. If you want a registered puppy, ask for the registration numbers of both parents. Also let the breeder know that you want the puppy to be registered with the International Sheep Dog Society with your name as the owner, and see that he sketches your puppy on the ISDS litter registration form before you leave. If the puppy has already been registered with the breeder as the owner (this often happens if the pups are over eight weeks old), then both you and the breeder will need to complete the ISDS transfer form. Whichever way registration of ownership is done, you will eventually receive the appropriate certificate via the breeder. If the certificate does not arrive within a few weeks you should take the matter up with the breeder or, if problems occur, with the Society, who will help sort things out.

Travelling with a puppy

Most puppies, when travelling in a car for the first time, will salivate copiously and are usually sick at some point. If you have a passenger in the car who wishes to have the puppy lying on a blanket on his knee and does not mind being covered in vomit at some point, then that's fine. I would be the first to admit that puppies, wrapped in blankets and held securely on somebody's lap, often travel very well and probably feel very secure, but it's not for me! An alternative is to put the pup in a travelling box of some kind—one in which he can turn round and lie stretched out when resting. Straw, wood-shavings or torn-up paper can be used as a bed and will help to soak up any fluids. Always have fresh water available in case the pup gets thirsty. It is wiser to avoid feeding him either immediately prior to the journey or during the travelling time, providing this is not more than twelve hours. It is a good idea to take plenty of kitchen paper, rubber gloves and a plastic carrier bag for waste—then, if the puppy fouls his bed, it is a simple matter to remove the excreta and to keep the puppy reasonably clean and comfortable. The car will also be kept sweeter smelling—an important factor if your spouse is not as crazy as you are about the new puppy. If you have children travelling with you, an even better idea is to persuade them to be the nursemaids—with luck, the novelty will not wear off until they get home!

Puppies are very much like children and have a marvellous, built-in resilience. Once the journey is over and they are out of the car, they tend to bounce back very quickly. Don't worry if your pup doesn't want to eat—he will soon catch up with his food tomorrow—and a thing which can help a puppy to settle very quickly in his new surroundings is a piece of old blanket, a hide chew or other article which you have brought with you from his previous home. Don't be afraid of giving the pup a lot of attention at this point; handle him frequently and talk to him to help build his confidence in you—this is a time when you *can* be soft with him and perhaps we do not do enough of this at this stage in a dog's life. After all, things will get much tougher for him later on.

CHAPTER 3

Foundations

Choosing a name

As far as my father was concerned, there were only two names suitable for a Border Collie and these were Jess and Jaff—so it was always a standing joke in our house, and when a new puppy arrived there was only one guess for a male name and one for a female—and we were never wrong!

Choosing a name for a puppy is an important and very personal decision and the final choice should be a name which befits a future champion! As the Border Collie is a working dog, the name should be suitable for command in any work situation. A name is a requirement for registration of the dog with the International Sheep Dog Society, so you will need to give the matter careful thought, as the names which may be appropriate to the show dog world are completely unsuitable for the puppy who is going to have to work for his living when he grows up. The names should be short, preferably of one syllable, and easy to pronounce—many people like to look at the puppy's pedigree in order to choose a name from one of his ancestors, others will have a name which is a personal favourite. Once the decision has been made, always use the dog's name when with him, speak to him by name when taking his food to him, when calling him to you, when playing with him. In no time at all the puppy will have learned to listen to you and (sometimes) to react appropriately when you speak his name—his first important lesson has been learned.

One thing of which the novice needs to be

What shall we call her?

aware is that, once a pup has been registered with the ISDS, his registered name cannot be changed. However, there is no reason at all why you should not use another 'work name' if you wish.

Early rearing and the foundations of training

Some people say that, as long as a puppy is well fed and warm, there is no need to do much else with him until he begins to show interest in sheep. All I can say to that is 'Rubbish'. Treat him in many ways as you would a child, have fun, be sympathetic in times of trouble but also be firm so that he knows his boundaries of behaviour. Rearing puppies reminds me very much of the time when we used to keep sows at Bwlch Isaf—if I couldn't see them they were sure to be up to some mischief!

There is also an old saying concerning sows to the effect that every time you pass a sow you should give it a kick because, if it isn't already doing something wrong, it soon will be. Whilst I don't agree with the kicking bit, I do think that you always need to keep a beady eye on a young pup, and if you do not have time to watch him, put him in his own place, out of the way of trouble until you have more time to spare—then you don't have too many confrontations.

Rear your puppy well and let him have a happy and energetic puppyhood for the first three to four months of his life. The women in our house always get this job because, in my opinion, they do it much better than I can—they have enormous patience with young animals, they play with them, give them a lot of affection and have the puppies around them all the time both in the house and around the yard. They are experts at house-training the pups with the minimum amount of hassle and encourage them to become self-reliant, confident and happy in a secure environment. During this time, Beryl and the two girls make sure that the pup learns its name and they begin the early basics of training the pup to come when called, making it a pleasurable experience; the pup also learns to understand

variations in the tone of the human voice—he has been praised, told off, growled at, trodden on, declared to be useless, told he's a good dog, a bad dog, a nuisance, a pleasure to have around—whatever the appropriate term may be at a given time—and he is learning to *listen*.

One word of warning here, however. Before the puppy ever sets foot in the house it is essential that the various members of the family who will be involved in the early training process have discussed, and agreed upon, the commands and methods to be used. The puppy's proposed physical boundaries within the house must also be decided, i.e. it is no good one person patiently teaching the pup that he must not go beyond the kitchen if another takes him up to bed at night! The puppy will get confused and worried if his boundaries are not consistently observed in the same way and by all members of the family.

We always house-train our puppies, even if they are actually housed outside at night-time, as I feel that a dog should be able to adapt to any circumstances indoors or out. After all, this puppy of yours may become an eventual champion, travelling around with you to trials where an overnight stay is needed; possibly he will need to spend his night(s) in the room with you if there is no alternative kennelling

Puppies at play.

for him so it is essential to be prepared for this. Beryl always says that the Border Collie pup is so intelligent that house-training should never be a problem—if it is, then it is the humans involved who are at fault!

The best time to have a young puppy around the place is in the spring and summer as the back door can be left open and he can wander in and out as he pleases for most of the time— in this way it is very easy to house-train him with few accidents and, when the inevitable happens, a swift exit is easy to achieve. At other times of the year it is necessary to adopt a routine of putting the puppy outside at certain pre-fixed times such as before and after food, on waking from sleep first thing in the morning, after sleep periods during the day, after drinking and after a play session and last thing at night. With this type of regime, the puppy soon learns that his lavatory is outside the house and he will eventually stand at the door and ask to be let out. Inevitably, in the early stages, the puppy will be taken short when he is indoors so it is important to have him on a floor which is easy to clean and disinfect. In our house the kitchen is the puppy's first home as we think it is a mistake to leave these youngsters fastened up in an outhouse with nothing to do and nothing to see—imagine yourself in this situation and I am sure you will agree—how can we expect a dog who has had little or no stimulation as a puppy to give us his all when he starts serious training later on?

It is important to remember during these early days with a young puppy that, although we are beginning to lay the foundations for his introduction to serious training later on, we should also be having enormous *fun* with him, and the whole family can be involved in this. I feel that shepherds and farmers have the ideal environment in which to rear sheepdog puppies, bringing them up to take part in the everyday life of the family and the farmyard; the pups in these surroundings become accustomed to seeing, and being amongst, different kinds of stock, they are part of the general hurly-burly which takes place in a busy farmyard and usually meet their first sheep in a very natural manner simply because the sheep are there. For others, it is still possible to enjoy rearing a puppy and introducing him to stock from time to time but it certainly takes more effort in making suitable arrangements for this.

Housing

The way in which the young puppy (and, later, the dog) is housed is an important consideration and is something which should be carefully thought out when planning the long-term care of a working/trialling dog. Remember that this dog will be spending much of his time working in the wet and cold and he will need somewhere dry, warm and free of draughts in which to rest and sleep.

Before deciding the indoors/outdoors question, remember that your dog will not always be squeaky clean and shining—much of the time he will be wet and muddy with an

A bed of straw and a heat lamp in an outbuilding.

amazing skill at spreading as much of the dirt as possible on walls and furniture in a very short space of time. Short-coated Border Collies are easier to keep clean and are perhaps more suited to being in the house although the long-coated type is more pleasing in appearance to many people.

If your dog is going to live in the house, he should be given his own bed or basket, in a quiet corner or under a table, so that he has his own place to go to. He should be able to rely on some peace and quiet when on his bed—after all, human beings like to have a place of their own so why not the house dog? I think it is a good idea to have the puppy indoors for the first few nights at least, until he has accepted, and feels secure in, his new environment. Once settled in, my puppies are housed in a stone outbuilding at night with a bed of straw and plenty of room in which to run around if they wake up before being brought into the house for the day. *Never* tie or chain a puppy to inhibit his movements—he needs plenty of freedom at this stage, and another point is that a puppy will quickly get tangled up in a rope or chain and you will find yourself with a corpse if he panics. If there are no outbuildings, then a shed in the garden is quite suitable—the main thing is that the pup has some means of keeping warm, can move around and has quarters which are clean and free of draughts. Wherever he is housed, there should always be a bowl of fresh water available.

One of the reasons why I prefer my dogs to be housed out of doors once their real training begins is that if things go wrong during a training session and the dog runs back to the homestead (because that is his 'pad'), he will find that his world has collapsed around him. This is because the family, which has previously picked him up and cuddled him, will have nothing to do with him in this situation—he will get no sympathy from them and will not be able to understand the change. If he is already living out of doors, he is unlikely to run back to the house for comfort and is, therefore, not placed in a confusing situation when times are a bit hard for him.

When my pups are about seven or eight months of age I begin to prepare them for their adult living quarters. I like my dogs to be able to see each other and also to see what is going

on around them but this presents me with a problem as the yard of my farm is also a public right of way which is hazardous when used by vehicles. So, I use kennels and train the dogs to being fastened on a chain when in their kennel—all the kennels are arranged in a semicircle and are situated near the yard where the dogs can feel a part of what is going on there without coming to any harm. I would be the first to acknowledge that this is not necessarily the best way to house dogs and I consider the ideal is to have kennels with separate covered runs for each dog—these give the dog plenty of freedom to move around and can be easily cleaned by hosing down at regular intervals.

Lyn chained to a well-worn but waterproof kennel.

(A word of warning here—if concrete runs are laid for purposes of hygiene, it is advisable to cover the concrete floor with movable wooden duckboards as dogs can get very sore pads from playing around on a concrete surface. The boards should be in sections for ease of removal and the spaces between the wooden slats should be no more than three-quarters of an inch.)

An additional bonus with this type of housing is that the dogs play and move around their runs thus exercising themselves in a very natural way, they can see each other and, even more important, they are very much aware of what is going on around them because they can *see* what is happening outside the runs. The snag is that kennels with runs are expensive, even if home-made, and it is not every-body who is prepared, or able, to invest in this type of accommodation.

There are plenty of different ways of housing your dog out of doors, and there are an increasing number of advertisements for ready-made housing and runs for dogs. The thing to do is to explore all the alternatives and then go for the one which you feel will be the most suitable for you, your dog, your situation and your purse.

Wherever your young dog is housed you will need to get him used to being fastened up for short periods from the age of six months or so. Choose a place from which he can see you as you are working or moving around and he will soon learn to sit and watch and will be content in the knowledge that the boss is still around. Again, these periods should be very short indeed to start with, gradually lengthening the time of restraint. This will stand both you and the dog in good stead later on both in the work situation and at trials, where it is often better for your dogs to be tied up outside the car where there is more movement of air and the dogs can see, and feel a part of, what is going on. Additionally, this is a good way of training a dog to the introduction of a lead and is much better than his being dragged around on the end of a lead while he gets used to the restriction imposed upon him. If he is used to being chained for short periods, the young dog is unlikely to fight against the lead when this is introduced—again avoiding confrontation with the handler.

The art of chaining a dog

As I have already mentioned, great care must always be taken whenever it is necessary to fasten a dog to a chain for short periods and you should always follow one golden rule—if you are not certain that the situation is perfectly safe and that the dog can come to no harm, then find some other way of keeping him under restraint.

DO use a light chain for young dogs and a sturdy chain for adult dogs.

DO ensure that the chain has two swivels—one at each end of the chain—and a sturdy clip to attach to a metal ring on the dog's collar. These swivels are absolutely *essential to the dog's safety* as without them the chain will twist and shorten surprisingly quickly as the dog moves around and thus can be very dangerous.

DO make sure that the metal ring on the collar will slip round the collar as the dog moves. Most collars have a *fixed* ring which I do not

(Above) *A sturdy chain with two swivels.*
(B. Collins)

(Left) *An augur spike.*
(B. Collins)

use as it can cause the collar to slip continuously around the dog's neck causing unnecessary discomfort. Additional metal rings can be found in most hardware or pet shops.

DO fasten the chain to a wall-fixing placed about eighteen inches to two feet above ground level, making sure that there is absolutely nothing upon which the chain can catch.

DO use an augur spike when chaining a dog out in the open field—even this must be used correctly and with care and must be pushed right into the ground so that there is absolutely nothing at all on which the chain can catch.

DO make sure that a chained dog is released regularly for exercise and that he either has a bowl of water available or, if he insists on tipping this over, as some of them do, that he has regular access to water.

DO NOT fasten the dog with a rope or leather lead—he will simply lie down and quietly chew his way through these!

DO NOT fasten the dog where there is a low fence for him to jump over and hang himself or from a point where he can reach a sudden drop in ground level—another way to self-destruction.

DO NOT tie the dog to a tree (or close to a tree) as he can run round and round this, shortening the chain and eventually strangling himself.

DO NOT chain a dog outside for long periods in bad weather unless there is some shelter available, and do not leave him in intense heat and full sun—make sure that there is always some shade available.

Beginning more serious training

I always think that training a dog is a bit like conducting a choir—the conductor needs to

A happy puppyhood.

know the basis of his subject and what he is after, then he gets the result he wants out of the choir by planning, patience, request, cajoling, repetition and being accepted as the boss. Training a dog is exactly the same, the only difference being that when training a dog to work with stock, we need to teach him to listen to us but not to watch us in the way that a choir watches the conductor—the dog should be watching the stock and that is what his eyes are for. If a young dog does look back during training it usually means that you are not maintaining adequate voice contact with him to help him to maintain his confidence.

When the pup has been reared as a pet for the first few months of his life, it can be very difficult for the novice handler to make the decision to introduce the family's new 'baby' to the type of life he is going to live when he starts serious training for work and/or trialling. You may, of course, have decided that the dog will continue to live in the house and many handlers' dogs are house-dogs and pets whilst training and eventually working. This can be very rewarding to both dog and handler, but I would strongly advise the novice handler, or the person new to training a young dog, to begin to take the pup over at the age of about four months in order to establish that important bond which is so essential in the relationship between the young dog and his trainer. This is what I always do, taking the pup with me and showing him to stock for short periods, interspersed with short sessions in the yard, getting the pup to come to me when called. Very soon, the pup comes to associate *me* (and not others) with something good, i.e. going for a run in the field with the sheep and being praised when coming back; going out in the pick-up with me everywhere I go and sharing with me in as many different experiences as possible. I take him to the market each week to get him used to seeing many different faces and hearing the animal noises and the general clamour of a busy beast market. Very soon, the bond with the family is broken and the bond with me has been established. From the beginning of this period in the puppy's life, he begins to live outside in his kennel when he is not with me, the daytime periods in his new home being short at first as he is with me all the time for most of his waking hours. He gradually begins to look upon his kennel as his own 'pad' (rather in the way human beings look upon their own homes)—a place in which to rest, relax and, we hope, to think about the day's events before going to sleep.

All this time, the beginnings of training are occurring without the pup realising it and without any confrontations between myself and the pup, who begins to associate work situations with the pleasure of being with his boss and something to look forward to. He has his own comfortable kennel to go back to at the end of the day, or when work and play are finished for the time being, and, a very important point, I am becoming the pack leader for the dog. From this time on, the rest of the family are not allowed to interfere with the training programme and it is not until much later that the dog will be taken into the house again.

By and large, puppies which show an early interest in sheep tend, in my experience, to do better than the ones which show late. Although there may be some exceptions to this rule, I have never found any and, at least if the interest is there early on, I know that I can do something with the dog. You hear of dogs that have taken no interest for twelve, eighteen or even twenty-four months and then they have suddenly taken off—all I can say to that is that

Four-month-old Mirk shows an early interest in sheep.

two years is a long time to wait to see if a dog has it in him or not! A lack of opportunities to see sheep can, I am sure, retard the development of interest, and I believe that the interest will develop sooner rather than later if a pup is taken out to sheep from the age of four or five months at least two or three times a week. Equally, if you have a young dog which is not taking much interest, there is no way that we can force the development of the herding instinct and great patience is needed at this stage. You simply need to keep taking your dog to sheep in the sure knowledge that the day *will* come when, hey presto!, a change in his behaviour signals the fact that it has finally happened—our dream has come true and we have a young dog which is now showing signs of starting to work with stock.

The three basics of obedience

'Come here'

By the time a pup is six or seven months old he should be lively, confident, interested enough to chase sheep and should have learned the basics of 'Come here', 'Lie down' and 'Stay there'. These are simple and *essential* obedience requirements in the early stages of yard training and, of the three, the 'Come here' command is the all-important one in my book—it comes into so many areas of stock-handling, be it singling, shedding or driving, and the dog needs to learn very young that he *must* come to you when required to do so. Always remember that you will want your dog to come *straight* to you so never teach him to come to heel—if you do, he will always try to come to your side and you do not want this when moving sheep. To teach a pup to come to me, I work at very close quarters to him initially, bending down directly in front of the dog and holding his collar, ready to welcome him and meet him halfway. I then give the command 'Come here', gently pulling on the collar, and he very soon gets the idea that he must come straight to me, quickly learning that this pleases me. Some people use

'*Come here*'. (B. Hamer)

food to get the pup to come to them but I have never found this to be necessary and I think that this type of reward system can lead to inappropriate behaviour in the working dog. It works very well for dogs trained specifically for obedience but not, in my opinion, for dogs that are going to have to work with stock, and I am firmly convinced that once the three 'basics' of obedience have been learned, training a dog for work and sheepdog trialling needs a very different approach to training a dog for more advanced obedience work. I think that we can learn a lot from the obedience world when teaching our pups to 'Come here', 'Lie down' and 'Stay there', but, once this is achieved, the two methods of training diverge towards their own particular specialist techniques.

One of the most common faults I see in the training of youngsters is when a pup that at first ignores the command to return is given a good hiding when he finally does return to the handler—the worst thing you can do, as he will then associate coming to you with something unpleasant. However long the pup has taken to come to you, you *must* keep your cool, praise him for returning and then *let him go again*! Do this several times before putting him back on to a lead. He then begins to enjoy coming back to you because he associates this with pleasure and the reward of being let go again. It takes a lot of patience but the rewards to both you and your dog will remain throughout your long working partnership together.

A word of warning is, perhaps, necessary

here as it is important to remember that you cannot expect your young dog to always come back to you when he is taken out to the sheep—this is an unrealistic expectation when he is out there having a whale of a time, running around and generally letting off steam—and do not keep calling him to you at this stage either, or he will simply get used to ignoring you! Just bear in mind that he will eventually get tired and you will then have some chance of catching up with him.

'Lie down' (the stop command)

This always starts off with lessons in the yard with the dog on a short lead. I make sure that I have the pup's full attention and that there is nothing going on in the yard which may encourage him to turn his attention elsewhere. I call the dog by name and, as soon as he looks at me I give the stop command, 'Lie down'. At the same time, I press firmly on the dog's back with the flat of my hand until he goes down, repeating this several times and praising him if he does as he is asked. Some dogs learn this very quickly but others are more difficult, flatly refusing to go down, and if the dog really objects to lying down I try to work out the reason why. Nine times out of ten I find that the dog is simply lacking in confidence and just needs a little more time before he is ready to accept this form of restraint. Sometimes a young dog simply dislikes the feel of the pressure on his back.

If the dog is being really bloody-minded I gain his attention once again (if necessary, holding his collar with one hand and cupping his chin with the other to make sure he looks at me as I speak his name) and then have another go. If I find that I have a really stubborn pup who wants only to play, I put him on to a lead and put my foot on the lead to keep his head down. Then I hold the front legs on and below the elbow and, on the command 'Lie down', I gently slide the pup's legs forward so that he is lying down. As soon as he is down, I put my hand along his back and then let go, still standing on the lead. This method ensures that

there is no real confrontation with the dog; he gradually gets used to the feel of a hand on his back and it is not long before he will respond to the first method. It is better to keep these lessons very short and give them several times a day than to have one long lesson when the dog will become bored and then lose concentration. After all, he is still only very young so you can take your time with him.

'Stay there'

'Stay there' means that the dog *must* stay wherever you have stopped him with the 'Lie down' command. Once he is down, you then tell him to 'Stay there' and, if he moves, place him firmly back to where he was before and start again. It is not that the position means anything in itself but simply that the dog *must* stay there until given permission to move. You want complete obedience at this stage so make sure that you only expect the dog to 'Stay there' for a couple of seconds to start with, gradually lengthening the time as he begins to know what is expected of him. Once the dog will 'Stay there' with you standing close to him, gradually lengthen the distance between yourself and the dog while he is lying down. Again, the length of time this takes will vary from dog to dog but you will get there in the end if you are firm, consistent and patient.

Some dogs take longer than others to learn at this time in their training but, after several weeks of consistent training in the three basics, we should finally have a young dog who is ready to begin his training with the sheep, and although at first he will forget most of his learning once he is amongst sheep, at least both you and the dog know that *he* does know and understand these basic commands. I always feel that, once I can stop a dog when there are sheep around, the worst is over and it gives both me and the dog the confidence to really get on with the job—in other words, we can go into a higher gear. This is when I start walking, walking, walking and explains why, after so many years of training dogs, I am an expert in the art of walking backwards!

CHAPTER 4

From Play to Work

WHENEVER I THINK of training a dog, I always remember Hemp 36879, a grand dog with a lot of natural ability bred by A. J. Bevan out of his bitch, Mist 19773, and by Brady's Buff 23069. When I started Hemp's training I decided that I was going to be his master, his friend, his eyes, his ears—the lot—and we got on splendidly. Hemp had considerable potential and lived for work, learning quickly and soon becoming a very useful dog indeed. We eventually represented Wales at the International trials at Towyn in 1968 where we won the Farmers Championship at the end of the qualifying trials. This meant that we were eligible to run in the Supreme Championship on the final day, and it was then that I realised that I had made a grave mistake—on that testing course, it is essential to have a dog who not only listens and responds to commands, but is also able to use his loaf and work things out for himself. I had taught Hemp to rely solely on my commands and *not* to use his excellent brain, and on that day I realised that I had spoiled him and that our failure was not the dog's fault, it was entirely mine. I had learned a salutary lesson.

There is now no doubt in my mind that a good dog, properly trained, will be able to differentiate between his farm work and trialling. For instance, when I go up on the mountain which provides my sheep with a lot of their summer grazing and send Bwlch Taff out, I know that, even if he is out of sight or cannot hear my whistles, he will *always* bring the sheep to me whatever happens, i.e. he is

using his brain. On the trials field, it is somewhat different as he then relies on me to give him correct commands and in good time to enable him to complete his task well. However, there are moments when he needs to think for himself on the trials field, even if it is only for that split second which can make all the difference between success and failure (this is particularly relevant when penning), and our training methods must take all this into account.

An example of Bwlch Taff using his brain on the trials field is when we are at the pen with difficult sheep. For instance, if there is one unruly ewe, Taff will stand with his eyes

With Hemp in 1968. (North Wales Press Agency)

31

glued on her, trying to anticipate her every movement—his head and shoulders will turn slightly with any small movement the ewe makes and, if she breaks, he is ready and in the correct position to move in whatever direction he needs to go to prevent her from breaking away.

This is probably a suitable place for me to state that I do not think anybody can say 'This is *the* way to train a sheepdog', and when people ask for teaching, guidance and help in the training of dogs I can only tell them what works for *me*. Training sheepdogs may not be a science but it is certainly an art and everybody who starts to train dogs will learn much from others, even more, perhaps, from their own experience, and will eventually distil all their knowledge and thinking into a method of training which works for them. One thing of which I am sure is that we must be very responsible and flexible in our breeding and training programmes and always have a clear idea of the end-product for which we are aiming. After all, we are trying to continue the development of an intelligent animal which has been with us for genera-tions past and is going to be with us for generations hence—if we breed from the best robots and train the progeny to become even more robot-like, where will it all end?

Anybody who says they can train a dog in a matter of a few weeks is up the creek, in my opinion—in such a short period they have not had the time in which to develop the contact with the dog which is necessary and the dog will not have the stability and confidence required to develop and maintain a continu-ously high standard of performance. This sort of thing takes time and cannot be rushed. Most of the good things in life are not easily achieved—you will hear people saying, 'He's a lucky man, having a dog like that', of many a successful handler but, of course, whilst we all need a measure of luck in our undertakings, there is far more to training a dog than that! These handlers have all spent many hours patiently training their dogs before reaching such perfection and it is little to do with lady luck. Whilst I accept that all dogs (and handlers) will not achieve the same high standard, even with similar training, it is the ideal for which we should always be striving—

PEDIGREE OF H. GLYN JONES' HEMP 36879
Rough-coated, black and white dog. Born 17/12/64

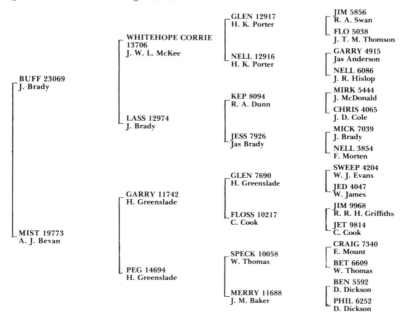

Bwlch Taff with daughter Lyn. (Neville Pratt)

The long rope

In general, I do not use a long rope as a training aid and one of the reasons I am so much against it is that I have seen it greatly abused in practice, although, if utilised with common sense, it can be useful in certain circumstances. In my opinion, the long rope should only be used by a very good trainer who has been asked to re-train a dog which has been allowed to develop bad habits—a type of training which requires very different techniques and controls and which should only be undertaken by the most experienced and able trainers. For the novice handler to use a rope in the early stages of training leads to its misuse, as once the handler realises that the rope gives him power over the pup and its movements, I think that he will come to rely on this to control the pup rather than on his own ability. Remember that I am talking now about the novice trainer who has reared his own pup, given him a secure, consistent environment and trained him in basic obedience in the first place; a need to use a rope in these circumstances stems, generally speaking, from the handler's lack of confidence—he needs to stand back and try to analyse where he has gone wrong if he feels that he has to use a long rope on this home-reared pup.

Those exciting things called sheep

When letting a young pup loose amongst sheep in his very early days, I just let him run in and enjoy himself for a while—he will probably scatter the sheep to the four corners of the field, chasing them and going generally bananas, so it is necessary to have some well-dogged sheep (it is worth the novice trainer's while to buy some in for starting off a young dog). The main thing is that the dog must associate stock with pleasure, be motivated to take an interest in them and, eventually, develop a desire to please his boss by bringing the sheep to his handler. I *always* make a great fuss of the pup when he (finally) comes off the stock and back to me. While all this is going on

we must never be satisfied with the mediocre and should always aim for that little bit (or a lot) extra in the performance of both ourselves and our dogs. There seems to be a general belief in the dog world that most handlers only ever have one really good dog and that when that dog goes there will never be another like it. To my mind, this is defeatist, and one should always think, when a good dog goes, that the next one will be even better. If we think constructively, we should be able to build on the experience gained with that good dog and use it to modify our approach to the next dog, which then has a better chance of becoming a champion. The perennial question is 'How do we do this?' and if there was any one answer I think that a lot of the fun and excitement would be taken out of the game.

I am assessing what type of pup I have: How much 'eye' does he have? Is he a gripper? Has he got a natural cast? How much natural ability does he show? This is a process rather like 'reading' the dog and, at this stage, I do not use any commands, preferring to find out what he likes to do and what he avoids doing—unlike my father who would have been demanding blind obedience in all things at this stage. I have no control at all over the pup at

both the young dog and the handler so it is better for the novice to stick with a smaller number which both he and the dog can manage.

Sheep which are used to dogs and their handlers will know that while they are with the handler they are fairly safe, but that if they pass him they are going to be chased. In other words, the sheep have been trained and the whole point of this exercise is that wherever I

Those exciting things called sheep. Thomas Longton with Bess. (Marc Henrie)

this point and do not want it as every dog has a different approach to stock and this is a finding-out time for both me and my pupil.

The ideal number of sheep for the novice handler is about ten and should never be less than five—I like to go to twenty or thirty sheep with a young pup and then when he has scattered them he will still have a small bunch left to bring to me. However, having spare sheep around in the field can be confusing to

go, the dog should bring the sheep to me once he has gone round behind them. I walk backwards so as to get the sheep to follow me and the pup to follow the sheep—an enabling process in which the pup will think that he is doing all the work, for which he can be praised mightily—and so we are off to a good start.

There are many people now training dogs for trialling who have no real work for their dogs, not being farmers or shepherds, and it is much more difficult for them to do the training. Things are easier for the farmer or shepherd who can introduce his young dogs to sheep at an early age in a very natural manner. The puppy will have travelled around with his handler, often in the company of other dogs, and will be a more free-range animal than the one which does not have this type of life. He may also have done quite a lot of farm work before he undergoes more formal training, so readers who are already in this situation may find some of the early stages I am describing to be irrelevant to their needs and may wish to move on to later chapters where more advanced training techniques are discussed. However, for the complete novice, whether he tends a flock of sheep or not, these first chapters are essential reading if he is hoping to do the job properly—and particularly if he is intending to go on to trialling when the dog has been trained.

Categories of pup

I have heard of pups who, the very first time they see sheep, have run round to the back of them to head them, but I have never had one myself—a pleasure still to come, perhaps. But most pups when introduced to sheep for the first time seem to fall into three categories or groups: the first group drop down as if shot and just stare at the sheep as though hypnotised; the second group will chase the sheep, scattering them all over the place, and then will lose interest and run back to the handler; the third group will drive the sheep away into the furthest corner of the field and hold them against a fence or hedge.

Of the three categories, the first and the third are the most common in my experience. These two types tend to be slightly more difficult to train in the beginning although this does not necessarily mean that they will not be as good as the others in the long run. The second type is relatively easy to cope with in the early stages once you have a good stop on them—at least they are moving and on their

feet all the time—whilst the others can be little horrors and the handler has to concentrate on getting them moving freely around the sheep. Remember that whatever the type, the first objective (and the first field lesson for the pup) is to get him on the far side of the sheep—in other words, to get the sheep between the handler and the pup.

Formal or field training begins

For the first few formal training sessions with the sheep, I carry the pup under my arm out on to the field—this is by far the best way to take a youngster, for if he is dancing about on the end of a lead he will spook the sheep and generally unsettle them.

Before a handler lets his pup go, he must

Carrying the pup under my arm—Mirk and Bwlch Taff.

ensure that the sheep are in the middle of the field, either by using a trained dog for this purpose or by doing the job himself. With my first objective firmly in mind, away we go—I walk as near to the sheep as I can and, when they turn and begin to move away, I let go of my charge and pray!

With the first category of youngster who wants to eye his sheep all the time, my prayer is unlikely to be answered, and if the little brute drops straight down to the ground, I put and keep myself in a position where I am on the opposite side of the sheep to the dog and then I encourage him to walk towards me. As the pup comes towards me the sheep will move too, providing I walk backwards to give them room to move forwards. By moving the sheep one way and another in a continuous move-ment I *will* get the pup moving eventually and in no way will I allow him to get to the same side of the sheep as I am. If he tries to pass the sheep then I will need to block him in some way, but the most likely thing is that he will keep sticking and 'eyeing' the sheep, particu-larly if they are not going fast enough to encourage the pup to move forward. This type of pup is less likely to move around freely because his great amount of 'eye' holds him back all the time, but one great advantage is that a lot of eye will help to stop him as he will invariably stop to 'eye' his sheep when he has headed them. If you have this type of pup and experience difficulty in getting him to move around, don't despair, as there have been many outstanding dogs who started off in this way. My own excellent dog Tweed (already mentioned in Chapter 1) also had a lot of 'eye', clapping down and staring at his sheep as a youngster, and it took a lot of time and patience to get him 'flowing' and to teach him to stand on his feet instead of spending half his life on his belly with his eyes glued to the sheep—but it was all worth while in the end and he became a very powerful, stylish worker who was as much at home on the trials field as on the farm.

'Loose-eyed' is the term we use to describe

the second category of youngster who likes to run in and scatter his sheep all the time, and although he is allowed to do this in the very early days when the handler is assessing the pup's natural potential, the time comes when this should no longer be allowed, as, once he gets into the habit of doing this all the time, it will be almost impossible to correct. With this type of pup it is essential to make sure that he fully knows his 'Lie down' and 'Stay there' commands during yard training as this will be the only way you can stop him from scattering his sheep.

Whilst I always prefer young dogs with a lot of determination and spirit, I must admit that the third category of pup presents a great challenge to my patience as they go forward with their heads down, rather like little bull-dozers, with just one thought in their minds, and that is to get the sheep against a hedge or a wall and hold them there, come what may. With these, I adopt similar tactics as with the first group, keeping myself close to the sheep and not allowing the pup to get too far away. As mentioned before, it is absolutely essential to have a bunch of sheep in the middle of the field when taking the youngster out, and at no time is it more important than with this type as

Getting out to the far side of sheep and bringing them towards the handler.

the very last thing you want is to work him up against a hedge where he can stick with his sheep and 'eye' them to his heart's content.

Whatever type of pup we have it is important to understand that, although there is some slight variation in the way he gets behind his sheep, these early lessons run on similar lines, with the main aim being to get the pup moving round the sheep, initially *following* them, as they follow the handler and, as the pup begins to get the idea, eventually *bringing* the sheep to the handler.

So now we have a youngster going out to the far side of the sheep (with a little help from the handler) and bringing them towards you whichever way you go. The lessons in the three basics in the yard are part of his daily routine and, most importantly, there is a growing measure of trust, affection and respect between teacher and pupil. Life for the dog is beginning to change from one of fun and play to one divided into times for work and play and things are beginning to get a bit more serious, although life should still be enjoyable for both handler and dog.

Use of the experienced dog when training youngsters

If you have an older, experienced dog, it is a good idea to have him to hand to round up the sheep from time to time, telling him to 'Lie down and stay there' when his services are not required (another example of the usefulness of the 'Stay there' command). A young pup does not, in my opinion, learn anything from working with an older dog—he needs to be on his own. However, it does help to build up the youngster's confidence if he is not losing his sheep all the time, and the use of the older dog to round them up whenever necessary helps the pup to maintain contact with his flock. For the novice handler without another dog, this early training time is going to involve some extra walking when the sheep have scattered or gone too far; with reasonably quiet sheep it is quite possible to get them together without

too much fuss, but with sheep straight from the mountain which have seen few dogs or human beings in their lives, it is virtually impossible to control both pup and sheep in this situation. The pup will get too excited and the levels of stress to which the sheep will be subjected will be unacceptably high.

Alternative method of introducing a young dog to sheep

For the novice handler who has neither an older trained dog nor his own trained sheep, there is an alternative way of introducing the youngster to stock for the first time. This is particularly useful if you are using somebody else's sheep and wish to reassure their owner that his sheep will be quite safe (and that you intend to behave in a responsible manner).

Put about five sheep into a small, circular pen in the middle of a field and close the pen gate. You can then take the young dog out to his bunch of sheep, which are safe in the pen, and when you let the dog go free he can see his sheep but he cannot do any damage. This manoeuvre achieves several things all at once: (a) the sheep will remain in one place, (b) the sheep will be less stressed than if being chased all over the field, (c) the owner of the sheep is more likely to allow the novice handler and dog to do their early training on his land, (d) the handler will be in a position to control his dog more easily and (e) the handler can concentrate on the dog.

Make no mistake about it: training a puppy is extremely hard work, requiring patience, time and the development of skills on the part of handler as well as pup. You will both get tired and dispirited at times but it is essential that you do not allow yourself to lose your temper with the puppy at any point—if there is any danger at all of this happening then stop the lesson, go home and have another go the next day when you are both more relaxed and rested and you have had time to simmer down, analyse the problem and work out what went wrong and why, so that you can avoid a recurrence. Never forget that losing your temper with any dog is invariably counter-productive, as one bout of bad temper can destroy all the careful work of several months by introducing an inconsistency which the dog is not able to understand.

Stopping the young dog on the field

Eventually the day comes when the dog, probably as much to his own surprise as mine, lies down on command when working with the sheep—then we *are* getting somewhere! It means that the dog is at last beginning to make some sort of a connection between his lessons in the yard and his time with the sheep. People always ask 'How long will this take?' or 'When will this happen?' and it is something which I can never answer because every dog is so different and they all progress at different rates. But a guide would be that, if you have a young dog out in the yard for very short lessons over a period of about four weeks, then by the end of that time you should be able to get him to come to you and to stop—not necessarily immediately but he should be beginning to understand what is expected of him and to listen to the command eventually and act upon it. Be patient here and do not fall into the trap of being too insistent on obedience too soon. Give the dog some time and then, if he is still refusing to do as he is asked when out in the field with the sheep, it means that you have not been firm and thorough enough in your lessons in the yard. Remember that the yard is the place where you can *insist* on the stop in these early days—so, if he disobeys on the field, avoid confrontations there and go back to the yard where, if you feel that the dog is deliberately disobeying you, you can be really firm with him. Once he is completely obedient in the yard, it *will* come eventually when out in the field with the sheep.

Probably the most difficult thing for the novice handler is getting a good stop on his dog. It is no use shouting 'Lie down' to a young dog who is hell-bent on getting to his sheep—all you will actually do in this situation is to teach him to disobey you as you would be asking too much of him. When I was discussing this with a young handler at a class recently I was pleased to hear him say, 'If I can anticipate the time when the dog intends to stop, I then tell him to "Lie down" and he stops as good as gold because he had been going to do that anyway.' By doing this the young man had achieved two things: (a) the dog obeyed a given command, earning praise from the handler and (b) the dog was not given the opportunity to disobey. A golden rule is to give your young dog time in which to let off a bit of steam *before* asking him to stop, and at this stage in his training allow him to head his sheep before attempting to stop him.

Going to the field for a training session

Often, when teaching novice handlers, I find that they are struggling to undo their dog's lead when it is their turn to go to the sheep. By the time the dog is free, the sheep have usually gone from the middle of the field, the handler is losing confidence and the dog may have lost interest or be so keyed up that he takes off down the lane back to where he came from. So, rather than a lead, I use a piece of strong string or baler twine, just slipped through the youngster's collar, with the two ends in one hand, and take him quietly to the sheep. When ready to release the dog, I simply let go of one end of the string and allow it to slide out of the collar, leaving him free of any constraints. This saves a lot of hassle—there is no bending down, holding the dog by the collar, and no struggling with a wriggling, excited pup in an effort to unfasten the lead. The dog soon learns that, once he is off the string, he is allowed to run out to the sheep and that, until the string is removed, he must behave himself. And there are no confrontations.

Going through a gate with a young dog

Invariably, you will have to take your dog

Using a piece of baler twine when taking the young dog to sheep. (B. Hamer)

through a gate to get into the field with the sheep and it is important that he does not get excited and uncontrollable at this point— again, the piece of string comes in useful and you should teach him to wait quietly while you get the gate open, walk through it and then close it behind you. If the dog begins to leap about with excitement at any point, simply stand quite still, speaking quietly to him until he quietens down and he will soon realise that, if he is to eventually get out to the sheep, he must behave himself. Once in the field, walk quietly to the position from which you want the dog to run out before releasing him.

Releasing the young dog

Before releasing a young dog in a field containing sheep (after the first few sessions when I carry him out), I always make sure that the sheep are in a group together *in the middle of the field.* We have already mentioned that some people advocate starting a young dog at the end of a long rope—and some also suggest that the sheep should be against a hedge or in a corner. Whilst this enables you to maintain firm control over the situation it does little more than teach you how to handle a dog fastened to a piece of rope and working at very close quarters to you and the cornered sheep. Neither you nor the dog is going to learn anything useful in this situation as the day *must* come when the rope will have to be taken off and the sheep be allowed into the middle of the field—so why not start there in the first place? Another thing worth remembering is that if you start by sending your young dog to fetch sheep from a corner or from against a hedge, you could be destroying what is often a natural instinct to leave space between himself and the sheep. If he has to rush at his sheep to shift them from a corner or a fence, then he is going to develop bad habits early on and is not being given the opportunity to develop a good instinctual movement which can be of great value in his work.

Remember that you have just been giving the young dog his basic lessons in the yard, so when you take him to the field on his bit of string, just tell him to 'Stay there' as he has already learned to do in a more controlled environment and he will soon get the message. As you remove the string from the dog's collar, take a step or two forward—the dog will do the same, realise he is free and take off, which is what you want him to do at this time. The important thing is that both you and the dog are relaxed when he sets off—and don't worry at this point if he goes straight through the sheep and scatters them to the four corners of the field—be pleased that he is taking notice of the sheep and is showing an interest in them. The really important thing is that we find a way of getting the youngster to the far side of the sheep at this early stage. If the dog persists in running straight through the sheep after the first few lessons, then you are going to have to do something to correct it—a fairly simple thing to do at this time. Just take the pup (still on his piece of string) much nearer to the sheep, stand slightly ahead of him so that you are between him and the sheep, allow the string to slide out of his collar and, as he begins to run off, you run with him, encouraging him to run out by remaining between him and the sheep until you want him to head them. Then, once he has gone far enough round to head the sheep, you can fall back to keep the sheep between yourself and the dog.

important that you do not attempt to send the young dog out too far too soon.

Distance between handler and dog

There will always be times when the young dog decides to test out the handler to see what he can get away with, so it is important to ensure that you are always in a position to correct him when this happens. Nobody can train a young dog when he is a hundred yards

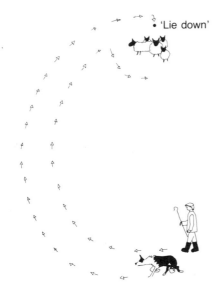

A Sending the young dog out to the left.

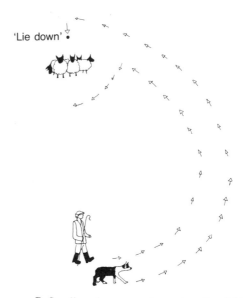

B Sending the young dog out to the right.

DIAGRAM 1   Teaching the young dog to get to the far side of his sheep. (Make sure you get this right before progressing further.)

It is necessary here for me to emphasise that the distance required between the dog and the sheep at the 'lift' is sufficient for the dog to maintain a contact with the sheep but not so much that this important contact is lost. Nor must the dog get so close to the sheep that he upsets them and sends them into headlong flight. You should be able to control this distance between dog and sheep right at the outset when you are running out with him and pushing him well out before you move to get to the other side of the sheep. It is also very

away—the handler must always be no further than thirty yards away from the dog in these early days of training and the distance of the fetch at this point must be no more than fifty or sixty yards at the outside; i.e. when he has picked up his sheep to head them to the handler, the distance between dog and handler should be no more than about thirty yards and adequate contact must be maintained.

Walking backwards

Once the youngster has been let loose in the

field with the sheep you *must not take your eyes off him for a single moment*—and the only way you can achieve this is to walk backwards all the time. The dog can see you at the far side of the sheep, he knows that you can see him and, believe me, the minute you turn your back on him, he is going to run straight at the sheep and scatter them, which is the opposite of what you want him to do—so try to avoid this happening in the first place.

To slow down the sheep (and the young dog) as they come towards you, move slowly backwards, holding both arms out and calling 'Steady'. For these times I take a rolled-up plastic fertiliser bag with me, and when the sheep are moving too quickly forwards, I bang the bag against the side of my leg to make a loud noise. I find this very effective in slowing things down, and if the dog does decide to chase the sheep past me, I can usually manage to catch him on the rump as he goes flying by in hot pursuit! This usually proves to be an effective way of persuading him to run round to head the sheep once again, if only to get out of my way, and I am then in a position to start the lesson once more. And we have not fallen out over it.

So, you eventually get to the point where, by watching the young dog, walking backwards and talking to him all the time (i.e. maintaining contact with him by the continual use of your voice), you can manage to keep things going without having mad scrambles, you and the dog have both achieved something, you can tell him that he has been a good boy and you both leave the field happy. Which brings me to another important point—when the lesson is at an end and you have eventually caught your young dog (this gets easier as time goes on and he has fully learned to obey the 'Come here' command in sessions in the yard), praise him and then put the bit of string back

through his collar and *lead him quietly from the field to his kennel*: this prevents the youngster from tearing back to get amongst his sheep for a game—a bad habit which, once formed, is very difficult to break. Again, the time will come when you will be able to say 'Come here', 'That'll do', and your dog will leave the sheep knowing that he is to stop work and go home with you, but this takes time and, meanwhile, you need to ensure that there is no hassle in this area. You will, at some point, feel confident enough to try taking your dog from the field without a piece of string but do not attempt this for the first half-dozen lessons or more—there is no hurry and you know that it will come in time. Your trainee still has his puppyhood and play times but *not* when he is in the field with the sheep; i.e. he is beginning to learn the difference between work and play.

During this early training I feel that it is better not to put 'Away to me' (right) and 'Come bye' (left) commands on the young dog. I send my youngster out from my side with a 'Shhhhh' noise, encourage him to come up behind his sheep with the words 'Get up' (to speed him up) or 'Steady' (to slow him down) and stop him (or attempt to) with 'Lie down'. Remember that, at this point, I simply want him to head the sheep and bring them *towards* me as I walk backwards, and he does not need any commands to his side until he is able to bring the sheep to me wherever I am standing— as I walk backwards I move from side to side, trying to keep the sheep coming to me but also trying to prevent them from getting past me. I also try walking backwards in a figure of eight to enable the young dog to become accustomed to using the whole area of the field and to change his sides whilst following the sheep without even being aware of it. At this point, the handler should be thinking ahead of his pup and planning his next moves.

CHAPTER 5

Getting Somewhere

Balance

SHEEP-SENSE is something else which our sheepdogs have to develop (and so do we) and the way we train our dogs can help them to develop this ability—it is what we call 'balance' and is something which we can help the dog to develop to the full. It is a word which is widely used in discussion about the working sheepdog; it has a specific meaning but is very difficult to explain to those who do not understand the term. One way of describing it is to say that balance is the distance at which a dog needs to be to maintain contact and control over his sheep without upsetting them or scattering them. You will find that some dogs can work closer to the sheep than others but what they all need is eye and an ability to flank squarely off the sheep when asked to do so. Some dogs have natural balance and others develop it as their training progresses.

Balance can be described in more than one context:

Lifting The point of balance here is achieved when the dog has completed his outrun to the far side of the sheep and the sheep begin to move forwards.

Fetching As he brings his sheep towards the handler, the dog will need to 'wear' or move from side to side in order to keep his flock moving forwards, together and in line. Some dogs have to move more freely from side to side than others in order to achieve balance in this situation.

Flanking and circling If the dog runs too wide

Gel demonstrates sheep-sense and the point of balance at the lift. (Steve Benbow)

or too tight he will lose the point of balance; i.e. the distance at which he can move away from his sheep yet remain in contact with them will set limits on how wide the dog can run.

Driving and cross-driving Again, in this manoeuvre, the dog needs to be behind the sheep and wearing to keep them together and going forwards. Whilst it is relatively easy to get a dog to flank when he is driving towards the handler, it is more difficult to get him to do this when driving away or cross-driving and many a trial is lost at this point because the dog fails to maintain the point of balance.

A dog needs to maintain the point of balance continuously in order to stop the sheep from straying out of line. A strong-eyed dog will always have his eye on the sheep which is most likely to break away from the bunch, whilst the weaker-eyed dog will invariably have his eye on the opposite side to the one where the sheep are pulling—he is therefore unlikely to make the correct flanking movements required to maintain the point of balance and thus check a sheep which wants to break clear.

A dog's balance is always in evidence when penning sheep and I had trouble with this at times in my early days of training dogs— particularly with Hemp. I never really understood why penning was a problem with him until I was handling Gel at his first trial—we were at the pen and I thought that Gel was in the wrong position so I gave him the command to move. He ignored this so I repeated the command and, when the dog obeyed me, we lost the sheep. I then realised that Gel had positioned himself (as he always did throughout a very successful trialling career) at the point of balance, i.e. in the correct position to control the leading ewe, whilst Hemp (the dog I had taught not to use his brain) would leave it all to me. With Hemp I had destroyed his instinct for the point of balance but not so with Gel and, after that one incident, I was very careful not to make the same mistake with Gel and other dogs which followed.

Beginning to assess your dog

Always watch your dog with a critical eye so that you see not only his good points but also any bad points which will need correction— the same rule also applies to yourself, and every time something goes wrong during training, ask yourself the questions, 'Am I doing something wrong?', 'Does the dog really understand what I am asking him to do?', 'Would a different approach work?'

From the very first time you take your pup out to the sheep, you should begin to notice which side he prefers to run out and the distance he likes to work from the sheep— Does he like to be close behind them? Does he prefer to work the sheep from a distance? Does he upset his sheep or do they tend to move quietly away from him? Does he like to remain on his feet when working or does he 'clap' down on his belly all the time? These and

Glen in the right position to control sheep at the pen. (Commercial Camera Craft)

many other questions will be raised as you walk backwards, always watching your dog and his various reactions and gradually building your knowledge of the way he moves and thinks—information upon which you will continually draw and build during the months ahead.

Direction of approach to sheep

When taking a dog into the field I always decide *beforehand* which side I intend to send the dog out from. I then go towards the sheep from the appropriate angle; i.e. if sending the dog out to his right, I approach the sheep from the *left* and with the dog on my right. Conversely, if sending the dog out to his left, I approach the sheep from the *right* with the dog on my left. By doing this, both the dog and I are facing the correct direction for the outrun right from the start and I am between the dog and the sheep when he starts off. By doing this with my dog I am, in fact, always giving him unspoken information from the minute we set foot on the field.

You will notice at the National and International trials that nine times out of ten the really experienced and successful handlers will walk out to the post from whichever side is appropriate for the outrun they have decided to use on that occasion. If we teach our dogs at a very early age to recognise the handler's intentions by correct positioning, when the

A Dog sent out to left.   B Dog sent out to right.

DIAGRAM 2   Taking a very young dog onto the field using a lead and correct positioning when lead is removed.

great day comes and you are running a dog at your first National trial, you will take your dog out with him walking on your right-hand side for an outrun to the right and with him on your left-hand side for an outrun to the left. And you will be confident that your dog will set out on his outrun well because he will only be doing something he has been taught to do right from those early beginnings. Both you and the

Mirk correctly placed to run out to his left.

dog, at a time of stress, will thus be able to rely on recall of early basic training (and habit) to help you not only to make a good start but to give a good account of yourselves over the whole course, sheep willing! There is nothing better than a little, stubborn or flighty Welsh ewe to bring even the most experienced and able dog and handler sharply down to earth.

Circling and flanking commands

Up to now I have been doing as much walking backwards as the dog has been running, but now that training has started in earnest I am going to make the dog do the work while I do *less* walking (and not always backwards!) and, at the same time, I am going to introduce him to the flanking commands for going to the left—'Come bye'—and to the right—'Away to me'.

To do this, it is important for the handler to keep *between* the dog and the sheep—this is so that he can control the distance of the dog from the sheep and it is also possible to have more control over the dog when he is asked to stop because he is not too far away. If the dog is twenty feet away from the sheep, it is only necessary for the handler to move a small distance as he also circles the sheep but in a smaller radius (see Diagram 3).

Being in a position between the dog and the sheep, and moving round the sheep to keep level with the dog, I can stop him from coming in too tight by telling him to get out and perhaps banging the rolled-up fertiliser bag (mentioned in the last chapter) against my leg to emphasise the point. The real point to remember is that the minute the dog tries to come on to his sheep he is prevented from doing so and, if necessary, he must be stopped with the 'Lie down' command and then, once the handler is in the correct position between the dog and the sheep, he can be sent out again to the appropriate side. It is a good idea to think of a circle and to divide it mentally into segments of a quarter or a sixth and then send the dog out, say, to his left, with 'Come bye', 'Lie down', 'Come bye', 'Lie down', and so on, stopping the dog at each segment and making sure that you keep yourself in such a position that, when the dog is sent out each time, he will run out properly to the appropriate side. And, as you see, we are now teaching the dog his commands. If the dog goes too wide, I bring him in with 'Lie down', 'Come here', 'Lie down', and then, when he has come far enough towards me, I give the appropriate command to run out once again. If he is too tight, I work nearer to the dog than the sheep, keeping the dog always on my outside as I move round the sheep.

The introduction of flanking commands is really a very simple procedure and can be done without the dog realising that something new is happening. The only two commands being introduced at this stage are those for left and right—you have already been using your own body position to indicate to the dog which side he is to go out on, running out with him until he is beginning to head his sheep. To introduce the verbal command, simply do as you have been doing and, as you release the string and

the dog begins to run out, say the appropriate word for left or right, as the case may be. You will probably be surprised at how quickly the dog begins to associate the given commands with his sides without any stress or confrontation involved for either handler or dog. As always, the emphasis is on remaining as relaxed as possible and reducing confrontation to the minimum.

In giving the 'Come bye' and 'Away to me' commands in these early stages, always make sure that you use the *full* command because, later on, when the dog is more advanced in his training, you are going to shorten these same commands in order to get more refinement of movement; i.e. 'Come bye' becomes a short, terse 'Come' when a *small* movement to the left is required, 'Away' or 'Way' for small movements to the right. In this way the dog will know whether you want him to make a big, wide movement or a small, shorter one and, although the shorter movements really come into later stages of training, it is necessary to mention it here in order to explain the importance of using the full commands in the early days.

Another point is that the teaching of the big movement must come first—if you teach small movements first it is unlikely that you will ever be able to get the dog to enlarge those movements, and if you teach the dog to flank using shortened commands, then you have no way of shortening them further. Similarly, when introducing whistle commands, the same technique is used—a long whistle at a certain pitch denoting the big movement and the same whistle, shortened, the smaller, similar movement. A well-known Scots handler who really excels in this is Jock Richardson, winner of the International Supreme Championship in 1965 with Wiston Cap, and I well remember his expert use and variation of the whistle.

Square flanking movements

When we are teaching a dog to circle his sheep in the manner described above we are not only

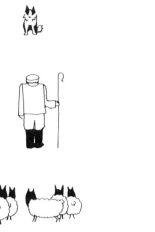

A Position of dog, handler and sheep at beginning of manoeuvre. The dog is in the 'Stop' position.

B Dog given command 'Away to me' and handler moves with him, indicating direction dog is to move by moving that way himself.

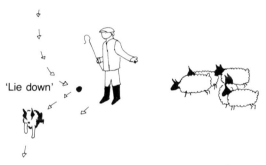

C Dog begins to move in to head his sheep. He is stopped and handler moves to stand between dog and sheep.

D Dog is given flanking command again and turns squarely out as handler moves with him.

E Dog moves in to head sheep and is again stopped.

F Handler moves round to dog and dog is sent out again.

DIAGRAM 3   Circling and teaching flanking commands for left and right. Diagrams illustrate the dog moving to his right ('Away to me'). Reverse the procedure for the left command ('Come bye').

teaching him the verbal commands for left and right; we are also teaching him to go left and right in a *square* movement. I happen to believe that the flanking movement should be square in order to ensure that the dog turns off his sheep correctly—to teach the dog to do this from the 'Lie down' the handler must be directly in front of him and between him and his sheep when giving the renewed command 'Come bye' or 'Away to me', making sure that he turns out squarely. Good, square flanking is very important in so many movements made on the trials field, and many trials are lost on the cross-drive because the handler cannot get the dog to flank properly.

never be allowed to happen. When he is in orbit the dog is not looking for his sheep and is simply running round in circles for the fun of it—a useless occupation and a bad habit to develop.

Once the dog is able to circle his sheep, you should practise this without running out with him. The handler stays where he is and the dog runs out round to the far side of the sheep, and lifts them to bring them towards the handler without help; this is called the 'fetch'. He should do this by coming on to his sheep in the twelve o'clock position, which is the correct point of contact for the dog to lift the sheep to bring them to the handler. When teaching this

A Correct.

B Incorrect.

DIAGRAM 4   Teaching square flanking movements.

In teaching a dog to circle his sheep we keep repeating the word commands for his sides and all the time we are walking round between the dog and the sheep, making sure that he turns out and keeps his distance. At no point must we send him out on a big circle where he loses contact with his sheep. One thing which can happen at this stage is that the dog may be allowed to run round and round his sheep in headlong fashion, not listening to his handler and completely out of control, having also lost contact with his sheep—a movement which is best described as going into orbit and should

manoeuvre, do it only two or three times before moving on to something else—one of the best things to do at this point is for the handler to walk round the field with the dog bringing the sheep all the time and gradually learning to maintain balance and contact with his sheep, flanking without commands and whenever necessary to keep the sheep together in a bunch.

The time has now come when you will find that you can turn your back on both sheep and dog as you go around the field—you will need to keep glancing back just to make sure that

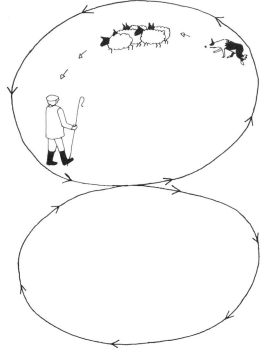

A Correct position for the dog to begin fetching the sheep to the handler, who is facing sheep and dog and is walking backwards.

B Handler's movement in figure of eight pattern when teaching the fetch.

DIAGRAM 5   Teaching the fetch.

things are going correctly, but as time goes on, you will be able to trust your dog more and more to keep bringing the sheep to you whichever way you go, and you will gradually find him to be flanking spontaneously to keep them from straying. This is always a useful exercise to use to vary training lessons as the dog gets a little more advanced and it helps him to learn a natural balance with his flock.

After you have walked for fifty or sixty yards, stop your dog at the far side of the sheep and give a flanking command to send him round the sheep until you tell him to stop. As I have explained before, the dog must not be allowed to go into the mindless exercise of orbiting at this point so it is still necessary to continue to stop him at segments of the imaginary circle before giving another flanking command, varying these more and more until

the dog will go whichever way he is asked as soon as the command is given.

All kinds of sheep

We must remember that, to be really versatile, a dog should be trained with all kinds of sheep, both flighty and heavy, to enable him to become flexible and really useful in all situations. Sheep are described as heavy when they are less responsive to a dog and tend to stand looking at him rather than moving away from him. These are usually Lowland breeds such as Suffolks, Dorsets and Border Leicesters. Flighty sheep tend to be quicker in their movements, skittish and unpredictable, more likely to bolt away from a dog. These sheep—Welsh mountain sheep, Swaledales, Herdwicks—are usually bred to live on the mountains.

Glen and Gel with all kinds of sheep at Bwlch Isaf. Watched by myself and Phil Drabble.
(Derek Johnson)

Of course, if a dog is going to spend all his life working heavy sheep and that is all he is intended for, then there is no problem, but versatility is an essential requirement for the trials dog, and I think it is better to train this dog on flighty sheep so that he gets used to the wider, bigger movements required when working with sheep which are likely to bolt all the time if the dog works too close to them.

Later, when he is working with heavy sheep, it is a comparatively easy matter to shorten the commands and to keep the dog working closer to the sheep in order to keep them moving. When working at the back of heavy sheep the dog does not need to flank as much as with the more flighty sort. He needs to pick up his sheep, head them and then start walking towards them to take them to the handler—he can be slowed down, stopped behind them, if necessary, or just brought slowly on, and as the sheep walk, the dog brings them on to the handler. Don't make the mistake of thinking that because a trained dog works well back from his sheep and flanks off squarely that he has no 'power'—he is doing what he has been taught to do and the 'power' soon becomes

evident when he is dealing with a stubborn ewe who stands to him or with a flock of heavy sheep when the handler calls him in to work closer to keep them moving. Llyr Evans and his International Champion, Bosworth Coon, were masters of the craft of flanking, and Coon's movements in turning away from his sheep were developed during his early training when he had a lot of experience with flighty Welsh sheep.

Remember that, right from the beginning of training, we have taught our dog to keep bringing the sheep to us without any commands, and we are not taking his natural gift away from him—we are harnessing it in such a way as to ensure that he will be able to cope with his sheep and vary his pace as required on command. In addition, he is also beginning to learn that, if no commands are given, what he has to do is to keep bringing his sheep to the handler. At this point in his training you will certainly notice how far a dog likes working from his sheep (if you haven't worked this out earlier). Every dog you train will be different—some notable dogs in the past could control their sheep from quite a distance and Wiston

Cap fell into this group. Others work really close to the sheep—one which comes to my mind was the famous little dog Ben, who was owned and handled by the late William Jones of Llanferres. Ben could work within just a few feet of his sheep without upsetting them and needed only short flanking movements to turn his sheep.

Once you are certain that your dog understands his right and left commands, the time has come when you are really going to insist that he does as asked. If he goes wrong, just stop him and repeat the command, and if he persists in doing wrong, stop him again, stand in front of him and go back to the stage where you were teaching him by staying near him all the time and, once again, consolidate his training from a position of control. A lot of the training is a mixture of taking two steps forward and one step backwards but the end result is that, from an overall picture over a period of a few weeks or so, the general trend is one of improvement.

The beginnings of driving

Once the dog is circling satisfactorily and knows his left and right commands, it is time to introduce him to driving away from the handler. This starts with an extension of the manoeuvre where the handler is walking backwards with the dog behind the sheep and bringing them to the handler, who is varying his pace (and therefore the pace of the sheep) and moving around in figures of eight with no verbal commands being used.

The next step is to teach the dog to follow his sheep when the handler is *not* directly in front of him. This is an important stage and, if not done correctly, can lead to problems later on when the dog is asked to drive his sheep and fails to do so. You need to remember that, for the dog, the difference between the fetch and the drive is not *his* position behind the sheep, which remains the same, but *the position of the handler*.

To get the dog used to this new situation,

William Jones with Ben.

begin to walk *towards* him to meet him as he brings the sheep towards you and then, as the sheep begin to pass you, start to turn towards the dog until you are facing the direction in which he is walking. By this time the dog will be alongside you and, for a few seconds, he will probably continue to move forward (this is the beginning of driving), but it will not be long before he thinks, 'I've gone past the boss. I'd better go round to the other side of the sheep and head them back to him.' The dog will then, 99 per cent of the time, veer away from the handler and try to get to the far side of the sheep to head them back to him (see Diagram 7). As soon as this happens, make sure that you get yourself level with the dog, then stop him and say 'Come here'. The dog should make a *square* movement and come directly

'Come bye'   'Away to me'

A Correct.   B Incorrect.

DIAGRAM 6   Square flanking when driving.

towards you. When he has got to the point where he is once again behind the sheep in the driving position, stop him. Then tell the dog to move forward; I use 'Get up' for this. As you move slowly forward, so will the sheep, and the dog will be alongside you following them; i.e. he is beginning to drive them again.

It will not be long before you will be able to walk around the field, the dog on a level with you, driving his sheep and, whenever he veers off to head the sheep, being brought back into the driving position with 'Lie down', 'Come here', 'Lie down' commands, as described above, before continuing his driving. It is important to stay level with the dog to maintain contact with him. He will see you out of the corner of his eye so will not develop the bad habit of turning to look back at his handler when in need of reassurance.

Once the dog has got the general idea of driving his sheep round the field with the handler a short distance away and alongside him to give him confidence, you are ready to effect the turn of the sheep at the far end of the field. When you are ready to change the dog's direction, stop him and then call him towards you with 'Come here'. When the dog reaches you stop him again and then send him round behind you, using the appropriate command

for the side he is to run to and turning yourself at the same time as the dog moves round.

If necessary, run alongside the dog, between him and the sheep, to keep him out until he is in the correct position for heading them, with you once again alongside him as you both go back up the field.

At this point, in addition to teaching the dog to drive, we are also teaching him to pick up his sheep as he will eventually be required to do at the end of his outrun—we are making sure, even in these early days, that he is learning how to make a good lift.

The cross-drive

Teaching the cross-drive is a continuation of teaching a dog to drive. Although the position of the handler is different in relation to the dog—i.e. he is facing the line of the drive and is not at the side of, or behind, the dog—the dog's position in relation to the sheep remains the same as when driving. Rather than teach the dog to drive his sheep across the field in the first instance, I find it better to start with me in the middle of the field with the dog driving the sheep in a circle round me. By doing this, the dog can always see me and, if I turn as he goes round, he is, in fact, driving the sheep across in

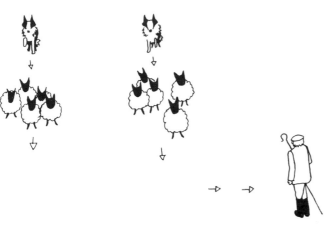

B Second stage.

C Third stage.

A First stage.

D Fourth stage.

E Fifth stage.

F Sixth stage.

G Back to third stage.

DIAGRAM 7 The beginnings of driving.

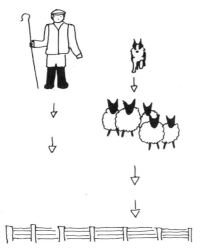

A First stage: Dog driving with handler at his side.

D Fourth stage: 'Away to me' command given and handler turns with dog.

B Second stage: Dog commanded to 'Lie down'.

E Fifth stage: Dog told to 'Lie down' when behind his sheep, handler still turning.

C Third stage: Dog commanded to 'Come here' and then to 'Lie down' when he reaches handler.

F Sixth stage: Dog has lifted his sheep and the drive begins again.

DIAGRAM 8 Changing direction when driving.

53

front of me all the time (see Diagram 9). When the circle has been completed and I want the dog to change direction, I call 'Come here' or 'Here' to the dog to get him to turn squarely off his sheep, immediately followed by the appropriate flanking command to get him to run round to head the sheep again and to drive them back in the opposite direction (see Diagrams 9B and D). Once again, you will notice that the dog is always called *towards* the handler in this manoeuvre and is never allowed to run round to head his sheep by going away from the handler; the dog must also flank squarely off his sheep before moving round to head them once again.

At this stage of training, it should be possible for the dog to take his flanking commands on the move without a 'Lie down' command first, but if problems occur, you may find it necessary to say 'Come here', 'Lie down' (when the dog has turned off his sheep towards you) and then give the flanking command. Dogs do vary in this respect but you should now be working towards giving more commands while he is still on his feet and moving. The stop command will, of course, be necessary when you want to correct a wrong movement made by the dog or if you simply wish him to stop.

Once your dog is able to complete his cross-driving in this circular movement, you should then start to vary the length of the cross-drive in a similar way to breaking the circle into imaginary segments as described earlier in this chapter when teaching the dog his flanking commands. Always remember that the dog must be called *towards* you each time he changes direction (as illustrated in the diagrams). As time goes on and the dog becomes more proficient at cross-driving, you can gradually increase the size of the circle to get him used to being further away from his handler when working this way.

You must remember that a young dog does not like having to move towards his handler in order to get sheep back on line, as his natural inclination is always to move away from the handler in order to head his sheep again. This can cause problems on the trials field if not dealt with sufficiently well in training sessions, and it is a common cause of failure in achieving a satisfactory cross-drive, with probably more trials being lost on this manoeuvre than any other. The most common fault in the cross-drive at trials is that the handler misjudges the position of the hurdles, usually bringing the sheep *below* them, and if he realises his mistake at the last minute, he will need to draw his dog squarely off his sheep in order to avoid moving them forward in a rush which would certainly result in their missing the gates altogether. Providing the training has been adequate, the dog will flank squarely off his sheep when given his command to move to his right and will immediately run to the side nearest the handler to move the sheep up towards the gates. If, when doing the cross-drive, the dog is driving the sheep *above* the hurdles, it is more natural for him to move *away* from the handler to bring them down to the gates again, so you should have few problems with this side. But, whichever way the sheep need to be moved to negotiate the cross-drive gates, it is important that the dog does not actually move forward until commanded to do so.

One of the reasons why I suggest teaching the cross-drive in the above way is that the dog learns to cross-drive in any direction and is thus prepared to cope with cross-drives from either the left- or the right-hand side of a trials course (and it is also useful to be able to do this in the work situation). As most trials courses in Britain run to a clockwise pattern with a left-to-right cross-drive, I think that too many people do this training only in one direction and then find that if they are faced with an anti-clockwise layout, the dog becomes totally confused.

There is a point here which I think is worth mentioning about obstacles in trials. The International Sheep Dog Society rules state that 'All gates must be negotiated'. If the sheep come below the cross-drive, for instance, and the handler, deciding that it is now too late to correct the error, commands the dog to

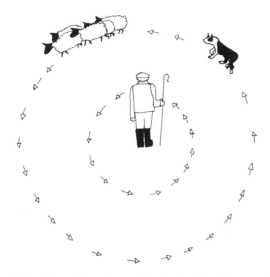

A Dog drives sheep in anti-clockwise direction round handler who turns so that he is always facing dog and sheep.

C Dog drives sheep in clockwise direction round handler who turns so that he is always facing dog and sheep.

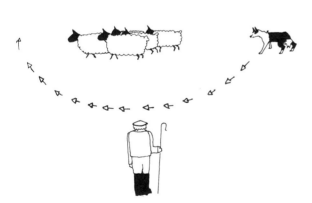

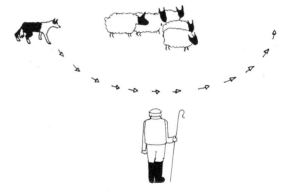

B Changing direction: 'Come here', 'Come bye' and dog flanks to pick up his sheep on the other side. Handler is stationary.

D Changing direction: 'Come here', 'Away to me' and dog flanks to pick up his sheep on the other side. Then back to diagram A.

DIAGRAM 9   Teaching the cross-drive.

head the sheep back towards him for penning or other obstacles to be negotiated, he *must* ensure that the sheep have actually passed the line of the gates even though he cannot get the sheep through them. If he does not do this he cannot, in my opinion, be said to have negotiated the hurdle. This problem and others associated with the cross-drive are illustrated below in Diagram 10 so that you can compare them with the correct cross-drive line and be aware of the difficulties you are going to face.

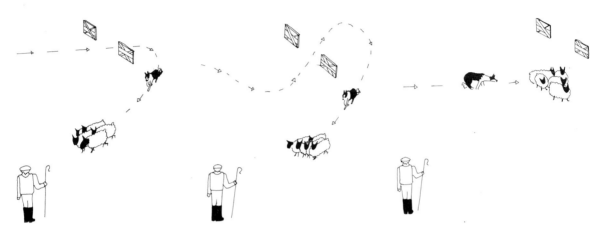

A Correct cross-drive line and gates negotiated satisfactorily.

B The 'banana' cross-drive. The line is poor but the gates have been negotiated. Points will be lost.

C Cross-drive line too low and the sheep are turning *before* the line of the gates. Can be corrected and sheep driven through the gates but points will be lost.

D Cross-drive line too low and the sheep are driven *past* the line of the gates. Cannot be corrected and competitor proceeds to next stage of the course.

E Cross-drive line too high and the sheep are driven *past* the line of the gates. Cannot be corrected and competitor proceeds to next stage of the course.

DIAGRAM 10   Negotiating the cross-drive.

CHAPTER 6

Widening the Dog's Experience

Beginning to use whistle commands

WHEN YOU HAVE GOT your young dog to the point where he knows his sides, will respond correctly to the full commands of 'Away to me', 'Come bye', 'Lie down', 'Get up', and is flanking squarely off his sheep when asked to do so, then you can begin to think in terms of widening his experience by introducing whistle commands. Although it is still too soon to begin shortening the verbal commands, you can think in terms of lengthening his outrun and teaching him to pick up his sheep not only from the middle of the field but from wherever they happen to be, whether loosely scattered or tight up against a hedge somewhere.

Before putting whistle commands on a dog, the handler should have planned and practised the whistles he intends to use until he is able to get a clear and consistent note every time because, if the handler is not clear in his own mind about the whistles, the dog will certainly get totally confused. There are many varieties of whistle available including the flat shepherd's whistle (metal or plastic) and whistles made of bone (often available from gunsmiths as they are used by the shooting fraternity); some handlers use the nose whistle, others are able to whistle best using their fingers in the mouth—it is purely a matter of personal choice, ability and inclination so take your pick! Whichever whistle you use, do try to develop sounds which have a piercing quality, as this can be essential when working in strong winds or when the dog is a long distance from

you. The novice may find it useful to go to trials and listen to the whistles used and to either copy these or develop modified versions for his own use. For the newcomer to the game, it is a good idea to tape-record various whistles and then play them back to evaluate general quality and clarity of sound.

This can be also of great help in making sure that the whistles used for each command are sufficiently different from one another to avoid confusion in the dog's mind (and, maybe, the handler's). I think that experienced handlers are so accustomed to using their own particular whistle sounds that it is easy to forget what a difficult area this can be for the novice. It is a good idea to *think* the whistle in your mind, using your imagination to provide variations, and then, having decided on the whistles to be used, have plenty of practice (better to do this out on the hill than to drive everybody to distraction by emitting piercing blasts in the house). Remember that, later in training, you will need to be able to shorten the whistle commands for 'Come bye' and 'Away to me' in the same way as the verbal commands in order to get refinement of movement (mentioned in Chapter 5 and discussed further in Chapter 9). Most handlers use a single sharp whistle for the stop command, and for the flanking commands, I always use a double whistle, i.e. — — — — — — ——, on different notes for each side. These can then be shortened to — — — — when the shorter command is required.

Always bear in mind that during training

57

sessions at home, you will be able to whistle clearly and consistently after some practice. But in the charged atmosphere on the trials field, things can be rather different when nerves can reduce even the best whistler to a dry-mouthed non-whistler in a space of a few seconds. This reminds me of my brother-in-law when he was running a dog in a trial for the first time—a nice little bitch who had been well trained by my father and who promised well. Unfortunately, in the excitement of the moment, my brother-in-law's whistle became non-existent and he ended up with the sheep in the road while he was still standing like a lost soul at the post, whistle-less.

It is important to help the dog associate each whistle with a different movement. The best way to begin is to take your dog to the sheep as usual and set him off with the 'Come bye' verbal command, immediately followed by the 'Come bye' whistle—the dog will not understand at first but don't let this worry you. At the point where the dog is most likely to stop, give the *whistle* command to stop, immediately followed by the stop command 'Lie down' and then repeat the whistle command. In my opinion, it is necessary to get the stop whistle right before any other, so concentrate mostly on this one in the first instance, gradually introducing the others. Again, we are concentrating on making sure the young dog stops before bringing his sheep to the handler. Some handlers are of the opinion that we should not make an issue of the stop command, stating that the farm dog's prime object is to go and fetch sheep to the handler—my argument is that I am going to need a dog who is precise in his stops, both for farm work and on the trials field, so we might as well start, right at the beginning, to teach the dog to react *immediately* to both verbal and whistle commands for 'Lie down'. I want to stress that we *must* get a good stop on voice *and* whistle—once this is achieved then it is up to the handler to decide the extent to which he uses it. The use of the stop can be compared with the brakes of a car—vital at times and used more sparingly when one gains in experience.

Getting sheep out of a corner

We know that the young dog can deal with sheep in the middle of the field so there is no longer a need to use the older trained dog to keep things under control and we can think of bringing a little more variety into the proceedings. With this in mind, I take the dog into the field in the usual way, quietly and under control by verbal command (my piece of string has now been dispensed with), and the dog is faced with a new situation, i.e. no other dog to keep the sheep in order and no sheep ready for him in the middle of the field. If the sheep are in a corner of the field, so much the better, because things are then all set for teaching a new manoeuvre, which will also come in useful later on when we are teaching the dog to pen sheep.

When I walk into the field and find that the sheep are in a corner, I keep the dog quiet and under control while assessing the situation and deciding what to do. I then send the dog from my side, going with him to keep him well out (as I did when first teaching him to run out to the other side of his sheep). I do this because he is in a new situation and he needs the confidence of my presence and voice to help him and to prevent him from getting over-excited and making mistakes.

Maintaining contact with the dog by voice alone, I encourage him to continue on his outrun, knowing that, almost inevitably, once he sees that there is no space to allow him to get behind his sheep, he will try to cross in front of them. If he does, stop him and, as soon as he has stopped, move closer to the fence on the right (see Diagram 11A). When you are in the correct position, give the 'Come bye' command in order to flank him squarely out to the fence on his left and, when he reaches the fence, stop him again (see Diagram 11B). It is important not to allow the dog to rush in and undo all the training done so far, so be very firm with your commands. If you look at the

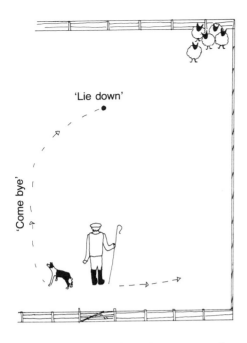

A Handler gives 'Come bye' command.

B When dog has stopped, handler moves to fence and repeats 'Come bye' command.

C Handler moves backwards out of the way.

D Handler and dog can keep moving around the field or get the sheep back in a corner and start again.

DIAGRAM 11 Getting sheep out of a corner.

diagrams, you will see that what the dog is going to do is to lift his sheep, but from a more difficult position than confronted with previously and from a position closer to his sheep. Give the dog another 'Come bye' command and stop him in the corner, and at the same time as the dog begins to move towards the corner and the sheep begin to move forward along the fence to get away from the dog you should immediately move yourself backwards out of the way (see Diagrams 11C and D) so that the sheep will keep moving.

You are now back in the familiar situation where the sheep are in the middle of the field, the dog is settled behind them and he is bringing his sheep to his handler in the way he has learned over the past months. Things are under control. This manoeuvre enables you to get the sheep in to the middle of the field without having given the dog the opportunity of undoing or forgetting previous lessons and the bonus is that your young dog is being helped to lift his sheep quietly and under control. To move the sheep from a corner with your dog on the other side, simply substitute the 'Away to me' commands to send him out to his right.

If you are using 'trained' sheep you are likely to find that, when the dog runs out to pick them up from the hedge or corner, they will see the handler standing some way off in the field and will begin to move towards him— this gives the dog the chance to move round between the sheep and the hedge, the dog thinks that he has moved his sheep out himself

and this gives him confidence to move them away from a fence or hedge the next time he is faced with this situation. It is when the sheep decide to stick that the dog needs a lot of encouragement and plenty of stops in order to eventually effect a movement away from the hedge.

Needless to say, things will not be all sweetness and light—some dogs seem to be able to learn to move sheep from a corner without too much trouble, others will take a long time over it, continually trying to move to the other side of the sheep to head them, but if you are patient and maintain contact with your voice to give him confidence, he will eventually get the idea. After all, if things start to go hopelessly wrong, you can always stop your dog, call him back to you and quietly start again. The great mistake the novice is inclined to make in this situation is to move in and try to help the dog—it is essential that, rather than moving in, the handler moves away to give the sheep the space they need to come out of the corner, thus enabling the dog to get behind them.

Talking about all this reminds me of an ATB class in which one of the students, with a nice, willing little bitch, was making a real hash of getting the sheep out of a corner. He was doing all the work, rushing about and flapping his arms in an attempt to move the sheep, and his little dog, on his command, was lying in wait for the sheep in the middle of the field. I could *not* get that man to understand that, to train his dog adequately, *he* must come

Teaching Ben to move sheep out of a corner.

out of the corner and teach his dog to move the sheep from it. Time and time again the same thing happened so at the beginning of one lesson I took a big, thick rope on to the field with me, the sort they use for a tug-of-war. 'Oh Glyn,' the man said, 'I don't fancy the idea of you putting that great rope on my little bitch.' 'Don't worry,' I said. 'The rope is not for the dog, it is going to go on you to keep you out of the corners so that the dog can do the job you should be training her for.'

think that in this situation, the dog should be allowed to have a small go at the sheep because we know that we can stop him as soon as we wish. I would rather see a dog go in to grip a ewe to get her moving than to have to go in to help him move her. When a trained dog is working a flock of sheep, there will be times when it is *essential* for him to grip to get a reaction. The important thing is that this is not just a random action but one which the dog is *told* to do and is also one which the trained dog

Encouraging the young dog to go in and 'rattle' the sheep a bit.

Teaching the dog to go in and move his sheep

Let us suppose that we have a different lot of sheep at this point and that they are really heavy sheep which *refuse* to move out into the field. What then? Well, we know that the dog will respond to all the commands he has learned so far so we do have control if we want it. There is, therefore, no reason why we shouldn't encourage him to go in hard on the sheep, if that is the only way they are going to be made to move. The sheep are facing the dog, refusing to move despite the dog moving correctly on command and varying his approach from side to side, so he is now told to 'Come in', 'Get in' and rattle the sheep a bit.

To grip or not to grip?

What do we do if the dog grips at this stage? I

will abandon as soon as he is asked to do so. There is a lot of controversy about the ruling in trials that a dog will be disqualified if it goes in to grip when dealing with sheep which will not move—I am in full agreement with this ruling because who is to say that another man's dog could not have moved that sheep without gripping it? But in the work situation, it can be an essential procedure, particularly when dealing with large numbers of sheep, and at lambing time it can often be the only way to stop a stubborn ewe who is in difficulty.

If you discourage the young dog from gripping on these occasions, there could be trouble later on in his working life when he will refuse to do so even when it is necessary. The golden rule is not to allow things to get out of hand. Another point is that once a sheep realises that a dog is frightened of standing up to it or going in to shift it, it will *always* stand to the dog in the future knowing it can get away with it, and

To grip or not to grip? Bwlch Taff and Ceri. (Daily Mail)

this causes the young dog to lose confidence and can permanently damage his willingness to work in awkward situations.

Power or character?

When sheep test a dog out by standing to him, it is often said that the 'power' of the dog is being tested, but I have a different theory. I think it is more correct to say that the 'character' of the dog is being tested, particularly in the youngster. There are dogs which, like some people, are quite willing to stand up and have a fight when the occasion arises. There are other dogs that do not want a battle, and if there is an easy way out, they will take the soft option—again like some people. These latter dogs may do very well in their early trialling life, but as things get more difficult and particularly if they reach National level, they will probably let you down when the going gets

really tough. They are certainly of little use as an all-round farm dog where character and determination can be invaluable—as at International level. So we must think carefully before using the word 'power' which I think is vastly overemphasised by many handlers. I have seen many 'powerful' dogs which just put their heads down and drive on but do not necessarily use their brains. It is the spunky dog with guile which I look for because I know that I can do something with him.

This is why I always look for a dog which shows evidence of being one of the world's survivors. There is a similarity between the rearing of dogs and bringing up children. Take a child who has been mollycoddled, babied and protected from all the nasty things in life—if he then has to go out into the cold, hard world to fend for himself, he is likely to go under. Conversely, the child who has been encouraged to be independent, to think for himself, to fight his own battles with his contemporaries, always knowing that there is parental support and guidance at hand, is likely to go out into the adult world with the confidence gained from having won some battles, lost a few, but *knowing* that somehow he will survive. And the same really does apply to our dogs.

Variation

Boredom can be very damaging to both handler and dog and should be avoided at all costs. Never keep on with one thing for long and always practise various movements and commands so that both you and the dog are kept on the alert. By this stage in training there are many things of interest to do, and at every lesson you should be going through the whole lot, just a short time with each, and if you have an area upon which you feel most work is needed, alternate this with something which the dog can do well so that he can earn praise and continue to enjoy life. Whilst the total duration of lessons has been gradually increased from the beginning and your dog is now very

The spunky dog with guile—J. Chapman's Snip.

fit, it is still better to train for several short periods daily rather than one long session, and, occasionally, for both you and the dog to have a day's rest from work. Remember what all work and no play did to Jack!

Additionally, there is the opposite situation to boredom when things are going particularly well and we are then in danger of being carried away by our successes and becoming so smug that we stop looking at the dog (and ourselves) with a critical eye. If we allow this to happen we will miss spotting faults as they are beginning to develop and our elation will soon be wiped out, so beware!

Shedding

One variation which we can begin to introduce now is shedding, i.e. dividing a group of sheep into two parts. Successful shedding depends as much on the man as on the dog—perhaps more—and the time has come for the handler to play his part to stop the sheep from passing him. It is also very important that your dog turns off his sheep squarely on the 'Come bye'

and 'Away to me' commands so that he will open out when asked to do so. People who do not advocate square flanking movements should ask themselves, 'What does my dog do when it comes to shedding?' My bet is that each time these handlers move their dog to left or right, the dog also moves towards the sheep who, in turn, will then look for a way out. This means that in the shedding ring on the trials field the sheep will try to get past the handler and run out of the ring—and how is the handler going to stop this if he cannot get his dog to flank squarely off his sheep? At trials, every time the sheep move out of the ring, points are lost, and every time the handler has to turn round in an attempt to control the sheep, more points go. When shedding, as in the circling exercises I spoke of earlier in training, make sure that your dog does not crowd you—if you want him to come forward, call him but do not allow him to come forward on his flanks. (See section on flanking commands in the previous chapter.)

Six or seven sheep are the ideal number to use when first introducing the young dog to the idea of shedding. I do not use a crook during this procedure, preferring to use my hand, but this is purely a personal preference and some people like to have a crook to lengthen their arm. When I run classes for novice handlers, nobody is allowed to use a crook as an aid for this or any other procedure—there is then no temptation to use the crook inappropriately.

Splitting the sheep

The bunch of sheep should be quiet and under control, having been brought to you by your dog. The dog has been stopped and the sheep then slow down and stop. The sheep should be looking at the handler (certainly in these early training sessions—on the trials field it does not always work out quite so easily!), and the handler makes a split between them after which he gives the 'Come here' command in a firm voice. The dog should come through the sheep and to your feet; tell him to lie down and

then allow the two packets of sheep to drift together again. The important thing in this lesson is that the dog comes straight through the gap to the handler's feet, and this cannot be emphasised enough. Eventually, as the dog gets more proficient, he will be able to come through the sheep when there is only a very small gap—as the handler's confidence grows, so does the dog's, and things begin to get very exciting. This is usually a very rewarding part of training but don't overdo it or use it to show off to your friends who may be watching over the hedge. Later on, we will teach him to turn back correctly to fetch a packet of sheep, but not just yet. After several lessons, the young dog will come straight to you every time and it will not be long before he is able to begin to anticipate what you are going to ask him and, as soon as he sees a gap, he will run through and straight to you, almost before he is asked—the dog is learning to think for himself.

Shedding the sheep.

A Dog, sheep and handler in correct position.

B Handler has moved forward to divide sheep into two bunches.

C Handler calls 'Come here' to bring dog through gap and to his feet.

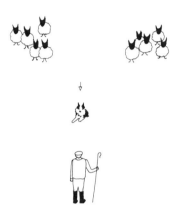

D Dog told to 'Lie down' in front of handler. Shed completed.

E Dog given flanking command (demonstrated here by 'Come bye') and stop command when in position to drive.

F Dog told to 'Get up' and drives the sheep together.

DIAGRAM 12 **Beginning to shed. NB Remember to practise both 'Come bye' and 'Away to me' flanking movements.**

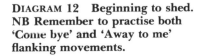

What do we do if the dog keeps hesitating and refusing to come through the sheep on the 'Come here' command? You can try to help the dog by moving slightly towards him as you give the command 'Come here', and if this does not work then you will have to acknowledge that the dog is not quite ready to learn this procedure and you will have to work on the 'Come here' command in the yard before trying again.

When teaching a dog to shed, don't overdo things by repeating the exercise time after time—do it once or twice and then go on to something else before coming back to it. Once the dog begins to understand what is required of him, practice in shedding can be included in all his sessions in the field. These training periods, by now, are beginning to build up in length but should never continue long enough for the dog (and the handler) to get tired and lose concentration. It is still better to have several short lessons each day than one long one.

Do not always practise shedding the one way. In coming straight to your feet, your dog will probably have a preference for moving in to you from either his left or his right; i.e. when you are flanking your dog on 'Come bye' or 'Away to me' in order to keep the sheep in position (good square flanking, remember), he may come in better after one of these commands than after the other. So, when practising, make sure that you do not make the mistake of always calling the dog in from the same side.

Turning the dog on to one lot of sheep
Once the dog will come straight through to your feet every time when shedding, you can then begin to teach him to turn on to one bunch and drive them away to keep them separate from the others. Do not rush into this and begin this part of training only when the dog is doing all his other movements satisfactorily.

To turn the dog on to one packet of sheep, call him in to effect the shed and, as soon as he has come through, but before he reaches your

A Dog called through gap and then stopped *before* reaching handler.

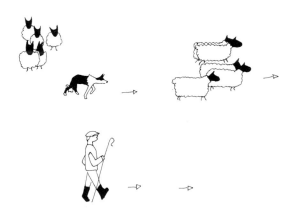

B Dog given 'Get up' command and handler moves in same direction to give dog confidence to drive away.

DIAGRAM 13 Teaching the young dog to take away a bunch of sheep after shedding.

feet, turn him on to one bunch almost bodily by moving that way with him and encouraging him to 'Get up'. As the dog becomes more experienced in this manoeuvre you will find that he can be commanded to turn on to the chosen packet of sheep without the need for you to accompany him, and, from this position, you will be able to start teaching your dog to 'Turn back' in order to get the two lots of sheep together again—a part of training which I will be coming to shortly.

There is sometimes a lot of criticism when a handler is doing most of the work in shedding himself, as can happen for a variety of reasons. My advice is to ignore this sort of thing as it really does not matter who does the most work in shedding—the man or the dog—as long as a shed is effected and the dog and handler are working as a pair. If you are at a trial and have to step forward to help split the sheep and call your dog in, then do so if you think this is going to be effective and decisive as, in my opinion, this is a much more business-like way to go about things than to stand dithering with the dog flanking backwards and forwards and the shed taking many minutes to complete. We must never forget that trials are (or should be) a test of the dog's working ability, and time, for any working shepherd, is a precious commodity.

CHAPTER 7

Singling and the Outrun

Singling

THE TERM SINGLING means the holding of one sheep from the rest of the flock. In sheepdog trials, the top-class judges usually decide that singling is a two-phase operation consisting of the dog shedding one sheep and then holding it from rejoining the rest of the flock. Singling is a dangerous phase of dog work—it can be carried too far, even in trials, but it can also be started too soon in training, and I like to think of it simply as an extension of the shed—this means that singling one sheep from the bunch is not started until the dog will come in to my feet *every* time he is asked to come to me between the sheep.

To effect a single, instead of shedding a number of sheep, just do the same exercise with one sheep and then let it take itself back to the others—in the same way as the two packets of sheep were at first allowed to drift back together in shedding. It is far too dangerous to ask a young dog in early stages of training to attempt to hold a sheep—this is because the ewe might beat him, i.e. stand to him and then run past him or jump over him. If this happens and the sheep gets away from the dog, he has lost her, and his confidence takes a knock from which it may never recover.

A good singling dog is one which has all the confidence in the world, a really cocky dog who will say, 'I'm the boss, I'm going to move up to you and hold you and you are *not* going to get away from me.' If the dog loses this sort of confidence and approach early on, it is a devil of a job building up his confidence again,

so if things go wrong with singling or shedding lessons, leave it alone for quite a long time (maybe several weeks or even months) until his confidence has had time to grow again.

If your dog is doing his shedding well and coming straight through the sheep when asked to do so, then concentrate on this rather than on singling, because if you have the shed right before the dog starts trialling and you find there is a single included in the run, all you have to do is to shed the one sheep.

Which sheep do we shed for a single?

In trials where collars mark the ewe to be singled, the decision of which sheep to shed has already been made, but what of the times when you have to shed or single from a number of uncollared sheep? In discussion on the trial fields, within the various societies, during panel question times and television programmes on sheepdog trialling, the question 'Which sheep should be singled?' invariably crops up and is usually answered by 'It must be the last sheep.' This answer immediately begs another question, 'If you have three or five sheep, with one at each end looking outwards, which is the last one?'

Many years ago, I was running a dog at a trial at Otterburn, Northumberland, where the judge announced that the last sheep must be singled and that the dog must come to the head of the sheep to do this; i.e. if the packet of sheep was beginning to go past the handler, the dog must single the last one in the line. If the singling was not done in this way, the

Singling with Glen at the 1952 Welsh National, Swansea. (Commercial Camera Craft)

judged shouted 'No single', and the handler and dog had to get the sheep back in the ring and do the single again according to the judge's previously announced requirements. To me, this sort of thing is a farce because, if you have failed to get your single once or twice because of this sort of rigid ruling, how many points have you got left? I would like to see singling dropped out of sheepdog trialling altogether, but not many people would agree with me. I feel that it is a phase of work on the trials field when a judge can make his own rules and I do not agree with this—there is an analogy here between judging singling at trials and the old ruling (since discontinued) that dogs should be marked for 'style'. The judging sheets at the National and International trials contained a place for marking the style of a dog—another area in which the judge can do whatever he likes. Style, like beauty, is in the eye of the beholder, so if a judge liked the look of a particular dog he would give him full points, but if not, he would subtract points accordingly. This section of marking was open

to abuse, and even if a dog had worked superbly with an almost flawless run, many points could be taken from him simply because one or more of the judges did not like his style. I think that this sort of thing makes a nonsense of what sheepdog trialling is all about, i.e. a testing out of the dog's *working abilities*.

Judging of singling is very difficult because if a ewe just splits herself off from the rest and walks off, the dog is called through and gets good points for something which was not singling at all, i.e. splitting off a single ewe and holding her. The next handler who eventually gets a superb single and holding may lose more points than the former simply because it has taken him longer to achieve—despite the fact that it is a true example of singling at its very best.

An example of such a problem occurring when judging the single happened to me some years ago at Machynlleth, North Wales. Elwyn Griffith and his marvellous dog Craig came into the singling ring, and almost before he had got the sheep together, one of the red-collared ewes just bolted. Elwyn took advantage of this and called the dog in to him, but it was not a proper single, so in the next few seconds I had to decide whether to tell Elwyn to get his dog to fetch that ewe back and re-do his single or just to give him fewer points because the sheep had literally singled herself. I opted to give him fewer points for a poor single and he was able to complete his run. But was my decision the correct one or not?

Elwyn Griffith with Craig (right) and Craig 2.

Singling in the work situation

I accept that the ability to single a sheep and hold it for the shepherd is an essential requirement for a good shepherd's dog (for instance, in everyday work, if my dog fails to hold a sheep when I have asked him to do so, I am less than pleased). Sometimes, to single and hold a sheep in the work situation, the dog is going to need to go in to grip—if, on the next day, he goes to a trial and has a difficult ewe to single and hold, how is he to know that he must not go in to grip? If he goes in, then he is disqualified, if he does not go in to grip, he will probably lose the sheep and the trial is lost. We are asking our dog to 'read' the difference in the two situations, and although the older, experienced dog will eventually often be able to differentiate between trials and his general farmwork, are we asking too much of him? And what of the younger dog faced with this

situation? Is it right to do this to him? I do not think so.

Penning

The movements of the dog in penning—manoeuvring a number of sheep into an enclosure—are no different, basically, from any of the movements he has been taught so far. The main thing at the pen is that the dog moves correctly in response to commands and *does not come forward on his flanking movements.* Catching a sheep in a corner during general farmwork is very similar to the penning situation, so this is where to begin practising penning movements as there is unlikely to be a nice, convenient pen available at all times in the fields where you train your dogs. If the dog does have to come forward in this situation it must be in very small movements when asked to do so (remember the shorter commands/whistles for the smaller movements) and he must be capable of flanking left or right *without coming forwards.* Practice in getting sheep into an actual pen will help to increase the novice handler's confidence before going to his first trial.

If you go round the sheep and find one which is lame, you are going to need to catch it in order to give it the necessary treatment—if you have a dog which is no good at holding a sheep, then he is not going to be any good at penning when he gets to the trials as he needs to be able to control the sheep without coming right forward himself. I always think that the dog has to be rather like a good full-back in football—he threatens to come forward but is always guarding so that nothing passes him.

Doing one's homework (again)

We are now at one of the points where we need to take a look to see if we have been doing our homework adequately and to ask ourselves if the lessons which the pup, and later the young dog, has been learning have really sunk in. My father's favourite saying was that a good poacher prepares his ground well before going out on an expedition, and the same really applies to dog training—it is not possible to place too much emphasis on the preparation for good handling by continually reinforcing the training of the basics in the middle of the field. Reinforcement of the 'Come here', 'Lie down' and 'Stay there' commands need not become boring to either dog or handler as they can be continually used in the dog's everyday life off the field—when out on walks, when

Sequence of manoeuvres now possible

We can now practise quite a number of different movements with our young dog and this keeps life interesting for both dog and handler, often being one of the most rewarding times in training, i.e. when you really begin to feel that you are both getting somewhere (and you *are!*).

Send the dog out to the other side of the sheep, he fetches them to you, you manage to

Michael Perrings penning with Lad. (Derek Johnson)

running loose around the yard or garden, when taken to the market, when other people are around or when only dog and handler are present. The dog's obedience to these commands becomes part of his everyday existence and he gets increasingly used to doing as he is told. And do not forget the advantages of rewarding the dog with 'Good boy' and a stroke or a pat when he does well—he will gradually develop a desire to please his handler and this can be used to advantage in all stages of training.

do a shed, then the dog drives the sheep towards the hedge where you can practise his flanking and standing to hold the sheep (as he will need to do when penning). The dog then moves the sheep from the hedge or corner and you do a single, the sheep are allowed to drift back together and the dog is sent out to fetch them to you once again. You can get him to bring the sheep round behind you, drive them away, cross-drive and back to the opposite hedge or corner to practise holding once again, with you close by and making sure that, as the dog flanks, he does not go in to the sheep but flanks squarely each time. By being close to the dog you are in a good position to maintain control, and when I deal with trialling at greater length, I will say more about positioning the dog correctly during the actual penning procedure. But we are not quite there yet!

The outrun

If you get to a point when you feel that things are getting monotonous then you can bet your life it is getting even more so for the dog, and you need to start thinking in terms of going on to the next stage to provide more variety and to begin to stretch the dog's abilities a little further. So what better than to begin developing your dog's outrun? I can guarantee that this will tax both you and the dog and boredom will go flying out of the window.

Up to this point, we have been teaching our young dog to get to the far side of the sheep before fetching them to the handler but we have not been teaching him his *outrun*—a more complex and refined action altogether.

Teaching a dog his outrun is indeed a very important and sometimes the most difficult part of training unless you are fortunate enough to have a dog with a good, natural outrun—an attribute possessed by many dogs who are related to Wiston Cap. Note that very wide-running dogs can be a problem unless you are able to draw them in adequately. Bwlch Taff will, if I am not careful, run out too wide at times when sheep are let out in the middle of a field, and drawing him in is far more difficult than turning him out.

Straight start
Teaching the outrun is an extension of the circling phase but we are now going to start off at a point which is further away from the sheep, and it is the pick-up end of the outrun which is the most important. Bearing this in mind, we are going to practise two outruns— one with a *straight* start and the other with a *square* start. The reason is that there are going to be times when the dog will need to (a) run out straight towards the sheep at first, to be widened out when the handler feels it is necessary to do so, and (b) run out wide from the very beginning of the outrun (see Diagram 14).

For the straight start, place the dog directly in front of you and encourage him to walk towards his sheep ('Get up') as though to drive them away. Then stop him and flank him out by giving either the 'Come bye' or 'Away to me' command, making sure that he turns out. If the dog is reluctant to do this after you have tried it a couple of times, walk up to stand near him and between him and the sheep, then send him out again, keeping him flanked out to make sure that he gives his sheep plenty of room at the top end of the field. You can achieve this by calling his name, followed by the appropriate flanking command, and talking to him to remind him that, although he is further away from you, you are still in contact with him and keeping your beady eye on him. If necessary, you can always stop the dog if he begins to come in too soon and walk up to him to flank him once again. It is most important to remember the need for a continual contact with your dog at this stage by using your voice or whistle to command him, praise him, curse him, talk to him and move up to help him when necessary in order to maintain his confidence.

Square start
For the square start, begin by having your dog on either your left or right side (depending on which way you intend to send him out) and getting him to stand with his head turned away from you and towards the boundary of the field. Send the dog out and, if he starts to draw in, stop him, walk over to him, place yourself in front of him and send him out again, turning him out as you have been doing in the circling exercises in earlier lessons. At first, it may be necessary to stop a dog several times on this wider outrun and walk up to him in order to flank him out again in the way

described before he eventually gets the message. Again, as with the straight outrun, maintain contact all the time with the dog to help him remain confident.

The major area of work must now be on the outrun and being able to stop the dog on command. A good test to see if the dog will do as you ask him is to stop him on his outrun and then to send him out to the same side from the place where he has stopped. He should turn out once again, thus widening the outrun. When you start to do this on a small field, do not send the dog out too wide to begin with, so that when you do stop him and send him out again, he has the room in which to turn out towards the field boundary. If the dog turns

out well in this situation it means that he really understands his 'Come bye' and 'Away to me' commands. You will remember that previously we were concentrating on the dog going out sufficiently to get behind his sheep and bring them to the handler; we were keeping him far enough from his sheep to enable him to get to head them but we were not sending him on a wide outrun. Things are now beginning to change and we are preparing for the times when a full outrun is going to be required. It does take some time for the outrun to develop adequately—several weeks or even longer— but he should gradually develop the ability to cast out wider to get behind his sheep.

Some dogs do have this natural 'cast' out to

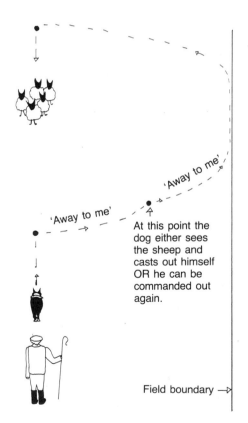

A The straight start.

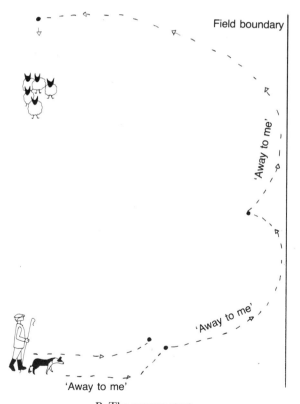

B The square start.

DIAGRAM 14 Teaching the dog to outrun and come back in on command.

get behind the sheep when they are some distance away from the handler and that makes life a lot easier. But, with the majority the trainer has to teach the dog to go wider and not to keep coming in on his sheep too soon. Whether on the farm or at trials, dogs need to be guided to pick up their sheep and to cast out satisfactorily. It is no good shouting 'Come bye, Come bye, Come bye' and expecting the dog to widen his outrun in this way. He should be sent out, stopped if he begins to come in, and then *sent out again* from that position.

The dog is at a point where he should be discouraged from looking back at the handler if stopped on his outrun. If his training when circling the sheep has been thorough, the dog will stop when asked to do so and will keep his eyes on the sheep, flanking off squarely when sent out again and thus widening out without losing contact with the sheep. He should now have enough confidence not to need to look back at you—if he does this, then you are going to have to take steps to correct the fault.

Back to earlier lessons and periods of rest

If the dog does keep looking back at you when teaching the outrun, then you are going too far too soon and you need to backtrack. Return to earlier lessons once again to increase the dog's confidence before widening his outrun. I have mentioned before that all training consists of taking two steps forward and one step backwards and these backward steps are absolutely essential from time to time so do not be afraid to take them—if you do so you are more likely to make a success of the training in the long term. Never be afraid of saying 'I'm not getting anywhere at the moment.' If you feel like that, don't keep trying to push on; it is far better to decide that you are both ready for a rest, leave the training for a few days, take the dog out for exercise and play but no work, and then, a week or more later, go back to training refreshed and eager. Believe me, both you and the dog will benefit and often the problem

Let out for exercise and play.

which you did not seem to be getting over will have disappeared anyway and you will wonder why you were getting so despondent. The great thing to remember after resting yourself and the young dog is that you must start from the beginning again and work (fairly quickly) through all the stages of training up to the point where you left off—in this way you may iron out the problem on the way. *Never* start off again from the place in the training programme where you had seemed to be getting stuck.

Reduction of command contact with the dog

Once your dog will outrun confidently to both sides, without looking back for reassurance and guidance, the time has come to try reducing the amount of verbal/whistle contact after he sets out on his outrun. You are going to try to get him to start using his brain and begin to look for his sheep without the need for your commands to keep encouraging him. You will also be testing his powers of concentration and finding out if he can work things out for himself. By this, I do not mean that you should give only the first command and then no others in one fell swoop but rather that the number of commands be *gradually* reduced over a period of time. Whilst doing this, you can, from time to time, test out how far he will run out before a repeated flanking command is needed, being prepared to give this immediately the dog shows signs of confusion. The need to do this will gradually lessen as the dog's confidence (and yours) grows, and the time will come when your dog will need only the initial flanking command for either the straight or wide outrun and you will *know* that you will be able to rely on him getting to the far side of his sheep to lift them every time with no further help from you.

Teaching a dog his outrun and trying to develop the pattern of him completing his outrun without the need for a repeated command takes quite a long time. Initially work close to the dog and very gradually make the distance from the dog (and sheep) a little greater if things are progressing well. If you find that this is not working, all you need to do is to go back to the beginning of training the outrun at close quarters (as when teaching circling) and then try to enlarge the situation some days or a week or so later. A lot of patience is required at this stage with nearly every dog you will train. With some dogs we get a bonus in that they do not hesitate on their outrun at this point, their confidence being sufficient for them to run and widen out naturally so that they get to the far side of the sheep without upsetting them—if this happens it means that the training can progress more quickly. If not, it simply means that the dog is not sufficiently confident and needs more encouragement from the handler to achieve a satisfactory outrun. It does *not* mean that the dog is no good.

Looking for the sheep and pattern of behaviour at the post

Most handlers like to tell their dogs to look for their sheep in a sensible and controlled manner before they are started off on their outrun. Some actually tell their dogs 'Look for the sheep', and I do this by making a small 'Whoosh' sound which, over the weeks and months of training, the dog comes to associate with the presence of sheep. Sometimes, especially at nursery trials, you see dogs that have no idea of where they should be looking and what they are looking for and, in addition, the handler may approach the starting post from the right but send his dog to the left, and vice versa. This means that (a) the dog has not received the unspoken message regarding the side he is to be sent on his outrun and (b) he has not seen his sheep because he has never been trained to suss out where they are before beginning to work. This means that the dog can be totally confused from the start of his run, so it is little wonder that he then crosses his outrun nine times out of ten. Always remember that you need to build a pattern of behaviour and approach which the dog will recognise when going out on to the trials field.

Look for your sheep. (Derbyshire Photographic Services)

Involved in the development of this pattern of behaviour is the use of the 'Stay there' command. This can be very useful when you go out to the post at a trial and then find that you have to wait for some time before sending the dog out—more often than not the problem being caused because there has been a hold-up in the letting out of the sheep for some reason.

If your dog attempts to run out *before* you have given him the command to do so, stop him, call him to you and then send him out when *you* are ready. It is important to nail this tendency for a dog to run out before being told to do so because, if he is allowed to get away with it, you are going to have all sorts of problems in the future when he needs to be well under control at the starting post.

A difficult outrun

Whilst on the subject of outrunning at trials, it is worth mentioning that we can often be faced

with problems such as the one every handler and his dog have to sort out at one of my local trials each year. This is at Vivod, Llangollen, which has one of the most trying outruns of any trial in Wales (and there is a real feeling of achievement to win this one). Two fields on a steep hill are used, and the sheep are out of sight of both dog and handler when let out. This means that the handler has to send the dog out to whichever side he has decided upon and, once the dog is out of sight, has to rely on the dog to lift his sheep and begin to fetch them towards the handler, who does not know where his dog is until the sheep begin to come over the brow of the hill. At this point, the handler once more takes over and begins to command the dog again to enable him to negotiate the various hurdles before reaching the handler (see Diagram 15).

This type of trial reinforces the need, as I have been stressing, for a dog not only to develop a good outrun but also to use his brain when necessary. At this particular trial there is no twelve o'clock contact on the lift—the dog has to keep going until he finds his sheep and then has to be able to remember the direction back to the handler. Mastering this manoeuvre is also essential for the handler and dog who gather sheep in hilly and moorland country— a dog who cannot think for himself is useless to the shepherd who works over this sort of terrain.

What I am saying here is that I try to develop my dogs' abilities and harness them by training and putting commands on the various movements the dog makes when working with sheep in order to have him working to my requirements but without turning him into a robot. I want the dog to learn that when I ask him to make a particular movement he must obey but that when I give him no commands he can use his own head to work things out.

Different outrunners

A dog does not need to be a natural outrunner

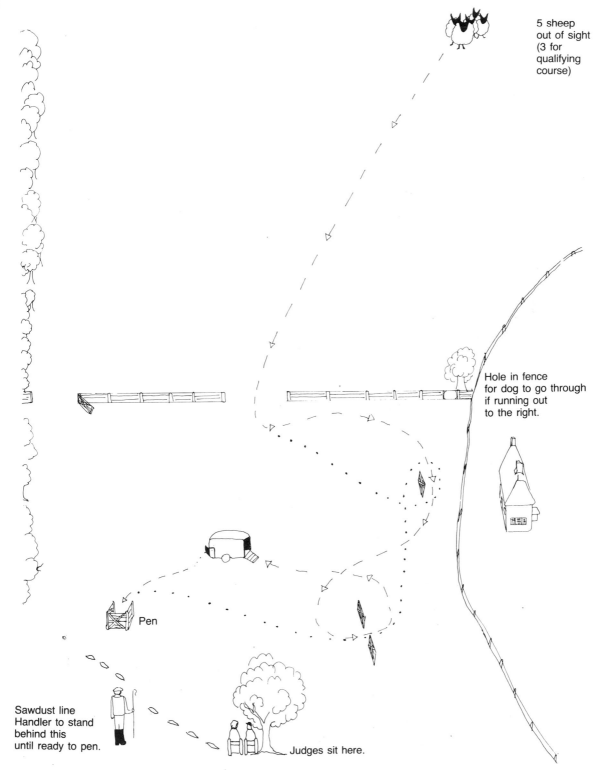

5 sheep
out of sight
(3 for
qualifying
course)

Hole in fence
for dog to go through
if running out
to the right.

Pen

Judges sit here.

Sawdust line
Handler to stand
behind this
until ready to pen.

DIAGRAM 15 Vivod trials course. Small dots show where the qualifying course is different to the finals course. Outrun to either side.

Gel, International Supreme Champion 1973.

to become a champion, as many outrunners are literally man-made. My dog Gel, who eventually won the International Supreme Championship at Bala in 1973, was never a natural outrunner and his outrun was made by practising on the mountain at the back of my farm. Even so, Gel would only go a certain distance before slowing down, so I always had to give him a second command to keep him going until he spotted his sheep and then there was never any problem, as he would cast out quite naturally to get behind them. A good thing about Gel's outrun was that he was always on the correct line so I never had to worry about that. The great beauty of the dog who has had to be taught his outrun in this way is that, when trialling, you are always confident that you can get your dog behind his sheep in all situations albeit with the loss of a few points for repeating the command.

On an open moor, this type of dog comes into his own because you can guide him to the sheep to be gathered (i.e. a particular bunch) from a particular point. This is a great boon when you think of the natural, wide outrunner who can get lost on open moorland—he just keeps going outwards to look for his sheep and gets lost unless he can be drawn in by command. Such dogs make excellent boundary runners for field work, but without boundaries they can present problems if they are not suitably trained.

I have already mentioned that Bwlch Taff is a wide outrunner. When on the open mountain he tends to run too wide and therefore too far, although I can always rely on him to bring sheep back to me—often mine *and* somebody else's as he has run so far! A wide-running dog who is working hard all day every day up on the moor with a shepherd wastes a lot of energy and often, for this type of work, a tighter running dog, trained well to commands, will get less tired. Taff, not being in full-time employment on moorland, is extremely useful to me in the type of work I do on fenced land on my farm.

Another dog from the past who had a completely man-made outrun was William Jones' Ben 11401, mentioned previously in this book. This dog had no natural cast at all but he did have a good brain and was a first-class listener. William Jones trained Ben himself and ran him early on but failed to win any prizes, so he agreed to sell him to Griff Pugh, another well-known Welsh handler, for the sum of £25 on condition that he kept the dog until the end of the week so that he could run him in his local trial at Llanarmon yn Ial at the weekend. He won the Local Class on the Friday and also the Novice and Open classes on the Saturday, and the outcome was that he never did sell the dog—and never stopped winning with him. Together, Ben and his handler won many top trials including the Welsh National in 1958, and they represented Wales four times when they qualified for a place in the Welsh team for the International Sheep Dog Trials.

The first Wiston Cap pup I had was Roy 41107 and he was a dog with a perfect outrun to the left but straight as a die on the right. Not surprisingly, I would send him on a left outrun whenever possible at trials but I always lost points if I had no choice and had to send him out to the right. Despite this, I did a lot of winning with Roy because, once he got behind his sheep, he was always reliable and very responsible to command, although, considering the higher standard of runs at trials today, I doubt if I would be as successful with him now.

Roy, my first Wiston Cap dog. (Farmers Guardian)

When watching dogs running at trials over the years, I have noticed that the vast majority of them are sent out on a right-handed outrun, and I don't really know the reason for this. Is it because most handlers are right-handed? Are the dogs right-handed? Is it just habit? Do novice handlers copy others, to be copied in turn as they become more proficient? Have we all got training fields which favour a right-handed outrun? Whatever the reason, it is important to make sure that, in our training, we enable the dog to develop *both* outruns and alternate them during training sessions, as it is essential for a dog to be able to run out to both sides for both work and trialling.

Strengths and weaknesses

Once again we come back to the question of assessments at regular intervals throughout training. People can grow and develop without losing their own individuality and personality, and we as trainers should recognise that every dog has his own character, inbred instinct, ability and potential, and it is up to us to recognise the strengths and weaknesses of our dogs and deal with them accordingly, using the strengths and correcting the faults. Present-day handlers such as Alan Jones, John J. Templeton and Thomas Longton (and many more) work with their dogs to realise their full potential—like wise parents, they have patience, understanding and an ability to give their dogs the confidence to learn well, knowing that no dog will give of his best if bullied into submission.

Periods of struggle

There can be quite long periods during the training of a dog when both he and the handler really have to struggle through problems in an effort to get things right. These times can be suddenly followed by realisation that things are beginning to go right again, but, alas, once one thing is put right, the struggle begins with something else! However, never underestimate the amount of learning you, as the handler, are

John J. Templeton with Ben (standing) and Roy (sitting).

Thomas Longton with Maggie (left) and Bess (right).
(Marc Henrie)

Alan Jones with Spot and Craig.

doing all the time and how your knowledge and skill are slowly developing as you continually assess progress (or otherwise) and the ways in which you manage, with patience, to solve what may have seemed insurmountable problems at the time.

With every dog there comes a time when you find that you are going to need to get a bit tougher with him. Have a good, objective look at all the moves your dog is making and ask yourself 'Does he move before I give him the command to do so?' 'Does he stop as soon as the command is given? Not a foot or so after the command has been given, but *immediately?*' 'Is he responding appropriately?' 'Does he understand what I want him to do?'

I mentioned my father's friend Jack Ellis in Chapter 1 (our chauffeur in his little Austin 7) and the problems he had in stopping his dogs, especially at the top end of the trials field when furthest away from the handler. Being young and foolish (instead of old and foolish as I am now), I tackled Jack on this point because I had noticed that he would whistle, not once, but three, four or more times to no avail. When I asked him, 'Why don't you *make* your dogs

stop?' he replied, 'I never can.' I then asked, 'So why do you keep on whistling?' and he answered, 'Because I just keep on hoping.' The truth of the matter was that, at home, he had got into the habit of whistling stop several times and then the dog would stop eventually because he was on home ground. But in any case, the stop was not so important there as on the trials field because there were no obstacles to negotiate. But the bad habit had developed and the dogs all learned to ignore Jack, by and large. I have mentioned before the need to look with a critical eye at ourselves and our dogs during training, a continual process in our struggle to reach perfection, and Jack Ellis' fault could be developing in our own training, so be aware of the ease with which we can fall into traps of our own making.

If you feel that the dog is not doing as well as you know he can do (is playing you up), then get back to basics, in the middle of the field, because that is the place where you can demand *perfection* at this stage. You still have your rolled-up fertiliser bag to bang against your leg, and if you feel that the dog is simply trying to test you out, you can hold him by the

The legendary J. M. Wilson with Whitehope Nap (standing) and Bill (sitting).

fur beneath his ears and give him a shaking to let him know you mean business. The dog will be so surprised by this treatment from a person who has always been such a nice, kind teacher so far, that he will bend over backwards to please you and you can then finish the lesson on a good note with a lot of praise.

Dreams

I remember how, in my early days at Plas yn Llan with sheepdogs, I would read glowing reports in the *Farmers Weekly* about one of the most famous handlers of all time—the late J. M. Wilson of Scotland—who used to sweep the board at all the big trials, whichever dog he was running, and I also remember watching J. R. Millar running double dogs at a Whit Monday trial in Greenfield Park, Liverpool, with his two smooth-coated black and white dogs, Drift and Speed. How I dreamt of the time when I would have their skill and be handling dogs of that quality! I remember J. R. Millar, who stood well over six feet, as a red-headed giant, and although I never did achieve his physical stature, I did eventually realise my dream of winning the Supreme title and of being able to handle double dogs successfully—there is no reason at all why you, the reader, should not do the same.

CHAPTER 8

Nursery Trials and the Turn-back

Dual-purpose dog

AFTER ALL THE WORK which you and your dog have been doing, there eventually comes a time when you look at the dog and ask yourself several questions (again!).

'Is my dog becoming a really useful working dog?' 'Does he do all his basic movements correctly?' 'Is he growing in confidence?' 'Am I growing in confidence?' 'Is my dog really fit, has he plenty of stamina?' 'Has he had experience of different flocks of sheep?' If your answer to all these questions is a definite 'Yes', then you ask yourself the question, 'Do I simply want a good, sound working dog or do I want to take him further?'

The working dog

If you are not interested in competing in sheepdog trials, then you will find that, by now, you have an extremely useful dog for your farmwork. Both you and the dog will

Bwlch Bracken—a useful dog for farmwork.

have benefited from the training routine, and after the addition of training in the turn-back (described later in this chapter), you will have a dog who will be invaluable to you in the years to come. It is still a good idea to reinforce training from time to time throughout your working years with a dog, however good he is at his daily tasks, as any dog with intelligence and spirit is going to try to test his handler from time to time. Sessions of routine training once or twice a week will help to keep both dog and handler on their toes and can prevent bad habits from developing at any age.

Whilst having a good farm dog is enough for many farmers and shepherds, there are an increasing number of people who, although they never compete in sheepdog trials, recognise the value of a highly trained dog on the farm and, even if they do not train dogs themselves will, when buying a dog, ask for one which has been trained to trials standard because they have learned from experience that these dogs can be worth their weight in gold.

Whether to sell your dog and buy in something better

When your dog has reached the stage where he is trained sufficiently to make a good farm dog, you, as the handler, must decide if this is the dog with the ability to be taken further in training and whether you want to do this anyway. If you are a farmer/shepherd and want a really good farm dog who will be of great help to you, you may decide to train the dog up to trials standard because you find the training to be interesting and you will then find him of even more use around the farm. If you are determined to carry on with training to trials standard and beyond and you are going to start competing in nursery trials, then the time has come for you to stand back and look at your dog with a really critical eye—and this is not always easy to do, especially for the novice handler who has invested so much in this, his first dog. You have spent many hours

with your dog, the bond between you will now be very strong, but, if you intend to be successful on the trials field, you must be able to make an objective assessment. Has he grown into the type of dog you really want? Has he the right temperament for trialling? Is he sufficiently intelligent to go even further in his training? Has he enough natural ability, combined with your months of training, to make the grade? If things go well, is he capable of getting right to the top with you?

If your answer to *all* these questions is a resounding 'Yes', then you can make plans to go on to the next phase of training. *But* if the answer to any of them is 'No', meaning that your dog is *not* good enough, then the time has come for you to part company. This is not really as harsh as it sounds and I am sure that if you think it through you will eventually agree with me. Suppose you keep the dog, carry on with his training, start trialling with him and then he continually lets you down— what then? How will this affect your eventual attitude to the dog? Is the dog going to be really happy if he is continuously put into a situation in which he does not feel comfortable, i.e. on the trials field? Would the dog not be happier doing what he does well—farm work and no trialling? If you are a farmer or shepherd you will be able to keep the dog as a useful animal for farmwork and he will be happy—but what if you have no work for your dog other than training sessions in the yard and trialling? Please, please do not consider allowing this dog to spend the rest of his life as a pet—he is now so used to work, loves nothing better than to go out to the sheep with his handler, and I think it is an act of extreme cruelty to condemn him to a life of relative inactivity simply because you cannot bear to part with him (pure sentiment and thinking only of oneself). The best thing to do in these circumstances is to sell the dog to a farmer who is looking for a well-trained dog to work on the farm—the dog will soon adjust to his new situation and handler (probably more quickly than you can adjust to the loss of his presence),

Three dogs that made the grade—Bwlch Bracken, Glen and Gel with Phil Drabble during the training of Glen for 'One Man and His Dog'.
(Derek Johnson)

your conscience will be clear and the money from the sale of that dog will give you sufficient funds to purchase your new young dog or puppy. In a way, you are making an end-of-term assessment and you are not being unkind. On the contrary, you are trying to decide your dog's future with his best interests at heart and *not your own*—an important point which is often overlooked.

You should always be aiming at something better all the time—how many times have I heard handlers say of their new youngsters, 'This is the best young dog I have ever had. I think he could be a champion one day'? We all tend to think this but, inevitably, many of these young dogs do not make the grade. The reasons for this are many and varied—it could be that the dog does not have it in him, maybe the training methods used are at fault, maybe the dog and the handler are not right for each other. Whatever the reason, the end result is the same and we go on to the next dog. But, every so often, we *know* that we have hit the

jackpot and when we do, *wow!*, it is a marvellous feeling, and continual optimism, hard work and the development of knowledge, skill and understanding all play their part in this exciting game.

Preparing for nursery trials

Never fall into the trap of trying to rush the training of a young dog in order to get him trained by a certain time. Occasionally you will see a handler who has a really outstanding, very young dog who is running in the nurseries at nine or ten months of age—if you are a novice, do not emulate this practice. Take your dog at a pace in training with which you are both comfortable and do not push him, or yourself, too far too soon. While some youngsters who do well at a very early age go on to great things (particularly if they are being handled by an expert), the vast majority fall by the wayside because too much has been expected of them at too young an age—usually because they showed exceptional promise and the handler was very excited by this and pushed the dog too soon.

If you decide that you do want to go further with your dog and would like to enter the trialling world, then now is the time to start— and what better place than in nursery trials which are run for novice dogs.

I have left discussion of preparation for trials until now because I think that, to start training a dog with the sole idea of running him in a trial is the wrong way to go about things. The concept of nursery trials is an excellent one, providing, as it does, keen competition for handlers and their young, inexperienced dogs, with, at the end of it, only small awards and no financial gains. But I do think that we often allow ourselves to get into a mad rush in an effort to get a dog ready for the nurseries and many good young dogs are spoiled in this way. If a dog is of a standard suitable to enter for a nursery trial, then enter him but not before he is really ready for it. If we are not careful, we can destroy what the dog has been bred for—herding sheep—if he is put in a stressful situation in strange surroundings too soon. The nursery trials should be used as a teaching ground for both man and dog, providing an extension of what has been happening in training sessions at home but now in a different environment.

Preparation for competing in trials is not simply a matter of training a dog nor only a matter of the level of confidence in both man and dog. Well before this time, the dog should have become used to travelling quite long distances in the car so that he is relaxed and happy when he reaches his destination—after all, a dog which gets car-sick cannot be expected to be on the top of his form when he arrives at the trials field.

Another area of preparation is that of sheep. By now you should have found some way of running your dog on different kinds of sheep and in fields other than his home ground so that he will have the confidence to work his small bunch on the trials field, whatever type they turn out to be.

What about people? This is something I have not mentioned since the chapter on early rearing and should have perhaps reinforced several times by now. If you live in a remote farmhouse where a dog is unlikely to see many people, it is important that, whenever anybody visits you, you let the dog get to know them and have him talked to and handled by them so that he is confident with strangers. Having the dog housed out of doors where he can see what is going on around the house will help a lot, but actual physical contact with as many people as possible is important. Don't forget that, on his outrun at a trial, the dog will encounter strange faces in the form of spectators (or the people at the top end of the field who are letting out the sheep) and the last thing you want him to do is to run away because he is frightened.

Can you take your dog to the starting post, well under control and *without a lead*, and will you be able to maintain control over him with verbal commands if he spots his sheep? It never ceases to amaze me when I see some handlers (not only novices but also more experienced ones) walking out to the post with the dog on the end of a lead—if they cannot control their dog in this situation, how on earth do they expect it to obey their commands when further away? In my opinion, if the dog

The Shropshire handler, Austin Bennett, who believes in 'Have pup, will travel'. (Barry Griffiths)

A dog well under control at the starting post. E. Wyn Edwards with his Supreme Champion, Bill.

has to be taken to the post in this way, then neither he nor the handler is ready to compete in trials.

Nurseries are held in the British Isles during the late autumn and winter months when the weather is usually at its worst. This will not worry the dog too much as he has a nice, thick fur coat to keep him warm, but what about the handler? Experienced handlers will have learned how to cope with all the hardships and difficulties of trialling (not to mention working) in less than perfect conditions, but the novice may need some advice so that he does not get caught out. Do make sure that you are adequately clothed in warm, waterproof clothing as it is impossible to keep your mind on the trialling if you are shivering, wet and miserable. You also want to keep fit and well enough to be able to go to the next nursery trial in a few days' time—you've really got the bug

now—so look after yourself. As most nurseries have no provision for supplying competitors with sustenance, it is essential to take picnic food with you and flasks of hot drinks, soup and even the odd noggin of medicinal whisky or brandy which will not only warm you up but can give a bit of Dutch courage too! (But don't overdo it.)

Even in winter, it is a good idea to take a supply of fresh water for your dog unless you are certain that there is going to be an adequate natural supply on the trials field—as the years go by you will learn which trials have water available and which do not. In any case, whenever a dog travels in a car, there should always be a canister of fresh water.

Stop and think

When you arrive at the trial, do not forget to go to the trial secretary with some entry money and book your dog(s) in for a run—novices can be so nervous that they completely forget that this is a necessary prerequisite to being added to the competitors' list. Find out what your number is and the number of the current run so that you will be able to assess the approximate time your run will be due.

Well before your run comes up, remember to let the dog out of the car or pick-up and take him for a walk to give him the chance to stretch his legs and to relieve himself. Keep things quiet and low-key so that the dog does not become overexcited, and it is a good idea, before putting him back to await his turn, to take him to the perimeter of the trials course and let him look for the sheep. Once he has spotted the sheep being let out for somebody's run, take him quietly back to the car.

Watch as many runs as possible before your turn comes in order to make an assessment of the course, to learn the sequence of hurdles to be negotiated and the hazards in relation to you and your dog—you will be able to decide which side to use for the outrun, you will see the type of sheep being used and you will see how the more experienced handlers cope with problems which arise. In other words, use the time available to advantage.

When your name is called, hand in your ticket and go steadily and quietly to the post with your dog at your side, and remember all that you have learned regarding the position of yourself and the dog in preparation for the side on which you intend to send the dog for his outrun, as previously explained in Chapter 5. Concentrate on your dog and the work in hand and this will help to allay some of the nervousness you will inevitably be feeling.

dog to complete manoeuvres he has done many times before. *You* can understand the reason for the change in situation and atmosphere, the reason why there are so many people around, why the sheep are to be found in a specific place—but the dog cannot, so concentrate on him and his need of you. Also remember that the nursery trial can be used as an extension of the training programme and, if your dog makes a mistake, *correct it in the way you would have done at home*. If this means that you have to walk up the field to be nearer to your dog in

Watch as many runs as possible. (Marc Henrie)

For the novice handler, in particular, it is worth mentioning that you should try to keep as calm as possible in your first trial—think of your dog and not of yourself and you may find that this will help. You are there to help your

order to give him confidence and put things right, then so be it, and if it costs you the rest of your run because you feel you should bring the dog off, it really does not matter. What does matter is that you have not allowed your dog to make an uncorrected mistake which could be the start of bad habits and you can make a fuss of him for having done his best and then go home to work on the particular thing which started to go wrong. Nursery trials can thus provide invaluable experience for both handler and dog by highlighting problems which may not have been noticeable on home ground. Unfortunately, many handlers now expect far too much of their dogs far too soon in the nurseries and would never dream of helping the dog out when it gets into difficulties because they feel that they will look foolish. Personally, I think that the latter look foolish anyway and the former group are the ones who will eventually make the grade.

There are many good dogs on the trials circuit today who started their careers by running at the nursery trials and who benefited from the experience gained there. Of the dogs of the past, one which sticks in my mind is Jim Cropper's Fleet 38813. This dog did exceedingly well all the way through his nursery season, gaining 23 awards in 31 trials, and Jim then went on to greater things, winning the English National Driving Championship in 1973 with Clyde 49960—another of his dogs which did well in his nursery season, won many Open Championships and gained a third and, later, reserve places in the International Supreme Championship. Both of these dogs had the same parents—and the same

Jim Cropper with Fleet (left) and Clyde.

handler—and the combination was formidable.

My father was very good with young dogs at novice trials and always used these as though he was still on the training field at home, with the result that his young dogs developed enormous confidence as the trials season progressed, and I think that this area of training was probably my father's forte. He always sold his young dogs at the end of their first season to make room for the next youngsters to be trained for trialling in the following year.

Nurseries as a market place

The nursery trials provide a good market for promising young dogs which handlers like my father may be prepared to sell at the end of the season. If you ever want to buy in a promising youngster, then go to as many nurseries as you can and watch all the dogs running. Over the season you will almost certainly find that one of the dogs continually catches your eye—if this happens it is a good idea to approach the owner to ask if you can have the first option of buying at the end of the season. You have to bear in mind, of course, that if a nursery dog does well, up will go the price and, conversely, if he does not do so well, down it will come. If you really want a dog you have seen, you can always make an offer part of the way through the season and take a chance on it continuing to do well—as in any market place, a lot of bargaining goes on throughout the season.

The turn-back

We are now at a point where we can start to train the dog to turn back to run out to fetch a second bunch of sheep—this is an essential working procedure when gathering large flocks of sheep and, in trialling, when you represent your country at the International trials or when you have qualified to run in the Supreme Championship on the final day, you and your dog will be faced with a turn-back and second outrun for another lot of sheep. It is no good trying to teach this in a mad rush during the

few weeks between winning a place in the International team and your appearance at this major event; if you do, then your dog is almost certain to let you down at the crucial moment when the big day comes and it will not be his fault, it will be entirely yours because you left the training for this particular manoeuvre too late. What is more, failure to effect a satisfactory turn-back at this level of competition will put the Supreme accolade completely out of your reach, however well your dog does over the rest of the course. Thirty years ago, I remember seeing many dogs fail to achieve a satisfactory turn-back in the Supreme Championship, but nowadays the standard is so high that it is unusual for a dog to fail in this movement, so be warned.

By starting to teach the turn-back at an early stage, we are giving ourselves and the dog plenty of time in which to get things right, there is less stress involved for handler and dog because there is no shortage of time, and, once learned, it can be put to good use in everyday shepherding so that it becomes part of the dog's working routine. If you are a handler who needs to rely on others to get a wider experience of sheep work for yourself and the dog, then you will need to make every effort to offer your help to farmers and shepherds in return for the opportunity of running your dog on their flocks. I know several handlers who do this and, believe me, there are not many stockmen who will turn down the chance of unpaid labour if they are convinced that the arrangement will be mutually advantageous—it is largely up to you to convince them that this will be so!

The turn-back really consists of two things: (a) the dog must learn to leave one packet of sheep and then (b) turn back to look for his second lot prior to the second outrun. In Chapter 6, when writing about shedding, I talked about teaching the dog to turn from one bunch of the separated sheep and to take away the others. I mentioned there that this manoeuvre is part of the turn-back training and you are going to find out why.

Beginning to teach Ben to turn back.

I now add the new command 'Turn back' to the basics of 'Come here', 'Lie down' and 'Stay there' which I am still practising with the dog in our yard sessions. I tell him to lie down, go up to him, give him the command 'Turn back' and physically turn him round so that he is facing the other way—this will bewilder the dog at first, so introduce the new command gradually, not necessarily including it in every lesson, until he begins to get the idea of what is expected of him. Your dog is older now, so will not take too long to learn what 'Turn back' means, and I very soon begin to put a whistle in for this command as the dog is able to assimilate these things more rapidly now. I want the dog to turn round with his back to me but not to move forwards until given the command to do so. Because the dog is uncertain at this stage, he will stand still after being turned around, or, if necessary, he can be given the 'Lie down' command to keep him in the place you have just put him. Another method of maintaining control at this point is to put a lead on the dog (in the yard only) so that he has to stay where he is.

When beginning to teach the turn-back

proper, I get the dog to shed the sheep and, as soon as he has come through the gap, I tell him to 'Lie down'. I then walk up to him and turn him round physically, saying 'Turn back' at the same time, so that he ends up on his feet with his back to me, looking up the field and stopped, waiting for the next command. We are now in exactly the same position as when teaching the straight outrun, where the dog is facing his sheep, has his back to the handler and is then asked to flank to one side or the other. From then on, the procedure for the outrun to one or other bunches of sheep is as described in Diagrams 14A and B (see page 73).

In the early stages of teaching the turn-back, it may be helpful for the handler to move the packet of sheep he has finished with to ensure that his dog concentrates on those which are on the side to which the dog is to be flanked. However, it is better, if possible, to get the dog used to leaving one packet of sheep behind him as this is what he is going to have to do eventually.

Teaching a dog just to go back when you ask him is a relatively simple thing; what is more difficult is to get him to go exactly where *you* want him to go. This is when the ability to stop a dog on his outrun and then give a renewed flanking command to open him out, if necessary, is of great importance, particularly when the dog may not be able to see his second bunch of sheep, as in the International trials or when working on mountains and moorland or even on very large fields.

As your dog becomes more experienced, when he is given the turn-back command he will be able to take the flanking command without stopping because he knows that, after turning back, he always has to run out to find more sheep. But at the very beginning the stop is essential to the turn-back training because it gives the dog the time to settle and await his flanking command.

CHAPTER 9

'Polishing' the Dog

WITH HIS FIRST nursery season behind him, the dog is now ready to advance further in his training through the rest of the winter and you can begin to prepare for the coming season of Second Class and Open Class trials. He has now learned all the basic manoeuvres he will ever need to know but there is still a lot of 'polishing' required. In addition, the handler will have to make some decisions which will refine his own movements and will have a bearing on the way he commands his dog in the future.

Most dogs will be around the age of two to two and a half years at this point but there are all sorts of variables, so if your dog is younger or older it does not matter. What is of importance is the level of the dog's maturity, his confidence, ability, response to command and general level of readiness to proceed further. He will need to have developed stamina and resilience and will have a great love of work which can be used to advantage in training sessions. At this point I always wish the dog could ask *me* the questions on things he is not sure about—it would save a lot of time and it would be so easy to work on *his* areas of concern which might be quite different from those on which I had thought extra work necessary. But stopping to think things through all the time and having regular times of assessment should help shorten the odds a little.

Method of commanding—decision time

In Chapters 5 and 6 I mentioned that both full and shortened versions of verbal and whistle commands would eventually be used; the time has now arrived when this can be done in order to get both large and smaller movements on command. The handler needs to decide on how he intends to use voice and whistle commands in different situations. For instance, is he going to use quiet verbal commands for close (inbye) work and the whistle for more distant (outbye)? Is he going to use only whistle commands? He must recognise that the use of verbal commands only is not a feasible proposition as the dog will be unable to hear him when working at a distance or in high winds and other bad weather conditions. In general, most handlers seem to use a mixture, retaining the voice command for times when the dog can hear without the handler raising his voice. One thing which I greatly dislike at trials (or in the work situation, for that matter) is the handler who continually bellows at his dog in an effort to get a response—I feel that this does neither the dog nor the handler any good and can certainly detract from the run from the point of view of the spectators. Of course, we all get exasperated with our dogs from time to time and let out a shout, but these occasions should be rare.

We should take a fresh look at the whistle commands and make sure that (a) they are easy for the dog to differentiate between, (b) they can be broken down into a smaller command on the same note(s) and (c) the sound is always consistent. Remember the usefulness of taping the commands to listen to them as described at the beginning of Chapter

6—this could be done again at this stage to ensure that the whistles have not changed out of all recognition. If they bewilder you, just think what they could be doing to your dog.

Lessening the use of the 'Come here' command

The time has now come to begin to eliminate the use of the words 'Come here' when the dog is working with the sheep, eventually using this command only for the shed and at other times when the dog has finished working. Up to now, this command has been useful in helping the dog to learn his flanking movements correctly, but once he knows these, the 'Come here' command gradually becomes less frequently used.

Dog on his feet or lying down?

Another decision to be made at this point is whether you want to have a dog who works on his feet or you are quite happy for him to clap down when he stops. Personally, as I have mentioned before, I prefer an adult dog who will remain on his feet all the time he is working, going down only when it is absolutely essential; but you may feel differently. So make your decision now so that you can plan your 'polishing' accordingly. There are no rights or wrongs in this—it is a matter of personal choice—but if you eventually want to have a dog with a lovely, flowing movement when working his sheep, then you need one who will stay on his feet. I think this is the trend these days. I cannot recall when this style became more popular, although I can remember the time, many years ago, when all dogs tended, or were encouraged, to clap down each time they stopped—making them look rather like big frogs moving around the trials field.

The 'Stand' command can be of particular use when shedding and penning, the dog's very presence, standing but not coming forwards, often being enough to maintain control over his sheep. I like it because I think that the dog on his feet is more or less on eye level with his sheep and they are more likely to take notice of him than if he is trying to hide behind a blade of grass! Often when working on the mountain, a ewe will give way to a dog moving towards her from the same level or above, but if that same dog approaches the ewe from *below* she is quite likely to stand her ground. Incidentally, you will hear people commenting on the penning of a particular handler saying, 'The man did all the work; the dog hardly moved/ was too far away/ did little to help.' They forget that the sheep feel the dog's presence and that it is instrumental in effecting the pen. Try penning without a dog and you will see what I mean. (This reminds me that I once asked the great J. M. Wilson which dog he preferred to pen with—the one on his feet or the one on the ground—and his answer was, 'The one on the ground has to get on his feet to move.')

A dog working on his feet. Llyr Evans with Chip.

Having outlined the advantages of teaching the dog to stand on his feet, I also have to remember that the handler (particularly the novice) may feel more comfortable and able to cope if his dog lies down every time he is stopped; if this is the case, do not attempt to go against your feelings by teaching the dog something which reduces your own confidence. It is far better to maintain the status quo and concentrate on 'polishing' what the dog has already learned. It does not matter if you never

Getting the dog to stand on his feet

If you decide that you want your dog to work on his feet and he has a natural tendency to do so, you can continue to train in this direction. If your dog tends to flop down and you wish to alter this, then the yard is the place to start the change. Start with the 'Lie down' command to stop your dog and immediately follow this with 'Stand' or 'Get up', lifting the dog to his feet as you do so. Keep him on his feet for a few

Tot Longton's wise old Rob working on his feet. (J. Ashworth)

get this dog to stand, as many of the top handlers have dogs which clap down every time they are stopped—they probably prefer things this way and they certainly win a lot, so take your choice.

seconds before saying, 'That'll do', and letting him go before calling him back and repeating the exercise. As the dog gradually gets the idea, you can slowly increase the length of time he stands until you feel sufficiently confident to take him out to the sheep and begin practising the 'Stand' when he is actually working. People who specialise in obedience training are extremely good at getting their dogs to 'Lie down', 'Sit' and 'Stand' (three different stationary positions), so there is no earthly reason why sheepdog handlers should not be able to get their dogs to stand on their feet to command.

Once the dog will stand to command in the yard *without moving forwards*, you can begin to practise in the field with the sheep. When you have got the sheep in a corner against a hedge call the dog to you and then walk beside him towards the sheep and, if he drops down when stopped, say 'Stand' and lift him quickly to his feet. You must make sure that the sheep are settled when you do this and that they do not attempt to run off. This combination of lessons in the yard followed by ones in the field will produce quite quick results in the dog who is now older, wiser and able to learn very quickly if he understands what is expected of him.

Refining movements

There is an enormous amount of inbred ability in the Border Collie, and by this stage in his training the dog will have demonstrated his inherent attributes (as well as defects) and the handler will recognise where his dog has the most ability. He may have a natural 'cast' (the ability to keep sufficient distance between himself and the sheep when gathering), good 'eye', be a natural driving dog and so on. All these things have a bearing on the dog's continued training and the 'polishing' programme. Is the dog a good outrunner with a natural, wide cast? If so, then it will be necessary to work on drawing him in when he goes too wide. Or it may be necessary to widen a dog's outrun if he has a tendency to come in too soon. Will the dog stop immediately? So look at all your dog's movements and work mostly on the ones where you are less than satisfied.

To begin to refine a dog's movements, work

very close to him in the middle of a field and give the shortened command followed by 'Lie down' after he has moved a short distance; i.e. if you want the dog to go to his left, you say 'Come', and when he has moved a short distance, 'Lie down'. Practise the same thing with the whistle commands, and once the dog will move short distances on his commands to both sides, you can gradually eliminate the need to stop him because you can keep him moving in smaller movements now and the stop is not needed once you have achieved this. The best place to practise these smaller movements, once the dog is able to respond correctly to smaller commands when further away from the handler, is on the drive and cross-drive once the dog has achieved the fetch. Do not attempt to use these smaller movements on the fetch until the dog is really expert with them on the drive (and nearer to you). Refining movements on the fetch should be left until you can rely on your dog to move, literally, one inch in any given direction.

If you give your dog the shortened flanking command and he does not respond, then you will need to immediately give him the full command and, as soon as he has moved a short distance, stop him because you only want a short movement. Then, once again, give the shortened command, followed by the larger one and another stop quickly afterwards. Gradually, the dog will begin to understand what is wanted of him with the smaller commands and, once this has been achieved, you should reserve the use of the full commands for the times when you want the larger movement as, for instance, when the drive is completed and you want to turn the sheep by sending the dog round to head them again. Gradually, the pattern will develop that, when given a shortened command, the dog will move just a short way to the side and wait, ready to respond to the next command. A fully trained dog, taught in this way, will know that the only time he is to head the sheep is when he has been given the *full command*. If you go back to the stage (described in Chapter 5) when teaching the dog to drive with the handler in the middle of the field, you can practise using the shortened commands while he is driving the sheep, using 'Come' or 'Away' until you want the dog to turn the sheep to go back in the opposite direction. At this point, use the full 'Come bye' or 'Away to me' to get the larger movement for the dog to head his sheep.

Keep practising these manoeuvres by adding them to the daily training routine. You should, by now, have a clear picture in your mind of what you require of your dog and you should keep persevering in getting him to move in the way *you* want him to move and not necessarily in the way *he* wants to move. Whilst there will be many times when both you and the dog want the same thing, there are also going to be the times when this is not so and this problem must be overcome—and you, the handler, will have to win this one so keep at it until you do!

There are some excellent handlers who never use the shortened commands and run their dogs in trials with considerable success, but I find that dogs work more consistently for me when trained as described. I think that, as the general standard of handling continues to improve, it will eventually be essential to 'polish' our dogs so that we can get these refined movements.

Alan Jones with his dog Lad 44675 was (and still is with any dog he handles) a master of these small movements. Lad used to be lovely to watch as he worked because Alan could get him to move one or two inches in any direction, with the result that he never needed to stop the dog and the whole run was rather like watching poetry in motion.

E. Wyn Edwards spent many hours training his tremendous, tough dog Bill 78263 and refining his movements over the years until, in his mature years, that dog was as near to perfection as one could wish to see and he became one of the few dogs to win the International Supreme Championship two years running. Gwyn Jones, Penmachno, reached a similar standard with his dog Bill 52654, and John Templeton of Scotland also has the same

skills with his dogs, maintaining continual contact with them by the use of voice and whistle—skills now being developed successfully by his son John, who has already become a young handler of repute. Another man who keeps a continuous contact with his dogs and keeps them flowing is the shepherd John Thomas, a Welshman who now lives and works in England and represents England at International level. Not only does John work his dogs in a flowing action, he is also able to do this with heavy lowland sheep, proving that continuous contact with the dog is necessary whatever the type of sheep.

Pacing the sheep

It is important to get the dog pacing the sheep correctly and smaller movements will help you to achieve this—so plenty of practice on home ground is needed. When involved in this refining process, it is necessary to talk to the dog all the time to keep in contact with him, and do not be afraid of overcommanding because, when the dog is working more than a short distance away from his handler, it is the only contact he has with him. In keen competitions, judges will be looking for a smooth, flowing run and this is where pacing the dog well (and thus the sheep) can come into its own. The aim is smaller movements at a slower pace.

If you watch most of the runs at a trial very carefully, you will see that, in the majority of runs, the dog is driving his sheep towards the fetch gates quite well and then, as the sheep get nearer to the hurdle, the handler will ask the dog to stop. If he does this and then asks the dog to move forward, the sheep will in all probability turn from the line they were on and miss the gates. If the dog has been trained to pace quietly behind his sheep there should be no need for a stop on the fetch. Amongst the best of today's handlers are Thomas Longton (the young English handler who won the English National in 1985 and the International Supreme Championship in 1986 with Bess

Gwyn Jones, Penmachno, with Bill and Shep. (Eileen Davies)

(Above) *John J. Templeton with A. R. Mundell.*

(Right) *John Thomas with Don, a son of Craig.*

101142) and Aled Owen (the young Welsh handler who won the Welsh National in 1985 with his grand dog Ben 129820). By voice and whistle these men maintain a lot of contact with their dogs, which work up on their feet and rarely need to be stopped because they have been taught the more refined movements thoroughly and thus pace steadily behind the sheep. It is not *continuous commanding* but more a *continuous contact* with the dog that helps him keep things right during the run.

ing, they should, I always think, be prepared to go out to the post on the trials field themselves before doing so. They would soon find out that it is impossible to have adequate contact and control over your dog if you stand mutely at the post, giving only one or two commands during the whole run. You will hear these people talk amongst themselves of marvellous dogs they have seen who have been able to run out for the 800 yard outrun, fetch the sheep, turn back for the second packet,

Aled Owen with Ben.
(Gerallt Llewelyn)

I think that this should be the aim of all handlers, and some of the runs in the International trials at Anglesey in 1986 were lovely to watch because the dogs were able to pace and respond correctly to commands for small movements. We must always aim at this sort of perfection rather in the way in which people in the horse world have done with their dressage horses, i.e. the horse is trained to move from the stop, to walk, to trot, to canter, to gallop and back through these movements without having to stop in between each phase.

When people who have never run a dog in their lives sit in the grandstand and continuously criticise handlers for overcommand-

bring all the sheep round the post, drive, cross-drive and so on with practically no commands being given. What nonsense! I have yet to see a first-class run where the handler has not needed to maintain a really good contact with his dog over the whole run.

There is, perhaps, a happy medium to be aimed at when commanding a dog—some people get whistling diarrhoea in the same way as others get the verbal variety. Even so, I prefer to hear a man whistling a lot to get small, quiet movements from his dog without having to stop him than see a handler who gives fewer commands (has less contact with his dog) but then has to keep stopping the dog to keep the pace of the run as it should be. Remember that driving should consist of the sheep moving forwards together and at a steady pace with the dog moving steadily behind them *with few, if any, stops*. Driving does *not* consist of stopping the dog behind the sheep and then moving him to correct the line of the drive when the sheep begin to veer to one side or the other. The dog should take the sheep at a steady pace in the right direction, making small flanking movements to keep the line correct as he and the sheep move forward— there is a subtle difference between a dog *following* his sheep and a dog who *takes* his sheep at a nice, steady pace. The 'stop and wait' system of working a dog is, to my mind, now outmoded and we should be aiming for something better than that all the time.

some will 'wear' quite naturally when driving, some will want to push on too fast all the time (the second category of pup), others will not push on fast enough (the first category of pup) but, whatever type of dog you have, you will have him sussed out by now and should be able to adjust the training requirements to the type.

Additional work for the dog

By now your dog should be taking commands from you up at 300 to 400 yards, and this needs to be gradually lengthened so that he will respond at any distance within earshot—up to half a mile or more. If at all feasible, some time spent on general flockwork would be of great benefit to both dog and handler at this time— not only does it help both to get used to

General flockwork. Bob Moore's Sally.

Some dogs are easier to train to refined movements than others; there are some natural driving dogs (the third category of pup mentioned in Chapter 4), some are natural 'pacers',

working at greater distances, it also helps in the practice of whistling to maintain contact with the dog when involved in outbye work.

It will be necessary to be able to stop your

dog even if he cannot see his sheep when he begins his outrun, so practise this. Another thing the dog will need to be able to do is to open out on his outrun, not only when he has seen his sheep but also at times when he cannot see them. This is where I learned a sharp lesson when running Bwlch Taff at his first International in Bala in 1980 where I was Captain of the Welsh team, Taff having won the Welsh National that year when he was fourteen months of age. Any big ideas I might

manoeuvre when the dog could not see sheep, and it was not until I stood there at Bala, wishing that the ground would open and swallow me up (and my dog), that I realised my basic mistake. Even after all those years of training dogs, I was still learning! Part of the problem was that Taff was too young to have been taken through the whole training programme adequately and the lack certainly showed up in front of all those people—a bitter pill to swallow.

The 1980 Welsh team. From left to right: R. Watkins, Mervyn Williams, R. E. Pritchard, E. J. Evans, R. Brooks, Mel Page, Alan Jones, Jim Dyson, Goronwy Edwards, H. Glyn Jones, E. L. Daniel, I. Jones, Lyn Lewis, Eifion Owen. (Alan H. Martin)

have had about myself and my dog were knocked completely out of me during our qualifying run when Taff, to my everlasting shame, crossed his course. I had sent him on his straight outrun, confident that I would be able to open him out when commanded to do so, and I was wrong—in the first season I had been able to open him out everywhere and was confident that there would be no problems with him on the International course. *But* I had made the error of failing to practise this

After that International, I certainly had something to work on over the winter months and, by his second trialling season, I could rely on Taff to open out on his outrun whether there were sheep in view or not—which demonstrates how one can put the winter season to good use when training the trials dog. Taff won the Welsh National again that year (1981) and once more we represented Wales at the International trials which were held on that marvellous, difficult course at Armathwaite in

102 A WAY OF LIFE

the north of England. Taff did *not* cross his course on that occasion and we qualified for the Supreme Championship on the Saturday. That was the first year that E. Wyn Edwards won the Supreme with his dog Bill 78263, the pair of them going on to win it again the following year at Blair Atholl in Scotland. Wyn and I had equal points at the end of the 1982 Supreme Championship so there was a re-run

and Bill won the Championship, with Taff in reserve place, so I was well pleased with him and, what is more, we had not let our country down. The above demonstrates that disaster can be used to advantage if we are prepared to learn from our mistakes and work with our dogs to eliminate the fault—it still does not mean that we will make it to the top but every fault removed will improve performance.

CHAPTER 10

Brace Work

BRACE WORK is great fun and I always have at least two dogs trained to totally different commands so that I can indulge in this pleasant side of sheepdog handling. It is also very useful to have a pair of dogs who will work together when gathering large flocks of sheep, and I think it is a great pity that more handlers do not run their dogs in brace competitions as it gives another dimension to the sport. Granted, it takes up additional time to train dogs in this area of work but the rewards are those of increased interest and enjoyment and, when competing, an extra chance of winning with your dogs. So why not have a go? The dogs you use *must* be fully trained before you introduce them to this type of work and I have found that, more often than not, they are more likely to be prepared to work in partnership if they know each other well. There are, of course, exceptions to every rule and some dogs will quite happily work with any other dog, whilst others will refuse to work when there is another dog around, even if they know it well.

A simple system of training

I use a very simple system when training dogs for brace work (there are other methods but this is the one which works for me). The first requirement is that each dog must have a totally different set of commands, both verbal and whistle, the only command which is the same for both dogs being 'Stop'. The second basic requirement is that, when I use a command for one dog, the other dog stops; i.e. I

practise using one dog on 'Lie down', 'Stay there' commands whilst working the other dog. I start this off with the dog who must not move being close by me, repeating 'Lie down', 'Stay there' very firmly each time I give a command to the second dog to move him. I alternate this exercise with first one dog, then the other, and as soon as I can rely on them remaining in one place whilst the other dog is working, I gradually lengthen my distance from the 'stopped' dog.

By training in this way, it is not long before each dog will immediately stop when he hears any commands which are used to keep his partner moving, i.e. he translates any commands which are not his own into a 'Stop' command. For instance, if No. 2 dog is moving too fast and I wish to stop him without stopping No. 1 dog, all I need to do is to give or repeat a movement command to No. 1 dog and No. 2 dog will stop. If, on the other hand, I want *both* dogs to stop, then I use the 'Stop' command which they have both been trained to obey. Once the handler has achieved this comparatively simple system, then he can continue to practise it with his pair of dogs, using it in flock work whenever possible and fining down all the movements in preparation for brace competitions on the trials field.

The only time that this system of training is likely to go wrong is on the outrun. If I find that, say, No. 1 dog is beginning to come in on his outrun, I have to repeat this flanking command to the appropriate side and, of course, No. 2 dog will then stop! The only way to get round this problem is to give the widen-

After winning the 'One Man and His Dog' brace championship at Crumock Water in 1979. R. Shennan (Scotland) on the right was the winner of the singles championship.

ing out whistle to No. 1 dog and immediately give the flanking command for No. 2 dog to keep him going—some points will be lost for this but not as many as if No. 1 dog had crossed his outrun. I know you are going to say that if I do this, my No. 1 dog will stop. You are quite right, of course, and it does sometimes happen—it is a time when I say my prayers and hope that the judges have dropped off to sleep. However, in general, if the brace outrun has been properly learned, this problem should not occur. The moral of the story is that outrun training for both dogs must be well practised, as discussed earlier in the book, and, hopefully, the times when there are outrun problems in the brace run with either of the dogs should be minimal. The great beauty of this system is that you never have to worry about getting your No. 2 dog to stop whilst sorting out something with No. 1 dog.

The brace outrun

Do not make the mistake of always sending the same dog out to the same side when teaching two dogs to work together. Brace work can spoil some dogs for singles work because they are being asked, most of the time, to work more to the sides of the bunch of sheep and, particularly if always used on the one side in the brace, they can develop the bad habit of trying to balance sheep continuously from one side. As I have said before, most dogs will have a preference for outrunning to one side or the other, and with my pair, Bracken and Gel, the former would always insist on going out to the right and I would allow her to do this because she was the dominant dog in the partnership and I found she would always run out better if given her own way in this respect. In her case, I was able to break my own rules because I had other dogs, including Gel, to run in the singles so I did not need her for that type of competition. Poor old Gel also preferred to run out to the right too but never got a look in when working with Bracken, and at least it had the advantage of not spoiling him by giving him his own way in the brace (he was my best singles dog at that time). I would use Gel for the first penning because Bracken, being such a madam, liked to have the last part of the action and thought that any applause (if it came) was for her alone. As you can see, I used Bracken's dominant, forceful and somewhat selfish personality to advantage in brace work.

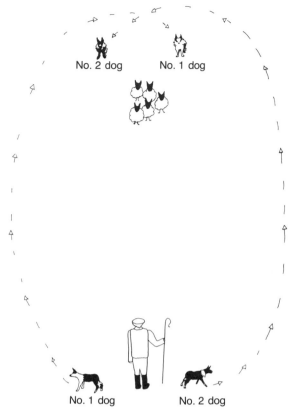

No. 2 dog   **No. 1 dog**

No. 1 dog   **No. 2 dog**

DIAGRAM 16   The brace outrun, overlapping at the top of the field.

Choosing dogs for brace work

When I first used Gel to work with Bracken, many people thought that he was the leader in the two-dog team but this was not so—Bracken was always the dominant dog and was the mainspring of my brace work. Gel had one great attribute: on the outrun he would never lift sheep before Bracken arrived to lift them with him, naturally slowing himself down so that he did not arrive first. This was one of the things which made my brace work with those two dogs so successful—not necessarily my training but a dog doing what came naturally. Of course, this is partly what brace work is all about—finding a pair of dogs who will work together in partnership with a 'feeling' between them. They were both about the same age but

there was never any doubt that Gel was the follower and Bracken the leader. I also used their individual inherent abilities when negotiating the various hurdles—Bracken was marvellous at driving in the brace and I would use her to drive the sheep through the gates and Gel to turn them once they were through because this was an area of work in which he excelled.

Using a dog and a bitch for brace work often eliminates the jealousy which can occur between two dogs of the same sex. As in human beings, jealousy can put them in competition with each other, affecting their ability to concentrate on the job in hand. My running Bwlch Taff and Ted in brace competition provides a prime example of this, Ted being the jealous member. An additional problem is that Ted is a 'busy' dog who wants to bustle around doing all the work, so I have to keep moving Taff to ensure that Ted will stop or slow down before he receives his own command for the next movement. I still haven't got this quite right, despite some measure of success in brace work with them, but I am working on it and should be able to get the act together before too long (I hope).

If one of a pair of dogs tends to run out more slowly than the other, then it is necessary to send him out first, assuming that the outruns to both sides are of similar length. Sometimes a

G. R. Jones' Glyn and Queen at brace work.

With Bracken and Gel at Loweswater.

course will have a shorter outrun to one side than the other and then it is necessary to do a balancing act based on the length of the outrun and each dog's outrunning style and speed. Get to the trials in plenty of time and you can have this all worked out well in advance of your run. Remember that the rules of ISDS state that, in the brace, 'both dogs should start together', but the really important thing is that the dogs arrive at the top of the field at the same time to effect a smooth lift together.

When training dogs for brace work it is a good idea to practise *overlapping* your dogs before they lift the sheep—the ISDS rules allow dogs which are running in brace competition to cross *once* and, by doing this at the top of the field, you will prevent your dogs from developing the habit of stopping short on their outrun in singles competition—an im-

portant consideration. Once a pair of dogs become proficient at brace work, I avoid giving the actual joint 'Stop' command as much as possible because I like to keep my dogs flowing, reserving the 'Stop' for emergency situations where things are beginning to get out of hand (as they are bound to do from time to time, even for the most experienced handler).

Some brace competitions

Talking of things getting out of hand reminds me of the time I competed in my first brace competition—this was at Vivod, Llangollen, over twenty-five years ago, and I was running Tweed and Glen (the dog my father handled in the singles class there). There were always great crowds of people at those trials and they were an appreciative audience and generous with their applause. At this particular time, the sheep were very wild and causing a lot of problems on a tough course of two hilly fields where the dogs had to go out of sight of the handler to fetch the sheep. I sent both my dogs out and they went well, vanishing from sight to find their sheep. Shortly afterwards, the sheep could be spotted coming over the horizon but my dogs were nowhere to be seen! I kept whistling for them and, in the meantime, the sheep just kept on walking steadily (everybody else's sheep had been almost uncontrollable) down through the gap in the fence in the middle of the course, straight through the fetch gates and still no dog in sight. At that very moment, the crowd decided to applaud and I stood there in acute embarrassment because the lovely, steady movement of those sheep down the course and through the hurdles had nothing at all to do with my dogs—it was sheer luck—and the run was at an end because I then had the humiliating task of going off to find my brace of dogs. The embarrassment of that day spurred me on to greater effort and did a lot to give me enough determination to carry on training dogs, to improve my methods of training and to improve my handling of double dogs in particular!

At that time there were many excellent brace handlers around such as the Longton brothers, Timothy and Tot, Ashton Priestley, W. J. Hislop, P. Hetherington, E. Wyn Edwards, Meirion Jones and many, many more.

I. S. Hadfield, a coal merchant by trade who lived at Prestatyn in North Wales, was a first-class sheepdog handler, being particularly noted for his achievement and skill in brace work. I think that he won more brace competitions than any other man of his day, wins which included the International Brace Championship on five occasions—in 1958 and 1959 with Jean 10216 and Roy 12127, in 1962 with Mick 13311 and Roy, in 1966 and 1968 with Ben 28220 and Tip 23558. He also won the Welsh National Brace Championship on six occasions—with Jean and Roy (1957 and 1960), with Ben and Tip (1966, 1967 and

G. L. Pennefather. (Derek Johnson)

1968) and with Ben and Lad 58962 in 1972. Quite a record and a real joy to watch.

I think that the general standard in brace competition at the present time leaves a lot to be desired. However, as with any sport, there are peaks and troughs, and I am sure that the art will peak again. All Irish sheepdog handlers owe much to their great mentor G. L. Pennefather, and there are currently some very good brace handlers in Ireland, Jim McConnell of Co. Waterford being one who has done well with his dogs recently and, of course, there is the handler with a very individual personality, Denis Birchall of Dunlavin, who won the International Brace Competition in 1985 with his two clever little bareskinned bitches, Kate 10140 and Mist 109678. Another classical handler in brace competition is G. R. Jones of Brechfa in South Wales, who runs his dogs along the same lines as one would work a team of horses, and with great success. There are, of course, other good brace handlers in the British Isles, and I hope that their numbers

Tot Longton with Jess, Supreme Champions in 1983. (Marc Henrie)

From left to right: Peter Hetherington, Raymond Macpherson, Tim Longton and Michael Perrings in 1974.

will increase noticeably. Perhaps trials organisers could do much to help to restore brace handling to the highly competitive and enjoyable sport it was in the past.

The indomitable Alan Jones.

Not only can brace handling bring more variety and competition to the trials field, it is invaluable in helping handlers to develop their timing to perfection, always a necessary asset when handling dogs at any level. I must admit that I have been very lucky to have a brace such as Bracken and Gel, who won the 'One Man and His Dog' competition the first time it was held twelve years ago and went on to win it three times in all. Because of those successes, the two dogs and I were invited to make a guest appearance at Cruft's Dog Show, having become television personalities and, therefore, well known in the more general dog world and with the general public. As we were introduced the roar of applause from the crowd was unbelievable, unexpected and exhilarating, the two dogs reacting quite differently, as I would have expected given the two diverse personalities involved—Gel was not at all keen on being the centre of attention but Bracken was in her element and, the more applause, the better she liked it, playing to the audience like the old trouper that she is and making it one of the highlights of her career.

Some time ago, the brace competitors at the International trials were faced with two packets of sheep—one in each corner of the field—when running at York in 1975 (I think it was that year) and everybody watched the proceedings with interest. However, the competitors got into all sorts of difficulties and subsequent brace competition has seen only one packet of sheep used right up to the present day. With the general improvement and high levels of skill in the handlers of today, I doubt if the problems set by two lots of sheep would prove to be too much of a difficulty and wonder if the idea of a 'turn back' in the brace might be put into practice once again in the not too distant future—perhaps it would help to rekindle interest in brace work and would certainly make runs at International level more entertaining for the spectators.

Brace work can also be great fun to watch if two handlers can run a brace competition together using their four dogs—I have seen this done in the past and it can be a most spectacular demonstration when things go well. Conversely if things go hopelessly wrong, it can cause a lot of fun and laughter for both handlers and spectators, so, either way, it is usually a success.

Sadly, with record entries at most trials nowadays, the emphasis seems to have shifted from one of a need to provide enjoyment to one of how to get as many dogs and handlers through as possible—this has resulted in a sort of down-grading of brace work which is now treated as being of secondary importance—not a little surprising as there is a real art in this type of handling. This is not really fair to handlers or dogs and certainly not to the spectators who are rapidly growing in numbers as the sport becomes more of a national pastime. I think that the time has come to impose limits on the numbers of entries to trials and the number of dogs one is allowed to run, in order to bring back just a little of the real 'fun' element which handlers and those who watch can enjoy and look forward to—many will not agree with me but I suspect there are also many who will.

CHAPTER 11

Trials at Home and Abroad

ALL HANDLERS DREAM of achievements and successes they would like to have in the future with their dogs and I have been no exception. However, even in my wildest dreams, I never envisaged that I would one day travel to the other side of the world as a direct result of my involvement with sheepdogs. Neither would my father have believed me if I had suggested to him that this might one day happen because of a remarkable expansion of interest in the Border Collie and in sheepdog trialling throughout the world. In his day, humble Welsh blacksmiths and others from the working classes rarely travelled more than a few miles from their homes, they certainly could not afford to go away even for modest holidays and only a comparative few had even been across the Border into England. But times have changed and, in 1984, I was invited to judge trials in Canada and America.

Judging in Canada

The first trial I judged was at Souris, Manitoba, in Canada at the invitation of Marv Brown, and it was there that I first encountered what I think must be the worst sheep in the world for trialling. Up to this time, I had always thought that our little, hardy Welsh ewes were the most flighty and unpredictable in the world, but I was wrong. The sheep at Souris were big cross-Suffolks and, I later learned, disliked dogs because they thought they were coyotes. Over there, the sheep have to be brought in to a corral at night to keep them safe from the wild coyotes which, even in the daytime, will

attack grazing sheep—this means that the sheep are always watchful, and the minute they see a coyote will run from danger like gazelles, or, if an ewe has a small lamb at foot, she will stand to the threat and fight to the death if necessary. So as soon as the sheep see a dog on the trials field, they immediately bolt, running around the perimeter fence at great speed. They either do this or stand to the dog and refuse to move, and, on one occasion, I saw a big ewe go for a dog and stand on him and would eventually have stamped the dog to death if the handlers had not been able to rescue it.

But, if I thought that was bad, we were in for even worse when I moved on to judge the two-day trial at a place called Markham. The trial was held at a sort of sports stadium where they were holding a sheep show at the same time as the trial, and here we encountered even bigger sheep—and could they run! It took about half a dozen men to bring the sheep to the starting post in a truck and to let them out—then, as soon as the sheep's feet touched

Taff, a son of Bracken, now with Harry Hobbs in Canada.

the ground, they would make back to the large shed they had come from. Again, as soon as the sheep saw a dog they equated it with a coyote and ran towards buildings which they equated with man and safety, I suppose. None of these sheep had ever seen dogs, I am sure, and they thought that anything on four legs and the size of a coyote was a killer. Holding a trial under these circumstances really was something of an achievement and I felt sorry for everyone competing against such hopeless odds.

In the British Isles, trials have been held for over a hundred years in every part of the land so all handlers know, by and large, what the trials course will have in the way of hurdles and in the sequence of the obstacles to be negotiated. In Canada and the States, where trialling is a relatively new sport, the judge always gets the competitors together before running commences and explains the course, what the competitors are supposed to do and how he will be marking the runs. This I found to be a novel experience but it did make me realise how much we take for granted over here and perhaps how blasé we tend to become when we have so many trials literally on our own doorstep at all times of the year.

Another thing which I found a novelty was the fact that, in a two-day event, it is the aggregate scores from the two days which decide who is to be the champion. I found myself disagreeing with this system as it certainly puts the more experienced handlers at an advantage over those who are less experienced and therefore not as skilled at working out a strategy for getting the highest marks.

For the third day of the Markham trials, my time was to be spent holding a training clinic, and in that particular clinic there was only one Border Collie present, all the other dogs being stock dogs of differing breeds including German Shepherds and a Belgian Sheepdog. The Belgian Sheepdog turned out to be the star of the day, not least because his handler was such an attractive French-Canadian girl but also because the dog demonstrated real ability by

the end of the clinic. The enthusiasm, thirst for knowledge, determination to succeed and application to the task of the people attending training clinics in Canada and America impressed me greatly at this, my first clinic, and continued to do so on other occasions, as did that of all the handlers I met over there. There is no doubt in my mind that, despite the fact that they began sheepdog handling and trialling nearly a century after we in Great Britain did, they will shortly be every bit as good as handlers over here, if they are not already. And they really are a joy to teach.

After the Markham trials, I went to stay at Blenheim, Ontario, for a few days with Jim Clark and his family. The first of Jim's Border Collies which I saw on arrival at his place was a little smooth-coated bitch who had come over to Canada from Wales. Watching Jim and others working their dogs (as opposed to trialling) made me realise that the type of dog they need there is the type I have already said that I like myself—the spunky, free-moving dog who will come on to his sheep and show them who is boss. The dog with a lot of eye who 'sets' on his sheep, drops flat on his belly when stopped (or before) and creeps about 'eyeing' the sheep all the time is of little use for herding those coyote-fearing sheep. The type of dog needed must have very good command on him and I think I saw more of this type of dog at Markham than anywhere else on my travels, and most of those Border Collies were home-bred, which says a lot for the way the breeders were planning their breeding programmes. The dogs seemed to be equally at home working either cattle or sheep and were really pushy but, with those awful sheep, it was impossible for even the best handlers to get the sort of polished performance at trials that we see from the top handlers in the UK. The only times when this was possible occurred when the sheep were re-run, possibly on the second day of a trial, and then sometimes they would behave more reasonably and give the dogs and handlers the chance to show some really classy performances.

Training clinics

It was while I was at Richard Tipton's place in Lone Pine, Alberta, that I had the best clinic I think I have ever held. There were about twenty handlers there with their dogs, the sheep were actually good, being Dorset-crosses I think, also some cross-Suffolks, but none as big or aggressive as those I had seen elsewhere in Canada.

The class was held on a good field, the weather was good and the handlers very attentive so I enjoyed myself greatly. They were all so keen to learn that teaching was easy but I did find that I had a major hurdle to get over right at the start. In Canada (and the States) all handlers seem to have had it drilled into their minds that the only way to train dogs is with a long piece of rope and a long stick. One of the handlers, who was, by profession, a trainer of cutting horses, had his dog well trained on the end of a rope and admitted that he did not know how to go further. When I eventually persuaded him to go into the centre of the field and let the dog off the rope he was really apprehensive and, afterwards, could not believe that it could be so simple to cope with a dog who was running free. I am sure that this man, providing he continues to train his dogs *without* that rope, will eventually become a first-class dog trainer because he had a good feeling for an animal. Part of his problem had been that he was used to training young horses on a lunge rope, first without a rider, then with a rider, eventually removing the rope for later training. The difference between training a horse on a rope and a dog is that the horse will always have a rider to control him when the rope has been dispensed with whereas the dog does not, his only contact with the handler being by word or whistle, so we have to get control over him *without* the rope right from the start.

There were a lot of female handlers at this clinic, all very keen and enthusiastic and really determined that they would achieve as much as the menfolk, and they found it difficult to understand why there are comparatively few

Clinic at Richard Tipton's farm 1986.

women in Britain who handle dogs at trials, particularly as the sport has been going for so long over here.

On the fourth day of this clinic, I decided that we would have a change and a rest from training in order to hold a judging clinic—this turned out to be most interesting, instructive (to me as well as the participants) and enjoyable, and convinced me that we should have more of this sort of thing ourselves. We all sat around in the sunshine, on bales of hay on the

With Clancy Clarke (left) and two of his brown and white dogs.

perimeter of the trials field. I became one of the class, and after each run, I would ask one of the handlers to give *his* version of the judging of the run. This done, all the others would pounce on what they thought was wrong and would ask questions about the number of points which should be deducted for various faults. By doing this, we were able to answer a lot of questions which were in the minds of the individuals present and it meant that I was not giving a lecture on what *I* thought was needed

(the two things could have been miles apart and the class would not have learned nearly as much). The groups judged about ten different runs which gave a great variety of good running and also of errors at the various obstacles, providing much material for criticism and comment. Discussion became, at times, really heated and the participants thrashed out points down to the last detail, working on the real nitty-gritty of problems, large and small. An additional benefit from a judging clinic like this is that it does give handlers more understanding of the problems which judges have to face and some of the difficult decisions they often have to make and usually on the spur of the moment. I kept a low profile during the day in the knowledge that each member of the group was learning really well without any help from the so-called 'expert'.

I would recommend this sort of judging clinic to anybody who is involved in teaching others the art of dog handling. It adds another dimension to the training programme and can be introduced quite early on even with novice handlers as it makes them become more critical, not only of others but also of themselves, and they learn greatly from the mistakes of others who are involved in both the running and the judging. It is worth mentioning that the judging clinic mentioned above was attended by both handlers and spectators, some of whom did not have a dog but were simply interested in trialling as a spectator sport, and having this variety of viewpoints added greatly to the success of that day.

State Fair trials in California

I have been invited to judge the State Fair trials in Sacramento, California, on two occasions (in 1984 and 1985). At the first one, there was a really good field and I set what I thought was an easy course but I was told by the handlers there that they thought it was a tough one. It was quite big but at least it gave the dogs a chance to get a hold on their sheep between hurdles. The field was large enough to have a full National course of the type we have in Britain; I set the course so that the cross-drive went up and away from the handler and the distance back from the cross-drive to the pen was longer than the distance from the post to the first drive—quite different from National-style courses in Britain which have become somewhat stereotyped of late, using a rectangular course with cross-drives going straight across the field in front of the handler. (Whilst this is quite a reasonable way to lay out a course, I do think that some variety is now needed to make trialling more interesting for handlers, dogs and spectators.)

The following year, this trial was held in a very different setting. The ground was encircled by a racetrack and there were two small lakes which provided natural hazards, so I set the course with the fetch running between these lakes and a long drive which encompassed one of them (see Diagram 17). The first drive away from the handler proved to be quite difficult and the course proved interesting and challenging for the competitors with the bonus of additional interest for the many people who were watching the trials.

Transatlantic differences

There always seem to be plenty of people around to help at American trials and they make judging a comparatively easy job. In Sacramento I was assisted by a clerk so that all I had to do was watch the runs and give the number of marks lost to the clerk, who did all the rest. This meant that I never needed to take my eyes off the handler and dog, and I am sure that, as a result, the judging must have been more fair than if I had been continually looking down to make notes myself as I do when judging at home. Another great advantage is that the judge is not tempted to look at the marks given to previous competitors or to make comparisons, and, at the end of the day, I had no idea who the winner was until the clerk told me, and I think that that was a good

thing. I think this is an idea we should put into practice for judges at our trials.

In both Canada and the States there are a number of prizes on offer at all trials with trophies such as for best command, best pen, best fetch, best lift and so on being awarded for things other than the actual run itself. This means that many handlers will go home with a prize and I think that this system provides a lot of encouragement. I felt that there was enormous rivalry between those two great countries which reminded me of the rivalry which still exists between Scotland and Wales— and I think that this can only be of benefit to the standard of sheepdog trialling world-wide because it really puts handlers on their toes and determined to do better all the time. At a Sunday trial in Ohio, I had a new experience when a short religious service was held before the competition began. It was well attended and the sermon was, appropriately, based upon 'The Good Shepherd' and contained a lot of humour, giving another dimension to Sunday trialling.

Bruce Fogt, shown here with Hope, is a first-class young American handler with a cool, quiet manner.

Trials in Canada and the States offer not only a day or more of trialling and clinics but they are also big social occasions with good sponsorship and always a get-together of all the competitors, families and friends at some sort of informal evening function. There is not usually a set format for these affairs but there

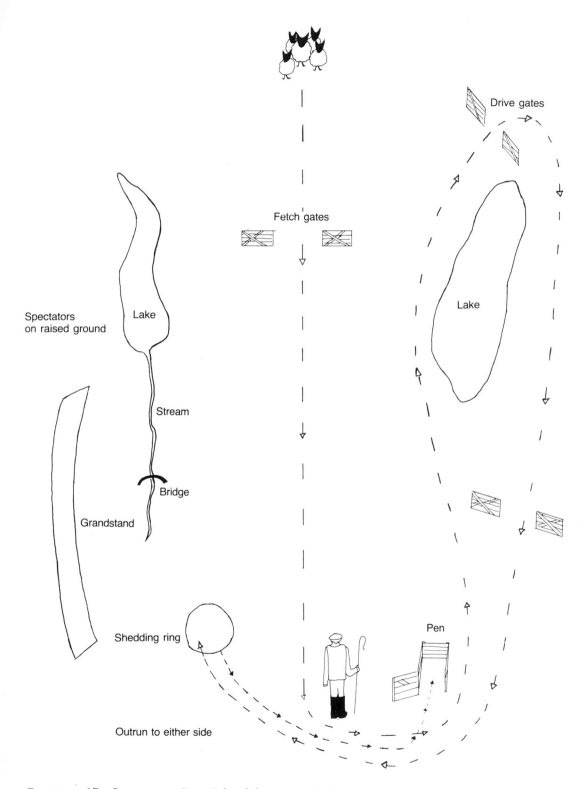

Drive gates

Fetch gates

Lake

Spectators
on raised ground

Lake

Stream

Bridge

Grandstand

Pen

Shedding ring

Outrun to either side

DIAGRAM 17   Sacramento State Fair trials course (1985).

115

With Ralph Pulfer (centre) and Guido Lombardi (right) at Sacramento. The dog is Ralph's bitch, Nan.

is always a lot of spontaneous entertainment which is most enjoyable and adds greatly to the sense of occasion. It took me back to my early days with sheepdogs when there were fewer trials and each one was a special event, a holiday and a time of relaxation—largely gone from the trialling scene here except for one or two very big trials such as the International, which has a formal dinner on one evening.

In general, I think that the American handlers are more relaxed in their approach to trialling than perhaps we are in this country, maybe because it is also more of a social gathering, I don't know, but the dogs also seem to be more relaxed too. It may be because there are fewer trials to get screwed up about.

In view of the complete mechanisation I saw in agriculture in both Canada and the States, it did surprise me somewhat to find that sheepdog trialling has become so popular both as a

hobby and as a spectator sport and is now well on its way to becoming a national pastime. The costs of trialling over there are enormous, involving travel over vast distances in specially equipped vehicular homes—many of the handlers use their holidays in pursuance of their sport and some of the most successful handlers can make a living out of it by winning the good prize money available; others are fortunate enough, financially, to be able to finance the hobby whatever the expense. But, whatever their situation, they are all enormously enthusiastic and there are some first-class young handlers now coming up to join the ranks of the top men.

A development in the States and Canada is holding trials for which only home-bred dogs are eligible, and this will do much to help them to improve their breeding and training programmes. I think there will still be a demand for dogs bred in Britain because there is no doubt that we produce some of the finest Border Collies in the world, but our friends across the Atlantic are catching up gradually and are breeding some first-class dogs from their own stock. I also think that as soon as they can get away from using the rope and long stick in early training of their dogs, we will see their standards of handling improve very rapidly and then we will really have to look to our laurels.

International Sheep Dog Trials

The International Sheep Dog Trials are held in Britain under the aegis of the International Sheep Dog Society. Competitors are selected as follows:

Single dogs The fifteen highest pointed competitors from each of the English, Welsh and Scottish National trials and the ten highest pointed competitors from the Irish National trials.

Double dogs (brace) The two highest pointed competitors in the National brace championships of the same four competing countries.

At Bwlch Isaf with Shep,
who was imported from America.

PEDIGREE OF H. GLYN JONES' SHEP A.B.C. 1779
Rough-coated, black and white dog. Born 20/9/84

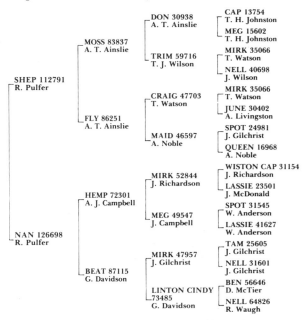

The trials are run over a period of three days. The top fifteen competitors from two days of Qualifying trials (single dog) then compete over the International Supreme Championship course on the final day for the top accolade. Diagrams 20 and 22 in Appendix 4 show the Qualifying and Supreme trials courses.

Other championships at these trials are the following:

Farmers Championship   Awarded to the highest pointed farmer in the Qualifying trials.

Shepherds Championship   Awarded to the highest pointed shepherd in the Qualifying trials.

Driving Championship   This is a separate contest in which competitors' dogs must drive sheep directly away from the handler in a straight line over a specified distance.

Brace Championship   Another separate contest in which competitors work with two dogs at the same time over a different course (see Diagram 21).

The return of the Dragon
Wales had a very lean spell at International level for some years from 1964 onwards, and in 1972 when I was judging at Machynlleth the handling was not as good as one expects to see in Wales. That same year my very good friend the journalist Eric Halsall wrote in his report

Eric Halsall with Gael. (Associated Newspapers)

on the International trial at Cardiff that 'Wales was in the doldrums'. My first thought on reading his comments was 'How dare he?' Being a Welshman I felt as though he had stuck a knife into the Welsh Dragon and I was furious. But it put us on our mettle and it was the best thing that ever happened to us because, with the centenary of the first sheep-dog trials in Wales being held the following year in 1973, it could not have been better timed. Eric's comments helped (perhaps 'pushed' would be a better word) the Welsh handlers into focusing sharply on the fact that their standards were falling and that it was necessary to do something about it—we had to face reality.

There was obviously a lot of hard work done by Welsh handlers as they trained their dogs through the winter which followed the 1972 season because, in 1973, the Welsh Dragon made a big come-back with Gel and me winning the Supreme title and Alan Jones winning the Farmers class in the qualifying round after a re-run against Peter Hetherington of Scotland. And since 1973 Wales has won the Supreme Championship seven times out of a possible fourteen, a vast improvement in performance. What we have to do now is to keep up the good work.

Griff Pugh with silver centenary medals which were presented to all the Welsh team members.

The following compilation by Eric Halsall is useful when considering the track record of the four countries in competition at International Sheep Dog trials held over the years:

- 70 Supreme Championships (from 1906): Wales 19; England 25; Scotland 26; Ireland 0
- 61 Farmers Championships (from 1919): Wales 23; England 16; Scotland 20; Ireland 2
- 61 Shepherds Championships (from 1919): Wales 10; England 9; Scotland 42; Ireland 0
- 43 Driving Championships (from 1937): Wales 11; England 15; Scotland 14; Ireland 3
- 51 Brace Championships (from 1929): Wales 20; England 13; Scotland 16; Ireland 2
- 53 Team Championships (from 1927): Wales 20; England 15; Scotland 18; Ireland 0.

It is interesting to note that, over the years, expatriate Welshmen and Scots have won trophies for England at the International owing to the ruling that handlers run their dogs for the country in which they reside, not from which they originate. So the English can consider themselves fortunate to have had handlers in their midst who have won various International championships on their behalf (I am talking tongue-in-cheek because the great rivalry which exists between the four countries is one of the marvellous things which keep us on our toes in the competitive field).

I am sure that handlers never think of their origins during their actual runs because they are part of a team and they are fighting to do the best they can for that team (and themselves). It does not matter who you are or where you come from—once you are in that team for the International you want to *win*. You sometimes hear competitors saying that

Alan Jones' Supreme Champion Roy in 1961.
One of the all-time greats and an outstanding 'class' dog.

(Left)
A group of Welsh handlers in the 1960s. Front row from left to right: T. O. Jones, E. Wyn Edwards, G. M. Jones, H. Glyn Jones. Back row: G. W. Jones (Tal y Bont), V. Humphreys, G. Pugh, G. W. Jones (Rhes y Cae).

(Bottom)
Three of my contemporary rivals in Wales. From left to right: Meirion Jones, former Supreme Champion, with Bill. Idris Morgan, a consistent winner, with Wag. Wilf Reed, former Supreme Champion, with Turk.

*Meirion Jones with his Supreme
Champion, Ben, in 1959.*

they are not in the sport to win, and I say that
if they are not out to win, they should not be
there because that is what the game is all
about. Without the desire to win no competitor
will do his team justice and he will be letting
them down.

You only have to watch the yachting competition for the America's Cup to see what
enormous achievement comes from the will to
win for one's team and country, and sheepdog
trialling is no exception. I always remember
Bill Shankley, the manager of Liverpool football team, who said, 'Winning is not everything, it is the *only* thing'. And if you lose, you
must be a good loser whilst being put on your
mettle to do better next time.

Bearing in mind that the construction of a

Channel Tunnel to connect the rest of Europe
with Britain is now becoming more feasible, is
the time approaching when the International
Sheep Dog Trials will become truly 'International', with foreign countries competing
alongside England, Scotland, Wales and Ireland
(the four countries at present involved at
International level)? What a great challenge
that would be for us all. Or perhaps the main
effect that the Tunnel will have on our collies
will be the introduction of that dreadful disease
rabies to the British Isles—what effect could
that have on the freedom of movement of
handlers and their dogs within these islands?
How would it affect the enormous choice we
currently enjoy when deciding which trials to
attend?

Young Handler Competition

Looking on the bright side, and assuming that there will eventually be freedom of movement for dogs from the Continent to Britain, there is no doubt in my mind that sheepdog trialling could only benefit from the increased competition we would face. I am sure that Wales (and the rest of Britain) is now very well prepared for any invasion by foreign handlers and we will be ably supported by the many young handlers we now see competing at all levels of trialling, an activity which has been actively encouraged by the International Sheep Dog Society in recent years. In 1973 the Young Handlers Competition was introduced at the International trials with a cup to be presented to the winner. This has done much to foster competition at this level and one of the major benefits it offers our youngsters is the opportunity to experience running dogs in the charged atmosphere generated by the crowds of people present at such a major event—good schooling and preparation for the future.

Each Affiliated Society may offer the ISDS Young Handler Award Rosette at its major trial each year, with an age limit not exceeding twenty-five years. For the Young Handler Competition at the International, a draw is made from eligible young handlers to compete for the coveted trophy. These handlers must not have attained their twenty-second birthday on the day of the International competition and their dogs must be ISDS registered. In North Wales, two of the trials which are affiliated to the International Sheep Dog Society for the Young Handlers Award scheme are the ones held each year at Glyn Ceiriog and Llangollen—two of the toughest courses in the country and offering a terrific challenge to even the most hardy veterans in the business, let alone the youngsters. Of course, any young handler who has run his dogs on difficult courses such as these is being well prepared for the time when he represents his country—a fact which is reflected in the high standard of the handling which they demonstrate each year at the International.

Robert Edwards, the young Welsh handler
who at age fourteen
won the Young Handler Competition
at the 1986 International with Max. (Marc Henrie)

CHAPTER 12

Agricultural Training Board Classes

CLASSES IN TRAINING sheepdogs have been run in all areas of the British Isles, wherever there is a demand for them, for some years now under the Agricultural Training Board (ATB) scheme, and full information can be found via the local National Farmers Union office, the public library or the local agricultural college. There is a small membership fee for joining the local group, and if you can collect four to six people who wish to request training on the same agricultural subject, including sheepdog handling, you simply contact the area organiser who will then make the necessary arrangements to run a course.

This really is a remarkable scheme and provides opportunities which should not be missed—there are always advantages from learning with a group of people, not least of which is the chance to learn from each other as well as from the instructor, and one of the good points about these classes is that each experienced handler who teaches has slightly differing methods and approaches to sheepdog training—this leads to added interest, discussion and controversy amongst those taking part. I think that handling and training can only benefit from this sort of activity, because a thing which all the instructors have in common is the desire to help others to handle their dogs better and to generally improve the standard.

These courses last for six weeks, and at the request of the students, a further course(s) can be arranged to take them as far as they wish to go in the development of their skills. They can also apply to attend ATB courses in other areas. What I find most rewarding from teaching these ATB students is that so many of them want to go further in the training of their dogs than the first six weeks allow. They also begin to develop an interest in furthering their other farming skills and may enrol for classes in shearing, lambing, general shepherding tasks, hedge-laying, tractors and other courses. As you can see, the system is very flexible, it presents all sorts of possibilities for those who wish to further their knowledge and skills and is available at minimal cost—unlike the United States where handlers usually have to pay quite large sums of money to attend training 'clinics' which are more or less identical to those offered by our ATB.

The main idea behind the ATB classes in sheepdog handling is to encourage handlers to train their own dogs rather than buy them already trained. As I have stated before, there are some distinct advantages in doing this, not the least of which is cost, and it has long been recognised that young shepherds do not earn sufficient money to enable them to buy the really good, trained dogs which are such an essential working tool for them. However, these same shepherds can usually afford to buy a puppy from sound working stock or may be in a position to breed their own but do not know where to start when it comes to training— the ATB has now filled this gap and it has done much not only to improve the standard of sheepdog handling in farmwork but also to encourage handlers to have a go at continuing the training up to trials standard, introducing them to this fascinating and absorbing hobby at the same time as improving their working skills. I have been taking part in these training schemes for the past few years, and as far as I am concerned, the main task of the ATB class is to teach the novice how to handle a sheepdog for use in his work with sheep. If that handler then wishes to take things further and start trialling when he feels that both he and the dog are ready for this, then so much the better—he is getting an added bonus!

In North Wales, where I live, we are very

However, in general, an increasing number of good handlers are prepared to take part in the ATB scheme and some also run private classes for those who can afford them or wish to have individual tuition. I know of novice handlers who first attended ATB classes and then went on to private tuition when the trialling bug bit them. With the increase in leisure time and the growing popularity of the Border Collie and his work, sheepdog trials are a rapidly growing sport and there is no doubt in my mind that

With the ATB class, Nant Clwyd, 1986.

lucky in that there are so many experienced sheepdog handlers who are prepared to help the serious novice handler—I do not know any of these people who, if approached by a novice with a request for advice, would not be prepared to give it. I have been told that there are still odd pockets of resistance to the idea of sharing knowledge in some areas of the British Isles and, if this is so, then I think it is a great pity that the people who class themselves as 'experts'—and, indeed, are acknowledged as such—will not give of their time and experience to help others with similar interests.

the requests for training will increase greatly during the coming years.

My involvement in the scheme

The first of the six ATB lessons which I give in the 'basics' of sheepdog training consists of a 'finding out' exercise with each student and dog and usually consists of a fairly mixed bag of problems, the most common one being that the handler cannot stop his dog, closely followed by the fact that he cannot catch him either. I have noticed that many novices at this first lesson are understandably self-conscious about handling their dogs in front of others—this can mean that, when their turn comes to go out into the middle of the field with their dog to show what they can (or cannot) do, their voices can change in response to their nervousness to the degree that the poor dog does not even recognise it, adding to everybody's problems! The dog feels that he is being handled by a stranger so he fails to respond in his normal way and the handler's first task is to learn how to overcome his own anxiety. Once he is able to walk out with his dog and forget everything else but the fact that he is *determined* to begin his dog's training, come what may, then we have a chance of getting somewhere because his voice returns to normal, the dog understands and recognises the voice and training can begin. I always point out, too, that I am still learning and that, during the course, I will learn as much from the class as they will learn from me. I find that people relax quite rapidly and we then begin to go through the stages of basic training for work with sheep as laid out elsewhere in this book. It is never difficult to know where to start. At the beginning of a series of classes in the basics, I say to each handler, 'Take your dog into the middle of the field and just let him go so that we can see what he will do', and the answer is, invariably, 'If I do that I'll never be able to stop (or catch) him', and I have my starting point: I say, 'Teach the dog to stop first and *then* you will be able to catch him', and we are away.

Farmwork or training first?

By and large, I think it is probably best for the young dog, where the facility exists, to begin developing as a farm dog first *providing* that he is trained to stop before he is allowed to go to work. This is absolutely essential but is often overlooked by the busy farmer or shepherd who only wants his dog to gather the sheep and bring them to him so does not feel the need for a stop command at this point. This is

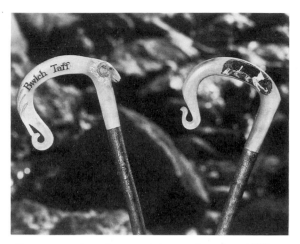

Two treasured crooks presented to me by recent ATB classes. They were carved by the North Wales crookmaker, R. G. Jones.

all very well but there are times when everybody who owns a dog will need to stop it, often for its own safety, and the stop should be taught with the other basics in the yard even if it is never used in the work situation until much later. I think that it is easier to train a young dog who is used to working on whole flocks of sheep by using his natural instincts to bring them to the handler than it is to train the young dog who is used to seeing only three or five sheep and is then faced with learning how to cope with larger numbers. Don't get me wrong—either way is possible but one way is probably somewhat easier than the other.

Many people attending ATB classes tell me, when they first come, that they only want their dog to be a good farm dog who will gather the sheep for them. Once they have learned to stop their dogs, they then think that they might as well teach him to go left or right on command and, if they achieve this, they tend to find that they want to go even further—they are beginning to get the training bug, of course. I have been asked what is the best age for the dog to begin training (and, sometimes, the handler) and my answer is always that the age of either does not matter; what is important is that the handler wishes to teach his dog more because he is finding it interesting and also because he is beginning to realise how much more useful the dog is becoming on the farm now that he is being trained in additional manoeuvres—and no dog or handler is ever too old to learn (I am living proof of that myself!).

It is important to recognise that it does not really matter if the student does not develop a high standard in handling his dog during his ATB course; the point is that he will have achieved more than he would have done if help and tuition had not been available. He has taken the first steps in improving his handling techniques, he has met other novices in the class and his knowledge and learning can continue for as long as he wishes. In this way, I think that these classes have been as instrumental in increasing the general interest in sheepdog training, albeit in a less dramatic way, as the television programme 'One Man and His Dog', which has now been running for twelve years and continues to grow in popularity.

I have noticed that an increasing number of handlers are going to ATB classes with their young dogs *before* they begin to develop bad habits, and this is really good to see as it can only result in happier and better-trained dogs,

whatever they are to be used for. The moral support which these classes give can be of great benefit and, from the dog's point of view, he meets the course instructor who has had a lot of experience with dogs and suddenly finds somebody handling him who will stand no nonsense, and that, in itself, can only be of benefit.

Various types of dog seen at ATB classes

When I started off with my first ATB class, the dogs which accompanied the handlers were invariably Border Collies, some registered, some not registered, but all of the same breed type. Nowadays things are changing and there is slowly increasing competition to be seen from other breeds such as Kelpies, Bearded Collies and Huntaways—a trend which I am sure will continue. Whilst I am firmly convinced that the Border Collie will always be unsurpassed for the type of stock work we have in the British Isles, I am pleased to see this competition from other breeds and feel that it should be encouraged.

Well-trained, all-round farm dogs at work in the market—Bracken and Gel. (Derek Johnson)

Kelpie owned by Don Wrench, Llandegla.

John Anderson's Beardie, Scot.
(C. Jones)

127

Kelpies

I have seen the Australian Kelpie in ATB classes in Wales and also when I was judging trials in Canada—the Kelpie I saw over there had been brought over to that country by his Australian handler who was attending a Woolgrowers Convention and he also competed in sheepdog trials in his leisure time there. That Kelpie had great difficulty on his outrun but, after that, his run was quite good and his work which I find myself liking. I think that the outrun problem may occur because I understand that the Kelpies are not taught to gather sheep in the way we teach our Border Collies, this being done by men riding on horseback and pushing the sheep forwards. I have read that the Kelpie has early origins in the bare-skinned Border Collies imported into Australia from the Borders and Scotland at the turn of the century, and I am sure that, if trained in the way we train our sheepdogs, it could prove

Kelpie at work in Australasia—Tim Austin's Elfinvale Daffy. (Elfinvale Stud Kelpies)

at the pen was really impressive—he did show 'eye' there when he was close to his sheep and was a first-class worker close to hand. I noticed that this Kelpie was used to hand signals because, when driving his sheep away on the trials course, he had to turn round to look at his handler to pick up his commands. The Kelpies I have seen over here have not demonstrated much 'eye' although they are dogs to be quite a competitor in trials in Britain. It is a tough little dog with a lot of guts and enormous stamina (we could do with a bit more of this in our present-day Border Collies), and I hope we will see their numbers increasing.

Huntaways
The New Zealand Huntaway is now being used increasingly by the farming community

and the one nearest to me is owned by John Anderson who works on the Nant Clwyd Estate where my father used to work as a blacksmith and where I was born. Although John's dog has a marvellous personality and is one of the most lovable dogs you could wish to meet, he is also one of the noisiest dogs on earth, being a great barker as he goes about his daily tasks, and that is something I cannot stand in the work situation. I think there is nothing the Huntaway can do which the Border Collie cannot do, the difference being that the well-trained collie can probably do even more than the Huntaway and, what is more, does it *quietly*! So why shatter the peace of the countryside unnecessarily? You have probably gathered by now that I feel that all other dogs which work with stock fall into the category of second-class in comparison with the Border Collie, and I would not give the Huntaway houseroom despite its pleasant personality and nature, but I am sure there are many people, particularly in New Zealand, who would disagree with me.

Bearded Collies

Beardies from working stock are the sheepdogs which I think come closest to the ability of the Border Collie, which is hardly surprising as they share some breeding lines from the not-so-distant past. They are tough and resilient with plenty of stamina and are good-sized dogs which can be trained to a high standard, although I do not think they would take any prizes for beauty unless it was in the eye of the beholder. John Anderson, the owner of the Huntaway mentioned above, also has a Beardie which has a lovely, natural cast, a good outrun and can really walk the sheep. He is a really grand farm dog and could, I am sure, be trained up to trials standard in a comparatively short space of time if his owner was so minded. He is a very intelligent dog who is able to use his brain and work things out for himself, and I would certainly like to see more Bearded Collies competing in trials because they would make formidable opponents indeed.

Maybe, in the future, we will, as I am quite convinced of their enormous potential.

The first Beardie I ever saw was at the Vivod trials near Llangollen and, at that time, I thought that it looked a really strange dog—there is certainly no doubt that the three sheep he worked with on his run thought that he was peculiar too, if their behaviour was anything to go by when they first clappd eyes on him; he upset the sheep even more when he missed the gap in the fence which he needed to go through in the middle of the field and he started to bark when he couldn't find his way. The sheep went hell for leather down the field and it would not surprise me to learn that they have not been heard of from that day to this.

My second encounter with a Beardie was at a trial in Otterburn in Northumberland—the shepherd who owned the bitch demonstrated his method of catching the ewe by her hind leg with the use of his leg crook (leg cleek in Scotland) and his Beardie coming up to hang on to the sheep's nose, making it all look deceptively easy. She was a tremendous Beardie and one of her puppies was later sold to a Mr Williams of Llandudno who eventually ran it in local trials in the North Wales area.

I would like to see the owners of Beardies and Kelpies training their dogs by the same methods as we use to train Border Collies to enable them to compete on equal terms at sheepdog trials. This would be a great challenge for trialling in this country and could only enhance the sport as it would put the Border Collie handlers on their mettle and would help to keep improving the standard. I say this in the sure knowledge that nothing, but nothing, will ever surpass the Border Collie in brains, ability and beauty of movement, but it would be nice to see other dogs attempting to reach the same standard.

Returning to ATB classes, one thing which always strikes me as being of interest is the collie which has been trained to a high standard of obedience (for obedience work) before its handler decides to have a go at training his dog for work with sheep. If the obedience handler wants to have a dog which is suitable for work in both the obedience ring and sheepdog trials, I think that he would find that the dog will develop better if he is trained for stockwork first before he is trained to the high level of obedience required in the ring. In my experience, most dogs which are trained in obedience beyond the three basics of 'Lie down', 'Stay there' and 'Come here' tend to have the herding instinct smothered (in other words, they become de-sheeped) and it is then usually very difficult to get them really interested in stock work. Again, there are exceptions to every rule and there will be the odd dog which excels in both areas equally. However, it is possible to have the best of both worlds if tackled in the right way. The same, of course, applies to handlers who wish to be involved in the beauty show ring and trialling.

CHAPTER 13

A Guide for the Novice Breeder

ONCE A HANDLER has trained his own dog(s) he may wish to have a continuation of the line of a dog or bitch with which he has been successful or he may have become interested in breeding for various characteristics. Whatever the reason, there is no doubt that breeding can be a fascinating and rewarding pastime but it is also demanding in both time and money and, therefore, should not be undertaken lightly. It must also be remembered that, if the pups produced are to be registered with the International Sheep Dog Society, both dog and bitch have to be registered and the owners must be members of the Society, the address of which is Chesham House, 47 Bromham Road, Bedford MK40 2AA. The telephone number is (0234) 52672.

Choice of sire and dam

Before breeding from a bitch, Beryl and I discuss which dog we should choose as the sire and we do this in advance of the time when the bitch is likely to come into season so that we can contact the owner of the dog to ensure that he will agree to its use. If, for some reason, the chosen dog is not available, we then have time in which to decide upon an alternative. There are many reasons why one should choose a stud dog (and the brood bitch) carefully but, for us, the one of prime importance is that of temperament, as a dog who is nervous, sulky or aggressive is of no use to any breeder and should be avoided. Our next consideration is that of bloodlines which should be compatible with those of our bitch and should contain plenty of outcrosses to other good dogs and bitches in addition to the lines which we particularly like—we have a preference for the Wiston Cap lines but this is purely a matter of personal choice. It is always nice to see a classy dog and we aim to maintain this in our breeding programmes, although the working ability of the dog is of paramount importance, and with a good-looking bitch you can hope for handsome pups even if put to a less attractive dog which has been chosen for working ability (or vice versa).

There are at least two main trains of thought regarding the matching of a bitch and a dog in order to get the desired result in the puppies. One idea is that you should breed from two opposite styles of worker—i.e. one being cool and steady, the other pushy and quick in movements—because it is thought that the two will blend together to produce a 'middle of the road' litter, easily managed but with a little more flair being introduced by the more lively of the pair. In my opinion, this does not work—what you are likely to produce are two extremes with some of the puppies being quick and erratic with perhaps too much 'eye' and the rest having insufficient 'eye' and push, making what I would refer to as plain dogs with little or no style and often lacking in concentration. At Bwlch Isaf we breed from pairs which have similar, classy styles and temperament; both dam and sire must be good listeners, be intelligent and have first-class working ability and stamina. We do not breed from close relatives (inbreeding can be fraught with hazards and may be instrumental

Beryl with Bwlch Bracken and one of her litters. (Bee Photographs)

in multiplying genetic problems) but we do like to have at least one line of breeding which is the same on both sides (this is where our Wiston Cap preference comes in). This is line-breeding but even here we take some care and like to have a four-generation gap before repeating the line.

Having decided which dog to use, it is then essential to ensure that both dog and bitch have been eye-tested for PRA and CEA (see Appendix 1) if over two years of age or that

they are from eye-tested stock if under that age. If you wish to have your bitch eye-tested, there is a list of approved eye-testing veterinary surgeons available from the ISDS.

The owner of the chosen dog, having agreed to accept your bitch, should be contacted again as soon as the bitch is seen to be coming into season in order to verify a date for mating. Also, before mating, the service fee should be agreed although, sometimes, if the owner of the sire particularly likes a bitch, he will opt to

Dogs in our breeding line that demonstrate the continuation of hereditary characteristics.

Wiston Cap.

Tweed.

Sheba.

(Far right)
D. Macdonald's Glen.

Bwlch Bracken, Gel and Glen, Bwlch Taff's father.

Bwlch Bethan, daughter of Bwlch Bracken.

Bwlch Tweed, son of Bwlch Bracken.

Bwlch Taff, son of Bwlch Bracken.

134

Lyn,
daughter of
Bwlch Taff.

Dolwen Dan, son of Bwlch Bethan.

Bwlch Taff with his son, Ted.

Bwlch Risp, son of Lyn.

take a pup in payment. It should also be established in advance that, if the bitch does not whelp, there will be a free return service at a later date—when all is said and done, the owner of the sire also wants to see the bitch in pup so this does not usually present a problem.

Preparation of the bitch

Before being put to the dog the bitch should be free from parasites (both external and internal) and this can be ensured by worming and by spraying her with a suitable spray (see Appendix 2), her coat and skin should be clean and she should be bright-eyed, in good condition and not overweight. Routine vaccinations for all the canine diseases should be up to date and, if there is any doubt as to the degree of immunity to parvovirus in the bitch, your veterinary surgeon can have a blood sample tested to see if additional booster vaccine is required. If *all* these criteria cannot be fulfilled by the time of mating, then the bitch should not be bred from until her next season, which will give time in which to put things right. You cannot expect good, strong, healthy pups if the dam is not up to scratch.

Assessing the readiness of the bitch

Most Border Collie bitches come into season once every six months from the age of about nine months onwards, although this can vary a lot within the normal range. Some bitches, but not all, show quite marked behaviour changes when their season is approaching and can become quite scatty and erratic, particularly in the work situation. The beginning of the true season is noticeable by a gradual swelling of the bitch's vulva which should then be inspected daily to determine the first discharge of blood, as the bitch is ready to stand to the dog in about ten–thirteen days, although this can be variable. By then the discharge is usually straw-coloured and the day has arrived! (For a full description of the bitch's season see Appendix 3.)

It is usual practice for the bitch to be taken to the dog for mating and, before you set out, remember to take with you your service fee (which is normally paid at the time of the service), the bitch's ISDS registration certificate and the eye-testing certificate so that the sire's owner can complete the mating card which it is his responsibility to send to the Society within twenty-one days of the mating. This will be acknowledged by the Society, and the owner of the bitch receives the litter registration folder which should be filled in with the requested information and sketches of each pup and returned to the Society *before the pups are six months old*.

The mating

Sometimes, owners rely on one mating; some arrange to leave their bitch with the dog for several days or a week in order to ensure that she is there at the right time for conception to take place; others who are lucky enough to be within easy travelling distance will take her back for a subsequent mating a few days after the first.

When you arrive at your destination, give the bitch some exercise—this will allow her to let off a bit of steam and then to settle down a little and will also give her the opportunity to relieve herself before being taken to the dog. If the bitch is ready for the dog she will probably flirt with him for a while before turning her tail to one side and standing for him to mount her and, with an experienced bitch, this will rarely present any problems. However, some bitches can be terrors, turning to snap at the dog when he attempts to mount her; if this happens it could be either that she is not quite ready to mate or that she has not been bowled over by the dog's obvious (to the owner) charms! In my experience, unless the bitch becomes too aggressive, it is better to allow the dog and bitch to play together for a time either in a large, closed building or out in the field (under supervision in both places so that mating can be seen to have taken place). The whole procedure seems to occur quite naturally under these circumstances with the vast majority of matings, but sometimes it may be necessary for the owner of the bitch to hold her steady if she continually refuses to allow the dog to mount her. Very occasionally the dog and bitch may dislike each other so much that no amount of persuasion will effect a mating and the whole thing has to be called off.

With a maiden bitch, initial penetration by the dog can sometimes be a little difficult but can be greatly helped by the application of petroleum jelly around the bitch's vulva—this will also make the whole procedure more comfortable for the bitch who is then less likely to rebel. Once mating has occurred the dog and bitch usually remain 'tied' together for up to twenty minutes or so, the length of time varying considerably, and, once the dogs have separated, the bitch should be taken somewhere quiet where she can relax.

It perhaps needs to be said that great care must be taken throughout the bitch's season to ensure that no other dogs have the opportunity to mate with her other than the chosen sire—some dogs (and bitches) can be very determined in this respect, nature being what she is, so you will need to be vigilant at all times until the season has ended, as the fact that a bitch has already been mated during a season does not preclude other matings from taking place.

After the mating

You now have sixty-three days (nine weeks)—give or take a week on either side of that period—to wait for the pups, during which time it is not necessary to mollycoddle the bitch, as she is not an invalid and is perfectly capable of carrying on with her work and trialling. However, when she is about six weeks in whelp and getting heavier, her workload should be reduced, particularly in hot weather, and it is also advisable to move her to her whelping quarters at about this time in order to give her time to settle in and consider the place as 'home'.

You should continue to feed the bitch as normal on a good-quality complete food, gradually increasing the protein level to ensure adequate development of the pups and to maintain the bitch in sound condition without putting on too much body weight. This can be done by adding extra meat, eggs, fish and milk to the complete dog food, and as she becomes heavier in pup, it is better to feed her with two smaller meals per day rather than one large one because there is less room for her stomach as the puppies grow. Fresh, clean water should be available at all times as the bitch will get very thirsty, particularly as her pregnancy progresses. (See Appendix 3 for a description of normal and abnormal signs of pregnancy.)

Whelping quarters

Whelping quarters vary considerably. If your bitch is used to living outside and you have a farm with outbuildings, she will probably prefer to produce the puppies in a quiet, dark corner of her own choosing, and we find that, if this is suitable—i.e. clean and where no harm can come to her or the pups—it is better to leave her alone, keeping a watchful eye on her, as long as she is in an accessible place (not under the hen-house!). Old Sheba always made a beeline for the hay shed where she knew it would be lovely and warm, and then when all the pups had been born, we would move them to the prepared quarters and leave them to settle down quietly after ensuring that all the puppies were suckling satisfactorily. The whelping area which we prepare is in a clean, dry outbuilding and usually consists of a bed of hay (we find this to be better than straw, being finer and softer) which is surrounded by clean bales to keep out the draughts. The area within the bales is about three feet square, initially, and is kept to this size to ensure that none of the puppies gets accidentally parted from the dam. Once the puppies are beginning to move around more freely and they have become strong enough to get back to Mum for food and warmth, the space between the bales is gradually enlarged—eventually removing one side of the rectangle of bales. We always make sure that there is a raised platform of some kind which the bitch can reach but which the puppies cannot get to—this ensures that, when she wants a short rest from her puppies, she has a place of her own which is free from disturbance.

In cold weather we always use a heat lamp suspended about three feet above the nest to ensure that the pups have sufficient warmth, and, used with care, it can be of great help in the conservation of body heat, which is rapidly lost in the young of most animals. Once the puppies have become really mobile (at around four weeks of age) the lamp is switched off for increasing periods until it is left off altogether by the time they are about six weeks old.

Never fasten the bitch up by a chain when she has a litter of pups—she needs to be able to move around freely to keep her offspring clean and to change her position as the pups suckle, and the chain can injure the pups or even cause their death by strangulation.

If you have no outbuildings and the bitch is used to living in the house, then there is no reason why she should not whelp down in a quiet corner indoors. For this purpose you will need a wooden whelping box with raised sides to keep the puppies in and the draughts out. This box should be of a size to allow the bitch to lie fully stretched out with about eighteen inches between her paws and the side of the box (any smaller and there is a risk of puppies being squashed, any larger and pups can become separated from the bitch and get cold very quickly). One side of the box should be on hinges so that it can be let down, when the pups become more mobile, to provide a ramp for them to walk up to get back to Mum. Clean newspaper makes a perfectly satisfactory lining for the box and has the advantage of being easy to replace as it becomes soiled. The whelping box should be placed in a quiet corner away from the general traffic of the household—our bitch Lyn had her last litter indoors in the kitchen where there is a suitably sized space between the solid-fuel cooker and the cupboards. She was warm, dry and out of the way in a place where it was easy to keep an eye on things and, as she is used to living in the house, she was quite happy to have her whelping quarters there. Once the puppies were big enough to become a nuisance around the kitchen they were moved outside into the prepared outbuilding which gave them more freedom of movement and us a bit of much-needed peace!

Whatever type of whelping area you (or your bitch) prepare, the main criteria are: cleanliness, freedom from draughts, suitable bedding material, a source of additional heat in case it should be required, quietness and an additional bed for the bitch which the pups cannot reach. If a heat lamp is not used, it is always a good idea to provide a source of soft light at night.

Some bitches tend to develop cracked and sore nipples when feeding their young, particularly the maiden bitch, so it is a good idea to keep the feeding area supple by applying a little cow's udder cream (available from the vet) daily from the sixth week of pregnancy onwards. This routine has the added advantage of providing a quick daily check on the bitch's general physical condition so that any problems which may develop can be nipped in the bud.

Birth of the puppies

Please refer to Appendix 3 for a veterinary description of the stages of normal birth, delivery of the whelps and difficulties which may occur.

Several days before whelping, the bitch may have a slight, straw-coloured discharge from the vulva—this is quite normal and is often associated with the secretion of a fluid (colostrum) from her nipples which is the precursor of the milk supply which goes into full production after the whelps are born. She is quite likely to become restless, vigorous nest-making may occur and some loss of appetite may be apparent—this may go on for a few days before the first contractions of labour cause even greater activity and the bitch begins to pant. When you notice these signs beginning, you should make a final check to make sure that the bitch has a clean, well-brushed coat, paying particular attention to her rear end and making sure that her belly and nipples are also clean. She should then be left in her whelping quarters with regular checks to reassure her and to keep an eye on her. Once the whelps start being produced, most Border Collie bitches like to be left to get on with the job themselves, but, as a precaution, we always keep checking, very quietly, to reassure ourselves as much as anything but also to encourage the bitch and to be on hand if things start to go wrong. Border Collies make excellent mothers and even a maiden bitch usually knows instinctively how to go about caring for her young—they rarely have any complications during the birth but, if things do go wrong or the bitch is becoming unduly distressed, veterinary help should be summoned without delay.

The first time you breed from your bitch you will find that you are probably far more anxious and restless than she is so be careful not to interfere with the natural process of birth simply because you cannot bear to stand by and allow it to happen without your help. A time when you can be of assistance is if the bitch fails to break the 'caul' (the membranes which surround the foetus) from around the face and nose of the whelp and you may need to do this so that the youngster can take its first breath—reasons for the bitch failing to do this herself are usually either lack of experience or whelps arriving so rapidly one after the other that the bitch has little or no time in which to perform the task. In all the years Beryl and I have been breeding puppies we have rarely needed to give our bitches any assistance when they have been in labour, and we never cease to admire their skill and expertise in completing their task.

The bitch will lick her puppies very vigorously after they are born—an activity which is essential not only to clean them but to stimulate them into activity and to get the bladder and bowels working. She will also clean up the afterbirths and then settle down for the pups to feed—this is the time when they will get the colostrum containing the antibodies which will give them the much-needed maternal protection so essential to their welfare; this is later followed by the milk, the supply of which should be good if the bitch has been suitably fed during her pregnancy.

It is a worthwhile precaution to have a supply of a suitable dried milk substitute (discussed in the section on weaning) available in case it becomes necessary to supplement feeding, along with a couple of baby feeding bottles and teats; the very small plastic bottles (sometimes called 'dinky feeders' and holding 50 mls./2 fluid ozs.) which are now widely available in chemist shops are ideal. Don't make the mistake of thinking that baby teats will be too large for a small puppy—they are just the right size, as pups have large mouths in comparison with their actual body size.

While she is nursing her pups, the bitch will need to be let out at regular intervals to relieve herself and to get some exercise, although, for the first few days at least, she will be in a hurry to get back to her pups. The time we always look forward to is when the pups' eyes are beginning to open: this occurs when they are about twelve to fourteen days old and it is then that their hearing begins to develop, they become much more mobile and interesting and their different personalities begin to appear.

Weaning

These days, pups seem to be starting on solids at a much earlier age than when we began breeding thirty years ago. I remember that when Sheba had pups, we never thought of beginning the weaning process before they were three to four weeks of age. Now, with Lyn's last litter of eight pups, they were fed small amounts of raw mince at fourteen days old even though their mother had plenty of milk for them. We encourage this early start on solids because we believe it produces good, strong, lively puppies which do not get too fat, and we also believe that it takes less out of the bitch in the long run. We start off with just a pinch of meat for each pup, feeding each one separately until they get the taste for it (this takes only one or two days), and then the amount is gradually increased. Fresh, clean water must be available at all times for both

dam and pups and, a couple of days after Lyn's pups started on mince, they were also introduced to Welpi, a proprietary brand of substitute milk for puppies which we have always found to be most reliable for puppy rearing. We have known this milk powder (made to a composition which is the same as bitch's milk) to be used by a farmer right from the start when he found his bitch had no milk whatsoever and was unable to feed her litter;

they were some of the best-reared pups we have ever seen, although the farmer and his wife had a fairly hectic few weeks with the feeding bottles! Welpi can only be obtained through a veterinary surgeon, and it is advisable not to leave ordering it too late because few vets keep it in stock, preferring to ensure that the supply is as fresh as possible. There are full instructions on the container for making up the feed, and it is essential to follow the maker's advice as to proportions and quantities.

As soon as the pups can lap, we gradually introduce Weetabix (any soft cereal will do) and we mix this into the Welpi to thicken it, giving this for the morning feed, and providing the bitch is still feeding them well, the pups are fed again during the afternoon with raw mince on its own. The amounts offered are slowly increased and if some is left in the feeding dish, the amount is reduced slightly so that it is all eaten each time. We have a butcher who supplies a good-quality pet mince—with not too much fat—for about a quarter the price of 'ordinary' mince, and most places have butchers who will do the same. If your regular butcher cannot supply it, then shop around and you should eventually be able to track down a good source. Failing this, there are some good-quality tinned dog meats on the market which are quite acceptable for feeding puppies—if you check the labels you will soon find the ones which have the highest protein content and these are the ones you should go for. Last thing at night, when checking that the bitch and pups are all right, we give a small drink of Welpi (increasing to about 50 mls./2 fluid ozs. of prepared feed each), and we continue this regime, gradually increasing the quantities of food as they grow older and more active. At about four and a half to five weeks we still give the cereal and Welpi morning feed and gradually introduce puppy meal, which is mixed into the mince with hot water to moisten it (and sometimes an Oxo cube) for the afternoon feed. The evening drink remains the same although the amount is slowly increased. By the time the pups are over five weeks, a dry 'complete' food is gradually introduced, along with a few small biscuits for their teeth, and this is left with the puppies for ad lib feeding. We use an old cast-iron preserving pan for a container, because if the mixture is placed in an ordinary lightweight bowl, it will later be found at the other side of the pen with the feed scattered everywhere. At this time, we stop increasing the quantity of the morning and afternoon feeds and at six weeks the supper drink is discontinued.

Overfeeding puppies can be as dangerous as underfeeding, so the amounts of food given during the weaning process have to be balanced carefully against the general progress and behaviour of the puppies. Their stools should be well formed and we have always found that they can provide a reliable guide during this time—small, hard stools can indicate under-feeding or lack of fluid whilst very soft or runny stools are often caused by overfeeding. A slight reduction in the amounts of food offered will often put things right. It is a sort of juggling act which calls for instant detection and appli-cation of the suitable remedy—as time goes on and experience is gained with subsequent litters, the adjustment of food amounts becomes almost second nature but, for the novice breeder, some guidance as to amounts of food required can be useful.

As the pups grow stronger there will in-evitably be fighting over food at mealtimes, particularly at the meal which has the raw mince added; therefore, watch to make sure that each gets its fair share. You can buy round puppy troughs which make this task much easier and they are difficult to tip over, an added bonus! Occasionally, if you have a pup which does not seem to be getting enough food, particularly in the early stages of wean-ing, it may be necessary to separate it from the others in order to give it a little extra meat. This will help the pup to continue to grow at the same rate as the others and it will not be long before it will be able to compete for its food on equal terms. It is important not to overdo this individual care, putting the pup

back to feed with the rest of the litter as quickly as possible so that it continues to develop the competitive spirit which is so necessary to survival and the growth of independence.

When the pups are six to eight weeks old, cod liver oil may be added to one of the daily meals, just a few drops at first and gradually increased to one teaspoonful each. From the end of the fourth week onwards the bitch spends less and less time with the pups and this is when the pup-proof area for her use becomes essential, giving her a place to escape from them. Nevertheless, she should still be left with them overnight until they are up to seven and a half weeks old and her milk supply has dried up. During this phase, as the bitch feeds her pups less and less, her own feed requirements also lessen and her food should be gradually cut down to normal portions to prevent her from becoming overweight.

Worming

Keeping worms at bay is a very important factor in the health of both the bitch and her puppies. Roundworms (see Appendix 2) are the type of worm which *all* puppies have in their intestines and it is essential that these be eliminated if the puppies are to maintain an adequate growth rate and, indeed, to survive, because heavy worm infestation, if not treated, can kill pups. We first worm our puppies at the age of four weeks and again at six weeks, always using a wormer obtained from our veterinary surgeon—these are most effective and do not upset the puppies' stomachs in any way; they do not cost any more than those obtainable from other sources and are, in our opinion, much more effective and specific in their action. I understand that many people now worm puppies more frequently, starting at the age of two weeks, so, again, I would advise you to consult your veterinary surgeon and follow his advice on a suitable worming programme.

As parvovirus disease is so prevalent, we have all our puppies vaccinated between seven and eight weeks of age or five days before they go to their new owners so that immunity is well developed. There are various vaccines available for this purpose and that busy man, the vet, will advise you about this. A vaccination certificate is provided for each pup and this should be given to the new owner who can then present it to his own vet for updating when the pup starts its full vaccination programme at twelve weeks of age.

Puppies which have been well reared and handled and have had plenty of fresh air, exercise and play are always a pleasure to see, and when they go to their new homes at the age of eight weeks onwards, you will know that you have done everything possible to give them a good start in life and can, perhaps, give yourself (and the bitch) a pat on the back for a job well done.

A successful method

Beryl and I fully realise that there are many different ways of rearing puppies and that all breeders develop their own methods based on their own knowledge and experience. What I have done in this chapter is to offer a method which has proved successful for us over the years, which has been continuously modified and enables us to feel proud of our litters. We always like to hear of 'our' pups' progress after they leave us and hope that we have bred a few champions—the Bwlch prefix is registered with the ISDS in Beryl's name as she is the one who is the breeder in the family, and it is her ambition (as with most breeders, if they are honest) to win the Breeder's Cup one day at the International Sheep Dog Trials!

With Ceri, Rhona and Beryl at Bwlch Isaf. (Bee Photographs)

CHAPTER 14

Full Circle

The old dog and retirement

THE WORKING DOG'S LIFE, like our own, runs on a cycle through puppyhood, adolescence, youth, adult life and old age. I feel most strongly that a dog which has worked faithfully all its life for 'the boss' should be given the opportunity to spend a happy and relaxed old age around the place where he has spent his life and which he knows so well—in other words, his home. To sell this dog to a complete stranger simply because the animal is no longer of working or trialling value seems to me to be the height of cruelty after years of good and faithful service—far better to have the dog put down than to condemn it to living out its life in strange surroundings or, perhaps worse still, to leaving it chained up in known surroundings with little or no exercise or attention other than being presented with food each day.

If you have kept your dog up to the age of about six years, I believe he should then remain with you for the rest of his life. At the time of writing, Bwlch Bracken is fifteen years of age and is now living out her retirement in the house where she started off as a young puppy. In cold weather she is in the warmth which helps to allay any arthritic pains in her old joints and she can snooze in front of the fire, dreaming of days gone by. In warm weather, she goes outside, finds herself some-where in the sunshine and basks there, half asleep but still keeping an eye on things going on around her. Living as part of the family in this way, Bracken gets a lot of fuss and attention from everybody around; she is also cussed at when she gets under our feet or plays deaf when we ask her to do something she objects to—like moving away from the fire so that others can benefit a little from its warmth. In some ways, she has gone right back to her very early days as a puppy, when she was brought into the house by Beryl and the girls before she started her working and trialling career. There is no doubt that Bracken now feels that she owns the place and why not? She has earned it, as far as my family and I are concerned. She still shows some interest in sheep but, as time goes by, this is lessening as her love of comfort grows and her eyesight becomes less acute. Surely it is the least we can do for a grand old lady who has been such a marvellous dog for both Beryl and me—she has done well in her work around the farm, she has been successful in sheepdog trials and she has also proved to be a first-class breeding bitch who, in my opinion, has passed on the attributes of her father, Wiston Cap, to her offspring. Being naturally biased, I feel that Bracken has few equals as a bitch who has carried a line so true, and her son, Bwlch Taff, also seems to be a good carrier of Wiston Cap's best points so that is also very pleasing to me.

Another thing at which Bracken excelled, but which is not widely known, is that she is a marvellous gun dog with a lovely soft mouth and has been the best retriever I have ever had out shooting, her only fault being that she will insist on dropping her trophies exactly one foot away from me and not into my hand. She has also been a first-class hunter in her own right,

Bwlch Bracken in her heyday. (Derek Johnson)

having caught many a rabbit, rat and the occasional pheasant in her time. She has always been, and still is, a guard dog par excellence—you can leave her in a car with the doors unlocked and the keys in the ignition and there is no way that anybody could steal that car—they would be eaten alive! A slight defect in this marvellous dog is that she does occasionally like to have a taste of blood and has been known to take the odd nip out of the legs of people who walk past our farm on their way up the mountain, but none of us is perfect. I live in hopes that I will, one day and before too long, have another bitch like Bracken and feel that this should be possible to find in one of Taff's future offspring—to have another bitch with such personality, flair and innate ability (and who would give me so much again) would be heaven indeed.

It is not every dog which can adapt to a change in lifestyle as suggested (a lot depends on how they were reared in their earliest days), and it is perhaps kinder to have these dogs put down when they reach the time that their creaking joints prevent them from even taking exercise. It is a very pitiful sight to see an old dog fastened up and completely out of things because the owner says, 'I am so fond of him, I cannot bear to have him put down.' It beats me how somebody can say that he is fond of the dog but is quite prepared to allow him to languish in misery to the end, and I cannot help wondering whose feelings that man is considering.

The Bwlch breeding programme

I find that I am very happy (although not complacent) about the breeding programme which Beryl and I follow, and, looking at the puppies which are produced in the litters at Bwlch Isaf, I can see evidence of the characteristic traits of our breed lines right back to twenty-six years ago when it all started. There is often an uncanny resemblance to the dogs which formed the foundation of our breeding stock and we usually have at least one or two replica Wendys, Hemps, Mosses, Tweeds, Glens, Wiston Caps or Bwlch Brackens running around the yard to remind us of their forebears.

Patterns occur in breeding programmes, some desirable, others not so desirable, but as time goes on, the responsible breeder learns how to maximise the good points and minimise the less desirable ones to increase the chances of achieving the ultimate aim. I am also convinced that luck plays a part in any breeding programme and perhaps we have had a fair measure of it in our time. We have always tried to produce dogs which are intelligent, have innate working ability and also that indefinable something which is vaguely termed as 'class'— the thing which catches the eye, causes heads to turn to watch and is found in those dogs with special appeal. My daughter Ceri is now able to train her own dogs, following in my footsteps and continuing a family tradition with the intention of breeding her own line of dogs with stock from the Bwlch line—this means that, long after Beryl and I are gone, there will be somebody still building upon the foundations which we have laid, and that is very pleasing.

My second daughter, Rhona, does not have the same interest in the dogs as her sister, horses being more in her line, but it has so happened that one of my dogs, Ted, has formed a tremendous attachment to Rhona and she to him. This is probably because he became very ill as a puppy and it was Rhona who nursed him carefully back to health— without the care which she lavished upon that dog I am convinced he would have died and, in return, Ted has repaid her with the development of an enormous bond and great affection. This has, of course, caused me some problems in the handling and training of Ted (in Chapter 3 I spoke of the need to remove the puppy from the household before he develops strong attachments with other members of the family). Although Ted has responded well to training, I think that he might have been even better if his No. 1 person in the world had been me and not Rhona—however, I confess myself beaten on this one and there is no way that the family will allow me to sell him, even if I wanted to, as my life would be made hell for evermore for having been such a 'baddy'. That is assuming that I would be left alive after Rhona had finished with me. If I ever sell Ted there is no doubt that I will have to sell Rhona as part of the deal!

Joking apart, whenever animals and family

are involved there always has to be a lot of give and take on all sides—you can quarrel, argue, whatever you will, but, most of the time, compromise wins the day whilst, at other times, one or other person has to give way in order to keep the peace. It all adds to the interest and helps to keep us on our toes.

The end of an era

I think that agriculture has now come to the end of an era and is entering a new phase with many changes in the offing which will inevitably have some effect upon handlers, their sheepdogs, their work and trialling, and it would be naive to think otherwise.

One of the most noticeable changes in recent years has been the introduction of indoor lambing and this, combined with the increasing use of motor bikes as transport for the shepherd in all but the most mountainous districts, will change the way we use our dogs at work. There is an increase in the use of the larger breeds of lowland sheep in preference to the little, hardy mountain ewes favoured for so long in many areas, and if sheep quotas are imposed there are going to be fewer sheep on which to work the dogs. How will all this affect us and what will it do to the high standard of sheepdog handling which we see today? Are we likely to see a reduction in the number of sheepdogs because there is less work for them or an increase because people have more time to spend on the sport of trialling? Does it mean that the Border Collie will eventually be bred more for trialling than for work? If so, will this result in a different kind of dog?

Some of us tend to think there will always be a need for sheepdogs on moorland farms, but is this so? With the rapidly increasing afforestation programme now gaining momentum in many parts of the British Isles which have previously been the shepherd's domain, how much longer will there be sheep grazing on the slopes? Will the lowland shepherds use motorised transport to gather their sheep, using their dogs only for working close to hand in the yards after the gathering? I wish I had a crystal ball to enable me to answer some of these questions but, like everybody else, I will simply have to wait to see what happens and, in the meantime, try to help towards continuing improvements in the training and handling of sheepdogs.

where they are beyond the reach of many people's pockets, and I think there are indications that this is already beginning to happen. Does this mean that sheepdog trialling will become a rich man's sport? I sincerely hope not. One of the reasons for writing this book has been to encourage people to buy their dogs in as

Typical moorland course for sheepdog trialling—Deerplay sheepdog trials. (Derek Johnson)

Wealth and its effect on the sheepdog

Originally the province of the farmers and shepherds, sheepdog handling, training and trialling is now undertaken by many who work in other professions, and it is important that they can learn to enjoy the sport and find it a stimulating area of experience and enjoyment— I can guarantee that it will become a most absorbing and time-consuming hobby for them if they stick at it, work hard and share the enjoyment of what they are doing with their dogs.

As the demand for well-trained Border Collies increases from would-be handlers who are taking up trialling as a hobby (a good thing in most ways), so the prices could rise to the point

puppies (or breed them themselves) when the cost is comparatively low and to learn how to train these youngsters to the desired standard. In this way, there is no major capital investment involved and the greatest area of expense is in the time and effort involved in the training process—this is available to most people, rich or poor, as leisure time becomes more widely recognised as a basic essential to healthy living. There is the cost of feeding the dog and keeping him properly vaccinated and wormed but I do not know of any hobby which does not involve some financial outlay. It will be a great pity, indeed, if the rich man begins to dominate the scene simply because he has a larger wallet and not because he is the more skilled handler.

Exportation and importation of dogs

So many registered Border Collies have been exported in the past few decades that many of our first-class bloodlines have gone completely, and although there are still many good lines left, they have become comparatively few in number. I think that the time is approaching when we should be thinking about introducing some new lines to our brood stock and, as we have strict quarantine regulations about importing dogs because of the rabies problem, I wonder if we should consider importing semen from some of the best working Border Collies to be found abroad; we do this with other stock for breeding purposes with great benefit so why not with dogs? Semen can be stored for many years and is often available after the death of a first-class sire, and I have no doubt that the ISDS will eventually find a way to approve this type of fertilisation in our bitches. In 1985, I imported a dog from the United States and I currently have two very promising sons of this dog at Bwlch Isaf. However, it is quite an ordeal for a young dog to spend six months in kennels and it is also risky, and I think that artificial insemination would be a better way of getting round the problem.

Increased interest in sheepdogs and trialling

If farmers, landowners and the public can sort out their differences about access to and care of the countryside, then I feel that sheepdogs, their work and trialling will benefit enormously from the increased interest which could result from the fact that people will feel more involved in the countryside and country pursuits. In this instance, I believe that the onus is on the sheepdog handlers and the various bodies involved in sheepdog breeding and trialling to make the moves towards a better relationship with the general public. After all, we rely on them for some of our income so why not try to get them more involved in the sport? We, as handlers, discuss our needs amongst ourselves and work for changes which we think will be

Penning at the International at Armathwaite, 1981, with Bwlch Taff. (Kevin E. A. Taylor)

beneficial to us, but perhaps we are making our world too closed and narrow in its thinking. There would surely be no harm in seeking the opinions of the increasing number of people who are becoming quite knowledgeable about sheepdog handling from reading about the sport and watching it on television over the past twelve years—we might come across some very refreshing ideas from those who are not hampered by tradition and what can sometimes be a somewhat narrow outlook. Many individual societies are looking for sponsorship of one kind or another for their trials these days—how can we get this (and keep it) if we do not consider the needs and opinions of those from whom we seek financial help?

As an example of involvement of the general public in sports which include animals, I think we should take a good look at the way the horse world goes about things. Take the Horse of the Year Show which is held each year at Wembley Stadium—not only are the horses, riders, trainers, grooms and spectators well catered for, but the general public is also encouraged to become greatly involved, both in watching the performance in the arena and in being encouraged to go behind the scenes to the stabling and preparation area where there are always some top riders, with their horses, available for discussion and exchange of ideas.

Sheepdog people, by and large, do nothing like this at all. They tend to gather in small, close-knit huddles on the trials field, discussing the merits of various dogs and handlers but rarely going out of their way to involve others in their sport. Just think what happens at our major trials, for instance. Many of the spectators have paid to enter the ground not only to see the dogs running but also to get a little closer to handlers and their dogs than they are able to do on the television screen. Would it not be a good idea to have some time set aside at each big trial where dogs (perhaps those which have already completed their runs) and their handlers could get together in a tent or small marquee with some seating? People could then meet handlers and their dogs and

would be encouraged to talk about the big thing they all have in common—love and admiration for one of the most versatile and attractive dogs in the world. I am sure that this would do the sport a lot of good and very little harm, people would feel more involved, their knowledge would increase and future sponsorship might become more readily available.

Efforts to involve more people in our sport does carry certain responsibilities and I think the time has come for us to improve the provision of refreshment and toilet facilities at major trialling events. Some are already well catered for but many are not and it does make a difference to the general enjoyment for spectators attending such an event. Perhaps even more annoying is the lack of information

Some members of the Llanelidan 1986 ATB class in front of the village church. John Anderson is on the left with his Beardie and Huntaway. Chris Jackson, one of the estate shepherds, is on the far right.

at most trials about the scores gained by individual handlers. The ISDS covers this very well by displaying the scores made by competitors at the four National and the International trials as they become available from the judges throughout the day, and I think that other trials organisers should follow this idea. More work is involved, of course, but I believe we should now be prepared to offer this sort of service.

classrooms in quiet, orderly fashion. But I am only dreaming, the harsher reality being the sight of the old empty school building which is no longer in use; the two village shops have long gone, the cobbler's shed is no more, the stone wall around the village playing field is crumbling away, many of the hedges have disappeared in the name of progress and the way of life has altered. The church remains, as does the old village pub, the Leyland Arms,

Bwlch Isaf with Offa's Dyke path just visible two-thirds of the way up the righthand side of the picture.

Back to the beginning

At the time of writing, I am running an ATB class in Llanelidan, the village of my birth, and as I wait in the field for the young shepherds to arrive for the training session, I look towards the village and in my mind's eye see children tumbling and fighting on the playing field so many years ago, a mixture of Welsh-speaking local children and wartime evacuees from Manchester and Liverpool, shouting and yelling at each other in two languages until the teacher comes out, getting them to form into regimented lines before marching back into the

which is still very much alive and where the 'shoot' (now syndicated) regularly spends lunchtime when shooting on the Nant Clwyd estate. The other day I looked for the old signpost which used to stand at the crossroads in the village, pointing the way to 'London 199 miles' but, alas, like so many other things, it has gone and there is only a small piece of the post left to record that it was ever there at all.

Much of the wildlife has disappeared from this area but, a few yards away from me, I can see a solitary rabbit grazing by the hedge where I chased so many of his kind with my father's lurchers in my youth, the birds still sing and the hills are covered with grazing sheep. The much-criticised bulldozing of houses and buildings belonging to the estate of my youth has now ceased and some of the remaining derelict cottages and houses have recently been sold for their new owners to renovate. The estate seems to have taken a new lease of life—there is evidence that attempts are being made to move a little towards the revival of the best of past traditions and, who knows, more changes may be afoot with the promise of some revival of village life in the future. I can only hope that this is so.

At the end of the day, the ISDS-registered Border Collie's brain remains as marvellous and outstanding as before because we have breeders, competitors, handlers and a governing body which will always ensure that the working sheepdog shall be bred pure and true, first and foremost for its working ability. This will ensure that the Border Collie will still stand supreme as man's companion and fellow-worker and, as I bend to stroke Taff's head, I think of the increase in the numbers of his kind over the past years, the developing interest and admiration being shown in the breed in all parts of the world, and, not least, of the adaptability and intelligence of these lovely dogs and I am well content with my lot.

The carved wooden plaque made by R. G. Jones and presented to Beryl and me by Ceri and Rhona at our Silver Wedding.

Inherited Eye Disorders in the Border Collie

By Gillian Hubbard BVetMed, CertVO, MRCVS

Inherited Progressive Retinal Atrophy (PRA)

Inherited means that the condition has been passed down from the parents.

Progressive means that the changes will get worse—although the speed of change is variable.

Retinal because the retina is involved.

Atrophy means a wasting away.

As a member of the eye panel, the worst thing I have to do is to tell an unsuspecting owner that his dog has got Progressive Retinal Atrophy and will go blind fairly shortly. It is not often that the owner is totally unsuspecting—frequently the reply is, 'Well, I did wonder; he doesn't see too well. I thought it couldn't be too bad as it doesn't seem to bother him all the time.'

To understand the changes involved, it is first necessary to understand the normal structure of the eye (see Diagram 18A). The centre of the eye is filled with various different structures and fluids but the actual globe is where we look for most of the changes in hereditary eye disease in sheepdogs. Of the many layers which go to make up the normal eye, the innermost is the retina. This is the layer which receives light messages and transfers them (via a main nerve) to the brain. It is also the layer most easily visible with an ophthalmoscope—the instrument used to examine the eye in careful detail. It is probably best for someone who has examined a lot of eyes to interpret the appearance of the retina, because there is such an enormous variety of perfectly normal patterns.

With an ophthalmoscope, the first change that is seen in an eye affected with PRA is an increase in reflectivity in one area (see Diagram 18B). This is where the highest concentration of cones is and is where most detailed, daytime colour vision is received. Because this is the first area of change, the first thing noticed by the owner may be loss of acute vision in bright sunshine. It is always possible that some distant and peripheral vision will be retained and only central vision lost.

The next change detectable is an increase in pigment. There are initially a number of spots of brown colouring, these later expanding to form larger nests. In due course, the blood supply to the retina becomes less and less, until there are no surface blood vessels at all. The changes in both eyes are bilaterally symmetrical, that is, the areas of change are of equal size and shape. These changes are first evident with an ophthalmoscope when the dog is somewhere between two and three years of age. By the time he is five or six years old, the owners are usually well aware that there is a severe problem with vision.

Aims of the eye examination programme

As no treatment is possible to prevent the condition of PRA from developing, the only way to lower the number of dogs affected is with a breeding programme. 'Inheritance is dominant with high, but incomplete, dominance.' This means that if any dog or bitch carries the disease from its parents, then it is almost certain to pass the condition on to its offspring. Checks with the ophthalmoscope can show whether any suspicious changes are occurring while the dog is still quite young and, by not breeding from registered dogs with PRA, the level of PRA in dogs registered with the International Sheep Dog Society has dropped from 11 per cent to less than 2 per cent. This means that, before the eye examination was enforced, more than one dog in ten was going blind before the age of six. This is a remarkable achievement and demonstrates the success which is possible with cooperation, in this case, between the ISDS and Dr Keith Barnett, who

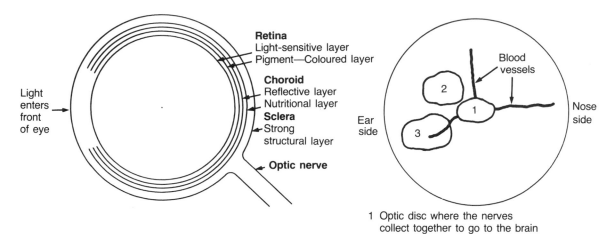

A Main layers.   B What is seen with the ophthalmoscope.

DIAGRAM 18   Eye of the Border Collie.

was instrumental in initiating the eye-testing scheme.

Collie Eye Anomaly (CEA)

Collie Eye Anomaly means a disorder or muddle of a collie's eye. The basic disorder is a poorly developed choroid (this is the layer which lies behind the retina and supplies it with nutrition, a normal choroid having a regular, sunray pattern of blood vessels of roughly equal size). Because the choroid is poorly developed, the retina above is starved and cannot function properly. In such cases a pale patch is visible with an ophthalmoscope (see Diagram 18B), with abnormal blood vessels running in all directions and of differing width. Also, because of the bad development of the choroid, the optic disc often has a coloboma, or hollow, in it. The hollow may be so enormous as to include an area around the optic disc.

CEA is non-progressive as a condition—this means that the amount of disorder will remain the same from birth and the owner may notice no problem at all with the dog's vision. But, because of that disorder, other changes may follow. There may be bleeding and haemorrhage may fill the globe, giving the appearance of a red eye. Or the

retina may detach because of the poor development of the choroid. Between 5 and 6 per cent of dogs with CEA eventually have one or both of these problems, and either of these may cause total blindness.

There is no treatment available for this condition and there are also many problems with trying to breed it out. A major problem lies with the diagnosis. Although in the majority of cases there is no doubt, there are some where a decision is more difficult. Examples of these are in blue merle dogs or where only one eye appears to be mildly affected.

A second major problem is that the condition is inherited with a recessive pattern. This means that unless *both* parents are carriers, the disease will not show up in the puppies. If one parent is affected, the puppies may still be carriers even if they themselves show no evidence of the condition. Because of this, full checks must be kept and any carriers must not be bred from, or more and more puppies will be born affected. This has already happened in the Sheltie and Rough Collie populations—to the point where at least 70 per cent of Shelties are affected.

Another problem is that of obtaining the co-operation of breeders. Because of the lack of progression and the frequent lack of interference with vision, few breeders appreciate the significance and seriousness of the condition. It is always a shame to hear of a working dog going blind, as this must always be after much effort, money and long hours of training have been invested in it.

It will take much effort, occasional disappointments and strict controls just to keep the incidence of PRA and CEA at its present level within the Border Collie population. The ultimate aim must be to actually *reduce* the problem but this will take time to achieve. The International Sheep Dog Society is very concerned and active in its work towards better understanding of these eye disorders; its requirements for adequate eye-testing of dogs are becoming more stringent and future policy changes will doubtlessly make the controls increasingly effective.

Canine Diseases Ectoparasites and Worms

By Ann G. Owen BVSc, MRCVS

Canine diseases

Routine dog vaccinations cover the four major canine diseases of parvovirus, distemper, infectious hepatitis and leptospirosis. Due to growing public awareness of the need to keep dogs protected, the incidence of all these diseases has dropped but cases of every type are still seen and these are outlined, with emphasis on clinical symptoms and modes of transmission.

Canine parvovirus

Canine parvovirus first appeared in the British Isles in the late 1970s. It had previously been recorded in Australia and North America and cases began to appear in Britain in 1978, spreading at a furious rate. Where did it come from? Outer space is one theory. However, a mutation of a related cat disease virus is the more popular theory given.

The cause of the disease is a very tiny virus which, despite its size, is very good at surviving outside the body, and this factor is important in its spread. It belongs to a family of viruses which include the feline enteritis virus and this relationship allowed the cat vaccine to be used to promote some protection in dogs against parvovirus in the early days of the outbreak.

The disease enters the body of the dog through the mouth. Infection can be picked up by dog-to-dog contact or indirectly from infected objects such as kennels, shoes and vehicle tyres. The virus attacks cells which multiply quickly in the dog's body such as the cells of the heart in puppies in the first few weeks of life when they are dividing rapidly, and this can cause terminal heart failure or massive scarring of the heart, which is irreversible and leaves the dog permanently handicapped.

The most common manifestation of the disease is gastroenteritis—inflammation of the lining of the gastro-intestinal tract. Dogs become depressed with acute vomiting which can last for days with an accompanying haemorrhagic diarrhoea. The animal can be ill for many days and, if it survives, can be left stunted. Dehydration is a big problem and it is important that the fluid balance is maintained either orally or by intravenous method by the veterinary surgeon. Treatment is often intensive and protracted and there is no guarantee of survival. The destruction of the lining of the intestine with bleeding can be very severe and death may occur from shock. This form of the disease is seen more in weaned puppies and adult dogs.

When the disease first struck in Britain it met a population of dogs which had no protection and this left every dog susceptible. This culminated in an epidemic, but now the situation has somewhat stabilised although it is still a major cause for concern. Many dogs are now vaccinated or have met the disease and either succumbed or overcome the challenge. The heart form of the disease has certainly decreased with many bitches being immune (usually from vaccination programmes) and passing protection to the pup for its early life. However, the gastroenteritis form is still seen in many areas.

Although the only vaccination in the early days was the cat vaccine, specific parvovirus dog vaccines have now been developed and have proved very effective. When puppies are born, they are protected, hopefully, by antibodies passed on to them by the dam. If vaccine is given when maternal antibodies are still high, the antibodies cannot differentiate between vaccine virus and disease virus and the vaccine is thus rendered inactive. Therefore one must wait for levels to drop, and this has been shown to be up to sixteen to eighteen weeks in some dogs. This means that puppies given a twelve-week parvo vaccine should be given an extra one at sixteen to twenty weeks. Levels of protection may then be maintained but it is important for boosters to be given yearly as protection is not lifelong. When the timing of the second puppy injection is uncertain, blood tests may be carried out for a guideline.

Thus, with better understanding of the disease and rigid vaccination programmes, the disease may be kept under control. Outbreaks occur where boosters have lapsed or where susceptible dogs have been brought into affected areas. This becomes relevant when groups of dogs are brought together from different areas to attend such events as shows or trialling. Dogs may pick up the disease and show no symptoms for five to ten days. Similarly, animals recovering from the disease can excrete the virus in the faeces for many weeks and can act as carriers. The resistance of the virus means that it can survive outside the body in faecal material for over a year and is therefore spread by shoes and boots.

It is, therefore, clear that vaccination is the only effective method of control for this virulent disease and the cost of this compared to fees for intensive treatment or the loss of a valuable dog is small. There is no doubt that parvovirus is here to stay.

Distemper
Sometimes also known as hard pad, distemper is the most well known of the four major canine diseases. It is still commonly seen in inner city areas where large numbers of dogs are unvaccinated and the causal agent is a tiny virus similar to the human measles virus. It is a weak structure and, unlike parvovirus, can be easily destroyed with steam or wet disinfection of the environment.

Transmission of the virus is by inhaling droplets from infected dogs; infection by mouth can also sometimes occur. The virus then attacks many different parts of the body, often producing a very varied picture of clinical symptoms. From infection to clinical symptoms may take over two weeks and signs can develop in stages. Symptoms include vomiting and diarrhoea, coughing, chest infections, red eyes and often a green discharge from the eyes and nose. The animal may be off its food or can be voraciously hungry. Nervous signs may develop from the fourth week onwards but they can take months or even years to show. Convulsions may occur or twitching of different muscles in the body. The virus also occasionally attacks the skin of the nose and/or pads and produces a thickening of these areas, thus giving the name hard pad.

In treatment of the disease, clinical symptoms are often treated as they appear and good nursing is very important. Nervous signs, however, may mean permanent damage and can be difficult to stop. Recovery does occur but can be with permanent twitching of the animal, and many cases beyond treatment are euthanased. The vaccine has proved very effective in control and can stimulate a response extremely quickly. The vaccine is given at twelve weeks of age when maternal immunity has reduced, and boosters are required at various intervals.

Canine infectious hepatitis
Canine infectious hepatitis, or Rubarth's disease, is caused by an adenovirus. When this is taken in by mouth, a very acute liver disease may be seen. The animal is extremely depressed with vomiting and bloody diarrhoea, and treatment is careful nursing and antibiotic therapy. However, onset of the disease is usually followed by death within a few hours. In less acute cases, if recovery begins, the glass part of the eye turns blue. However, this is a local reaction and often resolves within a few days. Other forms of the disease are sometimes seen, such as kidney or respiratory diseases. This virus can be passed in saliva, faeces and urine, and recovered dogs can pass the disease in urine for up to six months. Dog-to-dog contact is required for transmission and, again, vaccination provides an important control with immunity lasting for twelve months.

Leptospirosis
Leptospirosis is caused by bacteria and there are two different agents—*Leptospira ictero haemorrhagiae* and *Leptospira canicola*. The first is transmitted via rat urine and the disease should be suspected in sick dogs who live in environments where rats are known to be present. The organism attacks blood vessels in the body and acute bleeding can be seen in urine, faeces, vomit and sputum. Death may occur very quickly but less acute cases may respond to intensive treatment. It is important to note that this is a zoonatic condition whereby transmission may occur to man, in which case it is known as Weil's disease or sewer works disease, and it can be of great severity.

The second type, *Leptospira canicola*, is transmitted from dog to dog, again via urine. A common group to be affected are young, adolescent males who lick where other dogs have been. In this condition, the kidneys are affected, producing an acute kidney attack or a long-term renal illness.

Summary

The above information provides a short summary of the four major canine diseases. In mild cases, treatment may be successful but in many cases the outcome is fatal. All routine canine vaccinations given by a veterinary surgeon should cover all four diseases. A primary course is given around twelve weeks of age and two doses of leptospirosis and adenovirus are required where dead vaccines are used. The protection, especially for *Leptospira canicola*, is only maintained for a short period and annual boosters are very important. Boosters become particularly relevant in dogs such as farm dogs—these animals do not regularly meet other animals and, if taken to trials with no boosters, they are particularly at risk from the disease. Again, with sheepdogs, rat urine may be encountered and the first symptom may be death. Thus, with better knowledge of the diseases and their transmission it can be seen that prevention is definitely better than cure.

Ectoparasites

A dog's skin and coat are a paradise for many small living creatures, the warmth of the skin promoting activity and reproduction, causing great annoyance and irritation to the host. The parasites may cause damage in a number of ways: they can mechanically damage the skin surface by biting and burrowing, they may introduce damaging chemicals into the skin or the dog may produce his own reaction to the presence of the parasite.

Fleas

The most commonly known canine parasite is the flea, *Ctenocephalis canis*, which is probably the cause of over 75 per cent of canine itching. The flea, unlike the louse, is able to live away from the host for long periods and this becomes important in its control. Survival is not good if the environment is dry but when the humidity is high, fleas may live away from the host for up to four months, laying their eggs in the dust or dirt. Fleas are wingless creatures which feed by bloodsucking on the host.

They are usually visible to the naked eye and a red-orange colour. Flea dirt is seen as small black dots on the coat, this being digested dried blood.

The dog may be affected in two ways by the presence of fleas. Firstly, the biting and sucking action causes irritation to the animals and, secondly, there can be an allergic response to the flea bite. Many dogs will produce an allergic response in their skin when flea saliva is present in the blood stream. This means that a bite from only one flea can cause severe reaction with itching, usually along the back. The animal will often tear at the area, producing a lot of self-inflicted damage.

Treatment involves using one of a number of washes or sprays to kill the fleas. This should be carried out regularly during the summer season. Flea collars can also be used but are rarely sufficient alone. Where an allergy is involved, extra treatment is often required to suppress the allergic reaction. In the case of fleas, treatment of the environment is most important, the vacuum-cleaner becoming an invaluable tool, and sprays are now available for treating bedding and carpets in the house or the dog's kennel. All bedding such as straw or woodshavings should be changed and the old bedding burned.

Lice

The dog louse, *Trichodectes canis*, which is seen more in the winter when the coats are thicker, is also a cause of itching in dogs. Itching may be seen around the head and neck and a very severe infection could lead to anaemia in the host. The louse lays its eggs, known as nits, on hairs and they show as pale and translucent. If the lice leave the host they will only survive for a week. Again, washes and sprays are useful in the control of these parasites in conjunction with changing the bedding as described above.

Manges

Manges are caused by tiny little mites. The first type, known as scabies, is seen in all breeds and all ages. The mite burrows into the skin, producing a small tunnel. In this tunnel, the female may lay up to fifty eggs which will hatch in three to five days into larvae and these go to the surface of the skin; some will die but others burrow into the skin and change into nymphs. Of all the parasitic skin conditions, this one causes the most distress. Areas around the ears, elbows and hocks are often the worst affected and the animal may mutilate itself in response to this parasite. The condition is spread by close association with other animals, and humans in contact should also be checked for itchy papule-type lesions. Diagnosis may be confirmed by a veterinary surgeon carrying out what is known as a skin scraping and microscopic examination.

In this condition, one bath of a suitable product is not sufficient and repeated washings are necessary for a long duration. All bedding should be destroyed or suitably washed and drugs are sometimes needed in the early stages to relieve the itchiness.

Dermodex is a different type of mange which affects the hair follicles. There is very little itching but the animal may lose large areas of hair. Many dogs carry a small population of these mites and show the related clinical symptoms. It is a condition that is mainly seen in young dogs and short-haired breeds but occurs in many other breeds. Certain bitches may show this condition after rearing pups and it is thought that dogs acquire it through an insufficient immune system. The condition is not transferred by contact, and, again, several applications of a special wash are needed.

Ticks

Ticks are sometimes seen on dogs as small, grey, bloodsucking creatures and are common where sheep are in the area. They have powerful mouth parts and should be properly killed with a spray before an attempt is made to remove them, as otherwise the body only may be removed, leaving the head remaining in the skin. When this happens, it can be the site of abscess formation requiring veterinary treatment.

Harvest and forage mites

Harvest mites are seen in summer in certain pockets of the British Isles. They are often present in large numbers, looking like red pepper, and can be extremely irritant, especially around the lower limbs and the face. Forage mites are often seen in dogs that are bedded on hay and straw. Treatment again is with a suitable wash and a change of bedding.

Conclusion

There are now many preparations available for the removal of ectoparasites both from the animal and the environment. These come in the form of washes, powders, sprays, collars and tablets, and it is best to seek advice from the veterinary surgeon for the product most suitable for a particular condition. I feel that, when treating routinely, it is probably best to rotate the different types of product as this will help to decrease the breeding of resistant strains of the different parasites.

Worms

Tapeworms

There are many different types of tapeworm which can infect our canine friends. They live in the small intestine of the dog and seem to cause little harm unless they are present in very large numbers when loss of weight and illthrift may be seen. For the sheepdog owner, there are two of particular importance.

The first, despite being the smallest in this group, has the grand name of *Echinococcus granulosus*. An infected dog may carry several thousand worms in the intestine and one worm may shed a segment containing a few hundred eggs once a month. The worms may be seen in the dog's faeces and the eggs are left on the pasture and can survive several months, even over a winter period. They are then ready to be eaten by a suitable intermediate host where they may continue their development. In the case of *Echinococcus*, development may continue within sheep, cattle, horses, pigs and man. In the case of man, cysts can develop in liver and lungs and may produce a bizarre array of symptoms. Rupture of the cysts can cause death from shock, and treatment is surgical as no drugs are yet available for cyst removal. The egg, on entering the body of a suitable host, develops into a hydatid cyst. These are fluid-filled sacs which may grow up to ten centimetres in diameter and will live inside one of the organs of the body. Floating in the cysts are small particles and, if these are ingested from infected pasture by the dog, the worm may develop and the life cycle is complete.

Personal hygiene after handling dogs can be a relevant factor in the prevention of infection in man, and dogs should never be fed with uncooked sheep carcasses or offal. A regular worming programme should be maintained throughout the dog's life—this involves treatment every six to eight weeks with a suitable wormer such as Droncit which can be obtained from a veterinary surgeon and is very effective. Worming of dogs becomes particularly relevant during the trialling season when dogs will be together in large numbers. With control programmes relatively simple to follow and the cost of wormers inexpensive in comparison to a loss of condition and stamina in affected dogs, it is up to responsible sheepdog owners to keep their dogs regularly wormed and reduce contamination levels.

The second tapeworm which is relevant in sheepdogs is *Taenia multiceps* which, again, uses an intermediate host, and whole worms or segments of the worm may be found in the faeces. Control is the same as above with regular worming of dogs and other animals and observation of personal hygiene.

Finally, there are other types of tapeworms carried by the dog, using different intermediate hosts such as rabbits and hares. They all add to the burden on the sheepdog and, when not detected, could certainly contribute to poor performance from the dog. Treatment should clear the dog of all different types but needs to be given regularly.

Hookworm—the forgotten worm

The hookworm, *Unciniaria stenocephala*, can cause serious illness and possible death in groups of dogs. I believe that it is far more prevalent than is realised and that, possibly, many cases go unrecognised. Also, not all wormers are effective against this particular worm and dosing is required more frequently than for other worms, with the addition of extra controls. Many cases may be missed because the owners are unaware of the symptoms and believe that their dogs are under an adequate worming programme. The greatest incidence of the problem occurs where groups of dogs are exercised regularly on moist ground such as grass runs.

The cycle of infection is shown in Diagram 19.

Foxes may also be a reservoir of infection and contribute to the larval infection on the pasture.

Larvae that are left on the area over the severe winter months will die away and infection can then build up again, peaking in the British Isles in August and September.

Symptoms in the dogs can be classical. When the larvae enter the body through the skin, it is mainly, but not always, through the feet. The dog may have a shifting lameness and stand picking up his feet in turn. Careful examination will often reveal that the skin between the pads is red and moist and the pads themselves may show tiny, pinpoint holes where the larvae have entered. These small holes may ooze blood for a short time. The pads and claws can be affected and may eventually become deformed after repeated infection.

The larvae can also enter through the skin over the trunk of the body and this may cause itchiness. Whichever route, the larvae eventually make their home in the small intestine, growing up to 2 centimetres (¾ inch) long. The animal, if heavily infected, may then begin to have digestive disturbances, diarrhoea—often with blood and/or mucus present—and there may even be impaired absorption of food from the small intestine. The dog may become stunted in growth and the coat very dry and harsh.

Another important factor with this worm is its voracious bloodsucking nature. One worm alone can suck 0.1 ml. of blood every twenty-four hours and anaemia may set in with weakness and emaciation. Puppies may also be infected via their mother's milk and sudden collapse may occur at three weeks of age with severe anaemia, coma and death.

Diagnosis is usually by having an expert examine a sample of faeces for eggs through a microscope. When it comes to treatment, a 'dose and move' system should be adopted if possible, not allowing

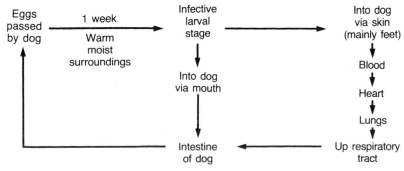

DIAGRAM 19   Cycle of hookworm infection.

the dog back into the affected area. If this is not practical, dosing is required every twenty-one days as this is the length of the cycle from egg to infection and this must be broken. Only certain wormers are effective in killing these worms: Panacur was very successful in a recent infection I treated, and Lopatol (nitrosconate) and Telmin KH (mekindazole) may also be employed. Where a dog has become very weak, a blood transfusion may be needed and bitches should certainly be wormed for hookworm as a pre-breeding measure. Where possible, if the problem is severe, grass runs should be concreted and cleaned regularly with salt and sodium borate to kill the larvae.

This worm is well known amongst greyhound people where groups of dogs are kept together and I believe that it is also causing problems in the Border Collie world.

Roundworms
These large worms—*Toxocara canis*—are commonly noticed in the dog's faeces. They can measure from 5–20 centimetres (2–8 inches) and sometimes appear coiled in a bunch like spaghetti. The worms live in the small intestine and the eggs are passed in the stools. These eggs then take a short period to mature and may remain alive on the ground for as long as two years. Once the eggs enter the dog by mouth, they hatch into larvae and these travel through the liver into the lungs. From there, some are coughed up, then swallowed and finally enter the small intestine whilst others remain in the blood, travelling around the body and being distributed in the tissues such as the muscle where they remain.

In young pups, virtually all the larvae go through the lungs and enter the small intestine while, in adult dogs, the larvae prefer to enter the tissues and lie dormant. However, with a pregnant bitch, the hormone levels after day forty-two of the pregnancy will wake up the larvae in the tissues and these cross the placenta and directly infect the pups before birth. Larvae from the bitch may also enter the mammary gland and can then infect the suckling puppies via the milk. These larvae then mature inside the puppies and eggs are seen at three weeks of age in the puppies' stools. Bitches can then be reinfected from their own puppies so it can, therefore, be seen that worming bitches is an important part of the control.

Although many wormers will not prevent infection from the bitch to the puppies while they are still in the womb, there are new strengths of certain wormers which are recommended for this and your veterinary surgeon may advise you. Once the puppies are born, worming from two weeks is advised to decrease the number of eggs. An early worm piperazine in liquid form is the best product at this age. This treatment should be repeated every two weeks till about three months of age and then monthly until six to eight months of age.

Attempting to remove the eggs from the environment is extremely difficult as the eggs are very resistant to disinfectants and only a flame gun may be successful. Another important aspect in elimination of roundworms is from a public health point of view. Ingestion of eggs, possibly by children handling young puppies, can cause problems, and cases have been reported of blindness caused by larvae lodging behind the eye. It can, therefore, be seen that regular worming of young puppies is absolutely essential and can only benefit puppy, mother and owner.

The Reproductive Cycle in the Bitch, Pregnancy, Birth, Lactation

By Ann G. Owen BVSc, MRCVS

The reproductive cycle

The normal bitch may show signs of her first season at any age from five to six months up to two and a half years, the latter group usually consisting of the giant breeds of dogs, but not exclusively. The seasons will then appear, on average, every six months, but, once again, vary enormously, with some breeds only showing once a year. In elderly bitches, the frequency of seasons often lessens and silent heats may occur.

The reproductive cycle in the bitch can be divided into four stages. The first part is known as *pro-oestrus*. Signs include swelling of the vulva, especially noticeable in the maiden bitch, and bleeding. One often sees signs of agitation in the few days prior to the onset of pro-oestrus with a first season. The bleeding then continues, on average, for nine to ten days but, again, there is great variation within a normal range. Some bitches only bleed for two to three days where others may bleed throughout the second stage. Normally, in pro-oestrus, the bitch will allow the male to approach her but will not normally stand to be mated.

The second stage is called *oestrus*. The bloody discharge usually disappears and is replaced by a watery, straw-coloured discharge. This again may last from two days to two weeks but, on average, is seven to ten days. It is during this phase that mating occurs. The bitch should stand to be mated and may show elevation and turning of the tail when she is ready for the dog. The eggs are usually shed two to three days into standing oestrus and this is the time mating should be encouraged or discouraged, depending on one's desires for the bitch. These first two stages together are known as 'the season' or 'heat'.

The bitch then enters the third phase which is known as *metoestrus*. In some other species, such as the cat, the animal needs to be mated to induce ovulation. However, the bitch will shed eggs whether mating has occurred or not and the hormones then produced create a pseudopregnancy or metoestrus. This lasts approximately the same time as pregnancy and the lining of the uterus undergoes the same changes as in a true pregnancy. This is a normal event in the cycle and is usually not noticed, as the hormones regress at eight to nine weeks. However, occasionally, events become exaggerated and a clinical false pregnancy is seen which will be discussed under 'Problems'.

The final phase of the cycle is a four- to five-month period known as *anoestrus*. The ovaries become quiet in their activity and everything settles down ready to begin the next cycle with pro-oestrus.

Problems

The first problem one sees associated with heats is mismating. The bitch escapes or, often, a determined dog breaks his way into a kennel or garden against all the odds. Fortunately a hormone injection may be given within the first four days, but preferably within the first twenty-four hours, which prevents implantation of the fertilised eggs in the lining of the uterus. This works by sending the oviduct, the small tube between the ovary and the womb, into spasm, thus preventing the fertilised eggs from passing down. The timing is, therefore, very important, as treatment must be given before the eggs' journey begins.

Another common problem, mentioned earlier, is that of false pregnancy. These are exaggerated signs in the metoestrus phase and symptoms are seen which can make the bitch very agitated. She may carry toys around and begin bed-making. Appetite may decrease or increase and mammary development with milk production is also quite common. The abdomen can occasionally swell and the bitch may even enter the first stage of labour with slight contractions. The symptoms normally disappear after around fifty to sixty days and tablets may be given to help suppress milk production. Unfortunately, once a bitch shows a clinical false pregnancy, this tends to recur in succeeding cycles and may lead eventually to a condition known as *pyometra*.

This condition of pyometra (literally translated it means 'plus in the womb') is mainly seen in middle-aged and older bitches, especially those who have never produced a litter. It is thought to be caused by hormones inducing glandular changes within the lining of the womb and is normally seen in metoestrus. The bitch may be dull and off her food and an increased thirst is often seen due to secondary kidney problems. The condition can become life-threatening with acute vomiting and toxaemia. The uterus becomes enlarged with a sticky or watery discharge. If the cervix is open, this is seen from the vulva, making diagnosis easier, but often the cervix is closed and further investigation is required. Treatments for this condition are varied but often the only option is to operate, removing the ovaries and uterus.

'To spay or not to spay' is often a dilemma for many owners of non-breeding bitches. Opinions differ and there are arguments for both sides of the coin. The advantages of spaying are, obviously, no more seasons, accidental matings and packs of dogs knocking at the door. In the older bitch, the dangers from pyometra are removed and, of course, false pregnancy will not occur. Another point to consider is that of *mammary tumours*. Many mammary growths in the bitch are known as oestrogen dependent. This means that they will grow in response to the hormone produced during oestrus, and a spayed bitch should thus not develop these. The anti-spay lobby talk of weight gains—there is certainly a tendency to this, but regular weighing and adjustment of food intake can certainly control it. Where spaying is not favoured, there are now various drugs available from the veterinary surgeon for control of seasons. They come in injection and tablet form and, when timed correctly, can suppress heat permanently or just postpone it.

There are many other veterinary problems which a bitch may encounter in association with her reproductive cycle but these are less common and more specific. I have outlined the more common problems encountered.

Pregnancy, birth and lactation

The time to mate a bitch is during oestrus when the eggs are shed from the ovary. This is usually eleven to thirteen days after the onset of bleeding but does vary. Pregnancy lasts fifty-six to seventy days and the best time for confirmation of pregnancy is between weeks four and five. At this stage, the foetuses may be palpated as small, spherical masses but this depends upon how cooperative and relaxed the bitch is!

Other signs of pregnancy include a change in shape from week five, with turgidity (enlargement) of the nipples. A tacky vaginal discharge is normally seen during pregnancy and anorexia with vomiting during mid-pregnancy is quite common. Bitches normally stay quite active during pregnancy and should not be allowed to become overweight. Calcium is not taken up till after day forty-nine and should not be added as a supplement to the bitch's diet until this time. Feeding should be little and often in the latter stages, and overfeeding should be avoided as this benefits the pups but not the bitch, sometimes resulting in oversize pups being presented at birth which might cause problems at whelping. If any abnormal signs such as bleeding or excessive swelling of the abdomen occur, one should consult a veterinary surgeon.

We then move on to the actual birth. The precise date of arrival is always difficult to predict, whatever the species, and although fifty-six to seventy days is the normal range given, I have seen bitches go through to seventy-two days. Taking the rectal temperature at regular intervals is sometimes a very useful guide. A dog's normal temperature is 38–38.5°C. (100–101.5°F.) but within twenty-four hours of parturition may drop briefly to 36–37°C. (97–98°F.).

The birth is divided into three stages. Stage one consists of a gradual opening of the cervix, the entrance to the womb, and may last up to forty-eight hours. Shivering and bed-making may be seen and the animal may appear very restless. In some bitches, especially if experienced, this stage may go unnoticed. The bitch then enters stage two, the phase during which the puppies should be delivered. The membranes may be seen and may break, expelling the 'waters'. A green discharge is quite normal and the bitch normally lies on her side to strain but this does vary. The puppies may be presented head and both front legs or both back legs normally, and problems begin when only the bottom is presented or one leg is stuck back.

When the puppy is delivered, the membranes may be over the face. These should be taken away by the mother and interference is needed if she fails to do this. Long resting periods between straining can be quite normal and make the event sometimes feel endless. Large litters may be born over a period of twenty-four hours and it can sometimes be very difficult for owners to differentiate between a normal birth and a problem. All I can advise is, in times of uncertainty, to ring your veterinary surgeon who should be able to put your mind at rest or take appropriate action.

Problems during birth are varied. The pups may sometimes be too big for the pelvis, especially if the litter size is very small. A condition known as inertia may occur: this is where the womb is relaxed and not contracting properly to expel the pups. It may be primarily due to a hormonal imbalance or can be secondary, due to exhaustion. These cases obviously need immediate veterinary treatment to save the puppies.

The third stage consists of further contractions to expel the membranes, and it is important that they are all expelled before the cervix closes. Past whelping, it is advisable to have the bitch checked. Within a few hours the mammary glands should fill with milk and the puppies should be suckling. The cords must be checked for bleeding and antibiotic powder applied to the ends. The green discharge sometimes takes quite a few days to clear from the bitch but should be checked if it persists.

Occasionally, in lactation, a bitch may suffer from *mastitis*. This is often caused by sharp puncture wounds from the puppies' teeth which allow infection to enter the gland. Symptoms include heat and swelling of the area and antibiotics are often required to settle things down.

Another condition one must be aware of during lactation is *eclampsia*. This usually occurs between days fourteen and fifty-six after the birth. The bitch may shiver and show nervous twitching symptoms and will eventually collapse and enter a coma. This condition is caused by a rapid fall in blood calcium, which is being lost to the milk, and needs immediate treatment by calcium injection, usually in the vein.

Whilst feeding puppies, the bitch should be well fed with an increased energy source. Plenty of fluids should be given and a high protein diet. All bitches will lose weight when feeding a litter and this should be minimised to 10 per cent of the original body weight. An extra source of calcium should be given but this will not necessarily prevent eclampsia from occurring. Regular checks of the bitch and her mammary glands should be carried out, especially as the puppies become older and can cause damage with their teeth and nails. Weaning is normally around six weeks when most pups have been on gradually introduced semi-solids for three weeks. As the pups leave the mother, the mammary area will shrink and the bitch should then be left to regain previous body condition.

National and International Trials Courses

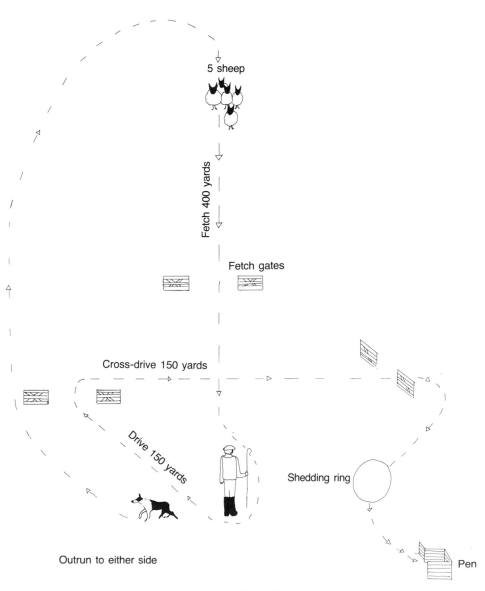

5 sheep

Fetch 400 yards

Fetch gates

Cross-drive 150 yards

Drive 150 yards

Shedding ring

Pen

Outrun to either side

DIAGRAM 20 Course for the four National trials and Qualifying course for the International.

National and Qualifying

COURSE—The responsibility for laying out the Course in accordance with the Rules rests with the Trials Committee and the Course Director.

(1) GATHERING 400 YARDS—In the outrun the dog may be directed on either side. A straight fetch from the lift to the handler, through a centre gate (7 yards wide) 150 yards from the handler. No re-try at the gate is allowed. The handler will remain at the post from the commencement of the outrun and at the end of the fetch he will pass the sheep behind him.

(2) DRIVING—The handler will stand at the post and direct his dog to drive the sheep 450 yards over a triangular course through two sets of gates 7 yards wide. A second attempt at either gate is NOT allowed. The drive ends when the sheep enter the shedding ring. The handler will remain at the post until the sheep are in the shedding ring. In the case of a short course, when the fetch is less than 400 yards, the drive will be lengthened when possible so that the total length of the fetch and drive is 850 yards, or as near to the length as is reasonably practicable. The drive may be either to left or right and shall be decided by the Trials Committee immediately prior to the Trial.

(3) SHEDDING—Two unmarked sheep to be shed within a ring 40 yards in diameter. The dog must be in full control of the two sheep shed (in or outside the ring); otherwise the shed will not be deemed satisfactory. On completion of the shed the handler shall reunite his sheep before proceeding to pen.

(4) PENNING—The pen will be 6 feet by 9 feet with a gate 6 feet wide to which is secured a rope 6 feet long. On completion of shedding, the handler must proceed to the pen, leaving his dog to bring the sheep to the pen. The handler is forbidden to assist the dog to drive the sheep to the pen. The handler will stand at the gate holding the rope and must not let go of the rope while the dog works the sheep into the pen. The handler will close the gate. After releasing the sheep, the handler will close and fasten the gate.

(5) SINGLE SHEEP—The handler will proceed to the shedding ring leaving the dog to bring the sheep from the pen to the ring. One of two marked sheep will be shed off within the ring and thereafter worn (in or outside the ring) to the judges' satisfaction. Handlers are forbidden to assist the dog in driving off or attempting to drive off the single any distance or by forcing it on the dog.

SCALE OF POINTS—Outrun 20; Lifting 10; Fetching 20; Driving 30; Shedding 10; Penning 10; Single 10. **TOTAL 110**

TIME LIMIT—15 minutes. No extension.

Brace

COURSE—*(1) Gathering*—There will be 10 or such number of sheep as the Committee decide upon, in one lot in the centre of the field at a distance of approximately 800 yards. Both dogs will start at the same time. Crossing at the completion of the outrun is permissible but dogs should remain on the side to which they have crossed and they should not recross. The fetch should be straight through a gate (9 yards wide) in the centre of the field. Should the gate be missed no re-try is allowed. Each dog will keep to its own side and the handler will remain at the post and at the end of the fetch will pass the sheep behind him.

(2) Driving—The handler stands at the post and directs his two dogs to drive the sheep 600 yards over a triangular course through two sets of gates (9 yards wide), back to the handler. No re-try is allowed at either gate. Each dog is to keep to its own side and the handler must remain at the post until the end of the drive. The drive is finished when the sheep enter the shedding ring.

(3) Shedding—The sheep will be divided into two equal lots by either dog inside the shedding ring; one lot will be driven off and left in charge of one dog—the other lot will be penned in a diamond-shaped pen with an entrance of 5 feet and no gate. This dog will be left in charge while the other lot are penned by the other dog in a similar pen approximately 50 yards away.

SCALE OF POINTS—Gathering 80 (Outrun 2 × 20 = 40; Lifting 20 and Fetching 20); Driving 30; Shedding 10; Penning (2 × 10) 20. **Total 140.**

TIME LIMIT—25 minutes. No extension.

Supreme

COURSE—*(1) Gathering*—Distance about 800 yards for one lot of 10 sheep (if possible unseen by the dog) which should be brought through the gate (9 yards wide) in the centre of the field to a post fixed 20 yards through the gate; the dog having reached the post will then be re-directed for another lot of sheep (if possible unseen by the dog) which should also be brought through the gate and united with the first lot. The first run to be right or left as decided by the Trials Committee before the Trial and all competitors will run on that side, the second run to be on the other side. Should the gate be missed no re-try is allowed. Both the dog and the first lot of sheep must be past the gate to the post 20 yards inside the gate before the dog is re-directed for the second lot. At the end of the fetch the handler shall pass the sheep behind him.

(2) Driving—The drive shall be for 600 yards from where the handler stands in a triangular course through two gate obstacles (9 yards wide), back to the handler. The drive may be right or left as directed. Should the gates be missed no re-try is permitted at either gate. The drive should be in straight lines and ends when the sheep enter the shedding ring. The handler will remain at the post until the drive is finished.

(3) Shedding—The 15 unmarked sheep to be shed off within a ring 40 yards in diameter. In shedding the sheep will be passed between the handler and his dog and the dog brought in to stop and turn back the marked sheep. Manoeuvring for 'cuts' is not allowed. Should any marked sheep leave the shedding ring and join any unmarked sheep already shed off the unmarked sheep with which the marked sheep has joined will be brought into the ring and shedding re-started. Until the 15 unmarked sheep are shed off penning will not be permitted.

(4) Penning—The five marked sheep must be penned and the gate shut. The pen will be 6 feet by 9 feet with a gate 6 feet wide, to which is secured a rope 6 feet long. On completion of shedding, the handler must proceed to the pen, leaving the dog to bring the sheep to the pen. The handler is forbidden to assist his dog in driving the sheep to the pen. The handler will stand at the gate holding the rope and must not let go of the rope while the dog works the sheep into the pen. The handler must close the gate. After releasing the sheep, the handler will close and fasten the gate.

(5) General—No points will be awarded for work done in the shedding ring or at the pen when either of these phases of the work has not been completed within the prescribed time limit.

SCALE OF POINTS—Gathering 100 (each Outrun 20; each Lift 10; each Fetch 20); Driving 40; Shedding 20; Penning 10. **Total 170.**

TIME LIMIT—30 minutes. No extension.

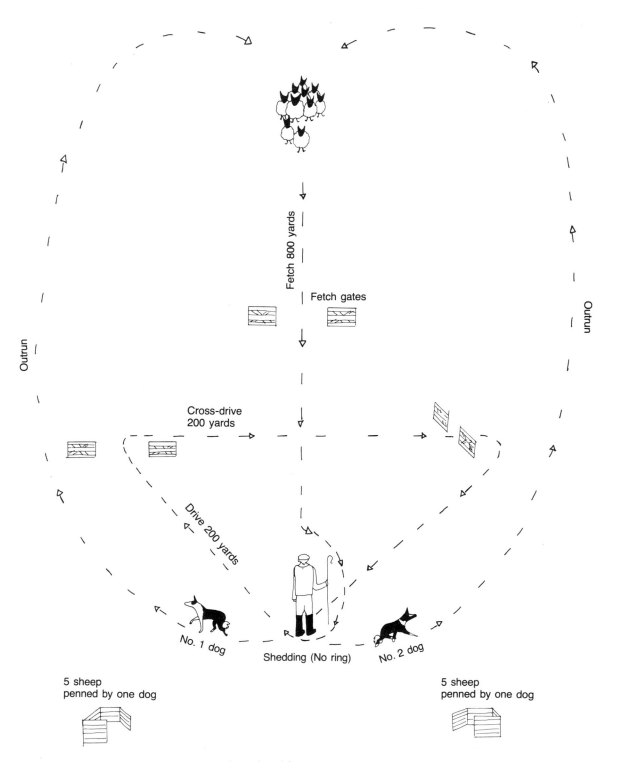

Fetch 800 yards

Fetch gates

Cross-drive
200 yards

Drive 200 yards

Outrun

Outrun

No. 1 dog

Shedding (No ring)

No. 2 dog

5 sheep
penned by one dog

5 sheep
penned by one dog

DIAGRAM 21   International Brace Championship course.

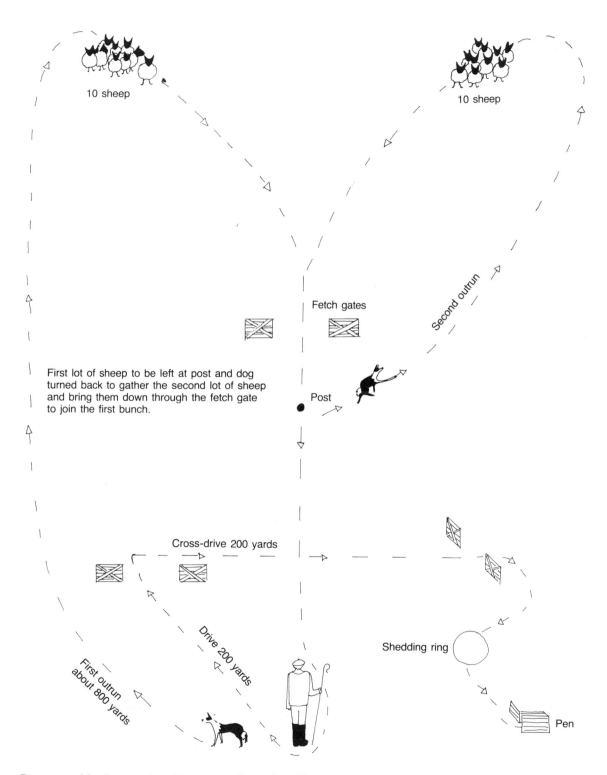

10 sheep

10 sheep

Fetch gates

Second outrun

First lot of sheep to be left at post and dog turned back to gather the second lot of sheep and bring them down through the fetch gate to join the first bunch.

Post

Cross-drive 200 yards

Drive 200 yards

First outrun about 800 yards

Shedding ring

Pen

DIAGRAM 22   International Supreme Championship course.

APPENDIX 5

Glossary

Agricultural Training Board (ATB) A body with local branches throughout the British Isles. Concerned with organising and running training programmes on any farming, agricultural or allied subject, including sheepdog training.

Away to me The traditional command for sending a dog out to his right.

Balance The distance at which a dog needs to be from his sheep to maintain contact with them and control over them without upsetting or scattering them.

Brace work Working with a team of two dogs.

Casting The dog's ability to keep sufficient distance between himself and his sheep when gathering them.

Chute See **Lane**.

Clap down The term used when a dog keeps dropping down on to his belly when working. It tends to prevent free-flowing movement of both dog and sheep.

Classes Critera for entry to the various classes at British trials vary slightly from one part of the country to another, so intending competitors are advised to check with the society running the trials they wish to enter. The following give a guide to requirements for most classes:

Open class A trial which is open to all dogs irrespective of age and previous successes (or otherwise).

Second class The usual criteria for entry are that the dogs have not had a first or second place in an open class trial.

Novice class Usually for dogs which have not been placed first or second in any previous trial.

Local class Entry is limited to dogs from within a specified radius of the trial location. Other criteria such as a limit on placings at other trials are also often applied.

Nursery trials Confined to dogs which have not been placed in any trial other than a nursery trial. The original idea of nursery trials was to provide an opportunity for inexperienced young dogs to gain experience on the trials field.

Collie Eye Anomaly (CEA) A genetically transmitted eye disorder which can be diagnosed by veterinary examination. Can result in eventual blindness caused by secondary problems associated with the disorder. Affected animals should never be used for breeding purposes. See Appendix 1.

Come bye The traditional command for sending a dog out to his left.

Crook A stick with one curved end which is used to catch sheep. Traditional crooks are made with a wooden shank and a curved horn head. The most common types of crook are the neck crook and the leg cleek (leg crook). The craft is thriving in the British Isles and ornamental crooks may be decorated with carving, painting and lettering. Some crooks are made completely of wood (usually hazel), with the root of the tree forming the head.

Cross-drive The dog's moving the sheep across the field in a straight line in front of the handler. On a trials course, the cross-drive ends when the sheep have been driven between two hurdles and the sheep have been turned and driven back to the handler.

Crossing the course   Instead of running out to one side and remaining on that side to get to the far side of his sheep, the dog runs across from one side of the course to the other and between the sheep and the handler. This is a bad fault that is heavily penalised at trials.

Dew claws   Rudimentary toes found on the front legs of the Border Collie. They rarely cause any problems, although some breeders have them removed. Dew claws are also found occasionally on the back legs and these should be removed shortly after birth as they become large and unsightly and catch on the undergrowth when the dog is working, causing injury.

Double fetch   Two groups of sheep, on different parts of the course, for the dog to gather. This involves the use of the turn-back command.

Down   See **Lie down**.

Drive   The dog's moving the sheep away from the handler. On a trials course, the end of the drive consists of moving the sheep between two hurdles.

Exhaust pen   The pen situated at the bottom of the trials field, at some point behind the handler, into which the sheep are driven at the end of each run.

Eye   An inherited characteristic in working dogs. The Border Collie uses his eye to control stock, the gun dog uses his eye when pointing his unseen quarry. Too much eye in the sheepdog can have a hypnotic effect on the dog and adversely affect his ability to work.

Eye-testing programme   A veterinary examination of the eyes (usually done when the dog is two or three years of age) to ascertain that they are free of inherited eye disorders (see Appendix 1). All dogs competing in the National and International trials are compulsorily eye-tested (or re-tested) by the veterinary surgeon in attendance at the trial, and any dog that fails the test is disqualified from running. An eye-test certificate detailing the condition of the dog's eyes is issued at the end of the examination and copies are given to the owner of the dog and the

ISDS. The examination may only be carried out by vets who have undertaken training, study and examinations in this field of work and who form an eye panel that acts in an advisory capacity to the ISDS.

Fetch   The dog's driving the sheep towards the handler after lifting them. On a trials course, the fetch includes the movement of the sheep in a straight line and between two hurdles.

Flanking   The movement of the dog from side to side as he drives his sheep.

Flowing   Steady, controlled forward movement of dog (and sheep) in a straight line and without stops.

Get up   The command to move the dog forwards towards the sheep.

Grip   The term used when a dog moves in to the sheep and uses his mouth to grab one, usually by the fleece but also by the nose or a limb. In general sheep work it is necessary for a dog to be able to grip on command, but in the British Isles gripping is forbidden at sheepdog trials and any dog that goes in to grip his sheep is automatically disqualified.

Heading   The dog's going to the front of the sheep.

Heat   See **Season**.

Heavy sheep   Sheep which are reluctant to move away from the dog. These sheep are more common amongst the larger breeds.

Holding pen   The pen situated at the top of the trials field containing the sheep used for the runs. A specified number of sheep are released from this pen for each run.

Inbye   The dog is working close to the handler.

International Sheep Dog Society (ISDS)   Chesham House, 47 Bromham Road, Bedford MK40 2AA. Telephone: (0234) 52672. Secretary: A. Philip Hendry. The governing body for registered working Border Collies of British stock. Has maintained the ISDS stud book since 1955, publishing a yearly volume recording all new registrations in that year. Is responsible for the four National trials and the International Sheep Dog Trials which are held each year in the British Isles and establishes rules and guidance for affiliated trials. The ISDS is responsible for the eye-testing programme and works towards the better management of stock by improving the shepherd's dog.

Lane An obstacle used at some trials. Usually formed by two or more hurdles.

Letting out Releasing a number of sheep from the holding pen for each dog's run.

Lie down This is the stop command. Some dogs remain on their feet when stopped, others will lie down.

Lift The moment when the dog has reached the end of his outrun and moves forward for his first contact with the sheep.

Light sheep Sheep which are free-moving and quick in their reactions to a dog. These sheep are often the smaller breeds such as the hardy Welsh ewe, which is a mountain breed.

Maltese cross An obstacle used at some sheep-dog trials. It consists of two lanes formed by hurdles in the form of a cross.

Outbye The dog is working at a distance from the handler.

Outrun The dog's run from the handler's side (to left or right) to reach the far side of the sheep.

Pen Driving sheep into a small enclosure, with or without a gate. Neither handler nor dog must touch the sheep.

Post A wooden post which is erected on the trials field to mark the handler's position throughout a trial until he moves to shed, single, pen or negotiate a Maltese cross. At some trials, there is also a post at the top of the field to which the sheep are driven prior to the dog being sent on his outrun.

Power An amalgam of self-confidence, fearlessness and the ability to master stock.

Progressive Retinal Atrophy (PRA) A genetically transmitted eye disorder which becomes apparent as a dog reaches maturity and can be diagnosed by veterinary examination of the eye. The condition is progressive and results in eventual blindness. Affected animals should never be used for breeding purposes. See Appendix 1.

Registered dog A pedigree Border Collie which has been registered with the International Sheep Dog Society. Registration with the ISDS must be effected within six months of the birth of puppies from ISDS-registered parents, and to register puppies with the ISDS the breeder must be a member of the Society. Very occasionally an unregistered adult dog can be registered on merit if it is an outstanding farm worker or trials dog providing it fulfils certain strict criteria as laid down by the ISDS. Dogs which compete in the National and International trials *must* be registered with the ISDS. Colours in the Border Collie which are accepted by the ISDS are as follows: all black; all white; black and white; white and black; black, white and tan (known as tricolour); all brown; brown and white; brown, white and tan; blue (a slaty colour); blue merle; red merle.

Season The term given to the period of time (usually twice yearly) when the bitch is fertile and ready for mating. See Appendix 3.

Shed Separating two or more sheep from the flock and preventing them from returning.

Shedding ring A marked ring, usually forty feet in diameter, where shedding and singling are carried out on a trials course.

Sheepdog Synonymous with the Border Collie. It is a generic term which covers both unregistered and registered Border Collies, and it is also sometimes used for other breeds of dog that work with sheep.

Shepherd's whistle The traditional flat whistle used by shepherds and sheepdog handlers. It is usually made of metal, plastic or bone and, once its use is mastered, produces clear, piercing whistles of varied tones which can carry over long distances.

Single   Separating one sheep from the flock and preventing it from returning.

Stand   The command for the dog to remain on his feet when stopped (as opposed to lying down when stopped).

Steady   The command used to get the dog to slow down behind his sheep.

Strong dog   A dog which is determined and fearless in his approach and will stand his ground when challenged by the stock he is working. These dogs can be difficult to stop.

Trials   A trials course is a man-made course for testing the shepherding skills of handler and dog (see Appendix 4). At a trial one or more judges allocate points on a prearranged system. The usual method of scoring is to deduct points for faults from the maximum possible. Runs must also be completed within a given length of time which varies according to the type of course. Usually sheep used at trials are from the same flock but sometimes mixed flocks are used, in which case all released for any one run should be from the same flock.
The National Sheep Dog Trials consist of the English, Scottish, Welsh and Irish National trials which are held once a year in each of the four countries under the aegis of the ISDS. The top fifteen competitors in the English, Scottish and Welsh National trials and the top ten in the Irish National go on to form the four teams which represent their countries at the International trials, usually held in September of each year. All dogs competing at these trials must be registered with the ISDS and are examined for PRA and CEA at the time of the trials.
The International Sheep Dog Trials are held each year under the aegis of the ISDS. During the first two days, members of the four National teams compete for the top fifteen places. On the third day of the trials, these fifteen handlers and their dogs compete for the International Supreme Championship.

Turn-back   The command given, after the dog has fetched one bunch of sheep, to leave them and turn-back to fetch a second bunch.

Unregistered dog   A sheepdog (Border Collie) which is not registered with the ISDS.

Weak dog   A dog that will turn away when challenged by stock.

Wearing   The dog's moving from side to side at the back of the sheep in order to keep the flock together and moving forwards.

Whelp   A pregnant bitch is said to be in whelp or in pup. Whelping down is the period between when the pregnant bitch goes into labour and the birth of the last puppy, and whelp is the term used for the young puppy from birth to the end of weaning.

Further Reading

Working Sheepdog News. (Barbara Collins, Ty'n y Caeau, Pwllglas, Ruthin, Clwyd, North Wales) A 40-page bi-monthly magazine devoted to topics of interest about sheepdogs, their handlers and allied subjects.

Practical books

All about the Working Border Collie by Marjorie Quarton. 152 pages. 51 photographs. (Pelham Books) Covers all aspects of the working Border Collie's life, health, breeding and training for farm work.

Border Collies by Iris Combe. 196 pages, 32 photographs. (Faber & Faber) A basic book on Border Collies with an excellent section on health, breeding and whelping. Good general formation.

The Farmer's Dog by John Holmes. 162 pages. 118 illustrations. (Popular Dogs) A sound book on the working dog, its rearing, general care and training for farm work.

Herding Dogs: Their Origins and Development in Britain by Iris Combe. 253 pages. 41 illustrations. (Faber & Faber) The author investigates the origins, characteristics and evolution of all the herding breeds, including the Border Collie. Well researched.

Key Dogs from the Border Collie Family, Vol. 1 (96 pages) and Vol. 2 (85 pages) by Sheila Grew (Payn Essex Printers) These two volumes contain valuable and detailed information, including pedigrees and photographs, about famous Border Collies and their handlers, past and present.

One Woman and Her Dog by Viv Billingham. 184 pages. 113 photographs. 20 wildlife illustrations by the author's husband, Geoff. (Patrick Stephens) An entertaining book, partly autobiographical, covering breeding, rearing and training Border Collies for work and sheepdog trials.

Sheepdog Trials by Eric Halsall. 224 pages. 122 photographs. 10 pedigrees. (Patrick Stephens) The author's second book on Border Collies, their handlers and sheepdog trials. Contains information which is complementary to *Sheepdogs, My Faithful Friends.*

Sheepdogs, My Faithful Friends by Eric Halsall. 256 pages. 121 photographs. 10 pedigrees. (Patrick Stephens) A mine of information on Border Collies, their handlers and sheepdog trials, ranging from the beginnings of trialling to the present day.

Sheepdogs at Work by Tony Iley. 71 pages. 16 photographs. (Dalesman Books) A good little handbook by a shepherd who has been competing in trials for many years. Illustrated with photographs, and covers breeding, rearing puppies, early training and anecdotes.

General reading

Don't Laugh till He's out of Sight by Henry Brewis. 153 pages. (Farming Press) A tongue-in-cheek guide to the would-be peasant and very amusing to anyone who sees farming as an interesting (if at times ridiculous) way to almost make a living.

Funnywayt'mekalivin' by Henry Brewis. 130 pages (Farming Press) A collection of very funny cartoons and verses which take the reader through the farming year with 'Sep', his wife, family, collie dog and farm animals, friends and others.

One Dog and His Man (108 pages) and *One Dog and His Trials* (91 pages) by Marjorie Quarton. Illustrated by Keith Henderson. (Blackstaff Press) Two very funny books 'written' by Shep, the Irish sheepdog, and telling of his life and experiences on the farm at Coolcoffin.

One Man and His Dog by Phil Drabble. 192 pages. 63 photographs. Cartoons and line drawings. (Michael Joseph) A humorous and well-written account of the 'One Man and His Dog' television series from its inception in 1976 up to the present day, by one of its presenters.

Red Sky at Night by John Barrington. 208 pages. Illustrated by Paul Armstrong. (Michael Joseph) Written by a Welshman who lives and works as a shepherd in the mountains of Scotland. The book is the story of one year in the author's working life, the natural history of the glens and the turbulent history of his part of Scotland.

The Shepherd's Wife by Viv Billingham. 270 pages. 56 photographs. (Viv Billingham, Tweedhopefoot, Tweedsmuir, By Biggar, Scotland) An account of the author's life with her shepherd husband and teenage son, their dogs, sheep and other livestock. The book tells of the hardships and grim realities, as well as the fun and pleasures of their lives together as a shepherding family.

New from Farming Press

The Blue Riband of the Heather by E.B. Carpenter is an attractive and informative pictorial account of the International Sheep Dog Trials winners from 1906 to 1988.

Index

Diagram page references are in italics. See also separate index of names of dogs and people. Photograph captions are not indexed.

Index of names of dogs and people